AVOIDING LEGAL LIABILITY

FOR ADULT EDUCATORS, HUMAN RESOURCE DEVELOPERS, AND INSTRUCTIONAL DESIGNERS

AVOIDING LEGAL LIABILITY

FOR ADULT EDUCATORS, HUMAN RESOURCE DEVELOPERS, AND INSTRUCTIONAL DESIGNERS

John Sample

KRIEGER PUBLISHING COMPANY
Malabar, Florida
2007

Original Edition 2007

Printed and Published by
KRIEGER PUBLISHING COMPANY
KRIEGER DRIVE
MALABAR, FLORIDA 32950

Library of Congress Cataloging-in-Publication Data

Sample, John, 1942-
Avoiding legal liability for adult educators, human resource developers, and instructional designers / JohnSample.
p. cm.
Includes bibliographical references and index.
ISBN-13: 978-1-57524-273-6
ISBN-10: 1-57524-273-7
1. Employees—Training of—Law and legislation—United States. 2. Occupational training—Law and legislation—United States. 3. Adult education educators—Law and legislation—United States. 4. Industrial designers—Law and legislation—United States. 5. Liability (Law)—United States. I. Title.
KF4256.S26 2007
344.7301 2592—dc22

2007016783

10 9 8 7 6 5 4 3 2

Dedication

This book is dedicated to the memory of the Honorable Judge Wallace Sample whose iron will and ethical principles sustain me daily.

Content

Appendixes

Preface

It is fair to say that one of the newest legal nightmares for employers is liability associated with the training and development function in organizations (Sample, 2007b). Legal issues run the gamut from federal and state regulatory compliance (employee discrimination; safety and health), to negligence (negligent training and experiential learning), intellectual property (copyright and trade secrets), and the criminal activities of organizations (Sarbanes-Oxley Act and the federal sentencing guidelines). Human resource managers will be familiar with most if not all of these issues. Not so for adult educators, human resource developers and instructional designers. Paying attention to liability is a new subject area for those who populate these positions.

This reference will be a valuable addition to the professional library of the following:

- human resource managers who have responsibility for conducting, managing, or documenting the results of the training function in an organization;
- chief learning officers and managers of workplace learning and organizational development programs who must be both strategic and compliant with the law;
- adult educators, human resource developers, and instructional designers who perform the variety of interconnected tasks that make learning in organizations a worthwhile enterprise, and who may be at risk because of these efforts;
- safety, risk management and compliance officers who must depend on effectively designed, implemented, and evaluated training;
- consultants and independent contractors who assume or share liability with those who employ them;
- corporate legal staff and other attorneys who do not understand the power of learning to propel organizations into the future,

and who must defend their clients the best way they know how; and
- faculty and instructors in special topics courses in human resource, management, training, and development in colleges and universities.

This reference text is not designed to be read chapter by chapter in sequence, although one might certainly do that if a general read of the subject is new to the reader. It is more likely that certain areas of potential litigation will announce themselves in untimely ways, thus requiring immediate and focused attention on a particular chapter. The recommended approach for engaging the content of this book is to (1) read Chapter 1, making sure that the principles underlying the civil justice system of the United States are generally understood, and (2) complete the short needs assessment at the end of the chapter to guide your further inquiry. Adopt a preventative approach to reducing the potential for litigation; focus on strategies that engage the whole system to reduce the threat of risk and exposure to litigation and liability.

Chapters 2 through 7 focuses on a specific area of liability, such as discrimination, safety and health, negligent training, copyright, or the federal sentencing guidelines. Each chapter includes explanations of underlying legal concepts in layperson's terms, several actual case examples from the annals of American jurisprudence, and recommendations for reducing the potential of liability and litigation. Legal terms in *italics* are defined in Appendix A. The remainder of the Appendixes include a variety of checklists, examples of useful forms, suggestions for the design and development for instructional materials, and summaries of federal laws that require or imply training. A short epilogue is included that raises questions and future issues.

Included throughout the text and the Appendixes, are references to various Internet web sites. Be cautioned that web site addresses, like fire flies, may have a limited lifetime, or change location unpredictably, so be prepared for dead links as time progresses. Also be prepared to visit certain federal and state regulatory web sites as necessary to stay current with changes in compliance regulations. Especially noteworthy are the federal EEOC and OSHA web sites.

For purposes of this reference text, the I will use the terms adult educator, human resource developer and instructional designer interchangeably. There may be an instance where, for example instructional designers, may be the focus of particular content (needs assessment, task analysis), or adult educators in their roles a facilitators of training programs. The reality is that no matter what role one adopts, it is likely that the full range of adult learning activities could be performed by a single individual, who may go by any of several training and development related job titles, any of which are susceptible to liability and litigation.

Acknowledgments

I want to thank a number of people who have provided helpful and critical feedback on various chapters in this manuscript. Dr. Jenny Grill labored over several chapters and her editing and continuing support in the development of this manuscript is greatly appreciated. Several attorneys read chapters for legal sufficiency, and I am especially grateful to Marni Pilafian, for her legal insights and excellent editing! Other attorneys who provided reviews include John Copeland, Michael Johnson, and Carl Zahner. Experienced consultants and faculty from several universities added their insights to several chapters: Dr. Rita Conrad, Dr. John Flynn, Dr. Marguerite Foxon, and Dr. Gary Green.

I am especially grateful to the following practitioners from a variety of human resource management, training, and development positions who gave of their energy to discern the practical implications for reducing or preventing liability: Robert Anno, Kari Ashe, Susan Dennett, Len Diptee, Doug Gaspardo, Ron Koenig, Dan Leavitt, Robert Lummus, Laneia McCrae, Heather Myers, Kimberly Pyles, Howard Rasmussen, and Susanne Szuch.

As much as I appreciate and have depended on the critical review and feedback of others, in the final analysis, any missteps are my sole responsibility.

John Sample, PhD SPHR
Tallahassee, Florida

The Author

John A. Sample is a retired associate professor and coordinator of the graduate program in human resource development program in the College of Education at Florida State University. He has published extensively on human resource management, training and development topics, including journal articles, chapters in books, monographs, and annuals. His 1993 American Society for Training and Development *Info-Line, Legal Liability & HRD: Implications for Trainers* was a seminal work that alerted the HRD community to a variety of issues related to training liability. Other publications have appeared in the *Pfeiffer HRD Annuals*, *Performance and Instruction* and *Training*.

Sample has over thirty-five years experience as a consultant, instructional designer, team-building facilitator and university instructor. His early interest in training and development occurred when he was the training director for the Florida Division of Youth Services. Other professional experiences included managing an instructional systems program for two nuclear power plants (Florida Power & Light), as a director of professional and business education at the Center for Professional Development at Florida State University, and as a contract manager at the Center for Needs Assessment and Planning, also at Florida State University. He is currently the principal in Sample & Associates, a Tallahassee-based consulting firm that specializes in issues related to training liability.

Sample received his B.S. degree (1965) in criminology and police administration from Florida State University, his M.S. degree (1975) in human resource development from St. Thomas University, and his Ph.D. degree in adult education, with a specialization in human resource development (1990) from Florida State University. He holds the designation of SPHR (Senior Professional Human Resources) from the Society for Human Resource Management and the RODP designation (Registered Organization Development Professional) from the Organization Development Institute.

Chapter 1
Liability and the Training and Development Enterprise

Chapter Objectives

Having reviewed the information in this chapter, the reader will have

1. a working knowledge of the civil court system in the United States, including key terms and concepts;
2. analyzed a court case that describes an example of negligent training by a large business;
3. identified the most common legal issues impacting the training and development function, including liable parties and the recovery of damages by the injured parties;
4. summarized the essential steps for avoiding training-related litigation;
5. explained what initial actions to take if a business is served with legal notice of pending litigation; and
6. analyzed a needs assessment survey that identifies potential liability associated with training and development.

The following additional materials will be found in Appendix A. Glossary of Basic Legal Terms, and Appendix B. Summary of Federal Statutes That Require or Imply Training

INTRODUCTION

In more pristine times, the primary reason for providing effective training and development was to increase the probability of correct and consistent performance on the job or to empower adults in their homes, communities, and neighborhoods. Managers of human resource development and adult education programs should be concerned for a second reason: the prevention of personal and organizational liability! In this sense, effective training and development become a legal defense to an allegation of failure to adequately train an organization's employees. If the primary reason were attended to by employers more consistently and effectively, the existence of the secondary reason would be significantly diminished (Feuer, 1985; Russell, 1984; Sample, 1993). The newest legal nightmare for human resource management, training, and development is liability associated with the training and development enterprise (Sample, 2007b).

The "Working Life" column from the May 1991 issue of *Training and Development* magazine cited an actual court settlement. It is reproduced here as a backdrop for appreciating the sometimes confusing state of our legal system in the United States.

> A man who threatened to sue himself for workplace negligence received a cash settlement of $122,500—tax free. The part-owner of a California manufacturing business was working in the factory one day when a maverick bolt snagged his sweater and yanked him into churning machinery. As an employee, the injured man hired a lawyer to sue himself as owner. As the owner, he then hired a lawyer to defend himself.
>
> The two attorneys (they're separate people) agreed that the "owner" had been negligent in allowing the bolt to stick out and that he should pay the "employee" compensation. As allowed by federal law, the "employee" got the money tax-free and the "owner" deducted the amount as a business expense.
>
> Makes you want to shoot yourself in the foot, doesn't it? (Working Life, 1991, p. 93)

This lighthearted view of our legal system may give way to a chuckle here and there, maybe followed by a series of bad attorney jokes. The fact is, we live in a society that reveres its personal freedoms, and therefore we must have a judicial system for righting wrongs. No segment of our society is immune from the potential of litigation. "Even more harrowing, in this fast paced world of computers where technology races faster than the law's ability to keep up with it, you could get yourself in trouble simply because the law is unclear" (Goldsborough, 1994, p. 18). It would be naive to believe that this phenomenon is a problem only within the United States. Similar issues are being litigated in Europe and elsewhere (Browell, 1996; Campbell, 1995).

Examples of Liability in Human Resource Development

Take for instance a contract trainer for a U.S. telecommunications business whom we will refer to as "Mr. Smith." Approximately 10 months after an accident of an employee that occurred during a training program, the contract trainer answered the door bell at his home one evening at about 8:00 PM. He was standing face to face with a civil process server who asked him, "Is this the residence of Mr. Smith, and what is your name sir?" The officer of the court then handed the contract trainer a summons. As he walked away, the civil process server told the contract trainer that he had 20 days in which to respond to the court concerning the allegations of the complaint and that he should hire a lawyer. The contract trainer was stunned to discover 14 allegations of negligence against him and the telecommunications corporation for which he was an independent contractor. He and his wife sat up late that night talking over the devastating news that had ominous personal, professional, and financial implications. Are you curious to know the outcome of this real example of litigation? Look for an expanded case analysis later in this chapter (Sample & Hylton, 1996).

A second example involves adults behaving badly in a sales-training program. A multi-state security business conducted a sales training program after which the employer was sued by previous employers for violation of California sexual harassment and gender discrimination laws, assault, battery, sexual battery, and intentional and negligent infliction of emotional distress. Both men and women sales personnel were routinely spanked by managers who conducted the training for arriving late and various other reasons. These spankings were administered with a sign from a competing security alarm sales business, caused bruising and tissue damage, and were used as a motivational tool in several offices over an extended period of time. Vulgar and sexist language by both managers and co-workers accompanied the spankings. The director of human resources for the employer, a certified California attorney, testified that if both men and women were spanked, it would not be considered sexual harassment! The plaintiff was awarded damages of $500,000 plus punitive damages of $1,200,000 (*Orlando v. Alarm One Inc.*, 2006; Sample, 2007a).

A third example involves a judgment in excess of $90 million dollars against one of the largest mini-market chains in the United States (*Stender v. Lucky Stores Inc*, 1991). The complaining parties alleged discrimination for not promoting women and minorities to managerial positions. One of the sources of information accessible to the plaintiff's attorneys through the discovery process was the notes and flip charts used by the trainers and the participants. Can you imagine having your flip charts and participants notes introduced as evidence? These facts became a civil rights case heard by a federal district court judge! It happened and you will learn more about this particular case in Chapter 2.

The fourth example involves negligent training provided by a vendor for large discount airlines. ValueJet flight 592 crashed on May 11, 1996 in the Everglades southwest of Miami, Florida. All 110 passengers and crew perished in the crash. The resulting civil trial determined that, among other findings, SaberTech, the maintenance contractor, had been negligent in training employees on how to maintain oxygen containers stored on the aircraft (*U.S. v. SabreTech*, 2001). In addition to the civil action, SabreTech received a 24-count federal criminal indictment charging three employees with (among other things) failing to properly train employees. An additional criminal case was brought by the Florida state attorney's office alleging 110 counts of murder! An expanded discussion of this case will be found in Chapter 3.

The fifth example highlights one of the most blatant examples of corporate greed in the history of the United States. Recent years have seen financial scandals that shocked the confidence of investors and government compliance agencies. Bernard Ebbers, former CEO of WorldCom Inc., was found guilty of an $11 billion accounting fraud scheme in 2005. A year later, Jeffrey Skilling and Kenneth Lay, former Enron executives, were convicted of a multitude of crimes. Skilling was convicted of conspiracy, securities fraud, lying to auditors and insider trading. A total of 28 guilty verdicts were amassed against the two toppled executives, and others involved in the scandal are being tried separately. Skilling could have received a maximum of 185 years in prison; he was sentenced in 2006 to more than 20 years in prison. Lay was convicted of conspiracy, wire fraud, securities fraud, bank fraud, and lying to banks. For Lay, the fraud and conspiracy convictions would have carried a combined maximum punishment of 45 years had he lived to see the inside of a prison. The bank fraud case adds 120 years, 30 years on each of the four counts; however, he died before actually serving any time.

The reality is that their sentences will be considerably less under federal sentencing guidelines. At age 64 at the time of conviction, Lay would likely have drawn the equivalent of a life sentence and Skilling faces 20 plus years in a federal prison. This case and others like it in recent years spawned the *Sarbanes-Oxley Act* which applies in general to publicly held companies and their audit firms. This law dramatically affects the accounting and legal professions and impacts not just the largest accounting firms, but any CPA actively working as an auditor for a publicly traded company. Do the federal sentencing guidelines come with training requirements? Find out when you read Chapter 7.

These five examples are only a few of the illustrative cases you will come to understand as you explore liability within the context of the training and development function. Whether you are a confirmed instructional designer, human resource developer, or an adult educator is really inconsequential to the treatment of this subject. A plaintiff's attorney who targets you or your organization will not care what professional role you adopt!

The purpose of this text is to inform human resource and adult educators about liability and its impact on training and development. Becoming knowledgeable and skillful about your craft is your best source of prevention. Learning more about the potential for liability, litigation and the legal process will add to your knowledge base and skill set.

At this point, an admonition is in order. The good news: it is highly unlikely that anyone reading this text will ever be sued for negligent training or other related legal actions. As professionals, we all have jobs to do and business missions to complete, and fearing potential litigation issues may diminish individual and team performance.

The bad news: litigation is typically a long drawn out process, fraught with bad publicity and the interminable disclosure of information prior to the first day in court. Our Mr. Smith lived with his dilemma for more than three years before the final stroke of the judicial clock stopped. As judges and attorneys have been heard to say . . .

- Even when you win, you lose; both sides have legal costs to bear.
- The names of the plaintiffs and defendants are emblazoned in print in case decisions for time immemorial.
- Negative publicity in the court of public opinion can be more devastating than any financial judgment.

The judicial system in the United States does not presume perfect people working in perfect organizations. There is, however, an expectation of reasonableness and foreseeability in the practice of our profession. As professionals, it is a reasonable expectation that we follow standard best practices in assessing, designing, developing, implementing, and evaluating programs for managers and employees. Knowledge of business and industry practices that have the potential for injury, death, or property damage and financial loss, is a reasonable expectation. Ignoring business practices that result in harm to employees and the public invites litigation.

Most Common Legal Issues in Human Resource Development

Table 1.1 summarizes the 10 most common legal issues associated with the human resource development (HRD) function. Table 1.2 summarizes who may recover damages, and Table 1.3 states who may be liable for those damages. Subsequent chapters provide explanations, case examples, and recommendations for reducing the threat of litigation. Most human resource management (HRM) personnel are very familiar with the statutes and case law that underpin these issues and many will have had experience with similar issues. It important that these two functions cooperate as strategic partners in responding to these threats (Robinson & Robinson, 2005).

It is unlikely that human resource development personnel and adult educators have a working knowledge of the legal system in the United States. The language and process for how the legal system works in our society is alien to most of us—unless you happen to become part of the system. The following short overview is designed to set the stage for understanding the remaining chapters. Note that terms in *italics* are defined in a glossary of legal terms found in Appendix A.

OVERVIEW OF THE U.S. JUDICIAL SYSTEM

The fabric of American culture has an underlying theme of individualism and self-interest coupled with a burgeoning diversity in our communities and workplaces. The potential for friction and conflict in all sectors of our society require rules for behavior and redress for harm committed one upon another. Such pronouncements are *laws* which can be defined as a "body of rules for human conduct, enforced by a governing power, as the means by which the control of society is achieved" (Henzey, Myers, Phalan, Bagby & Sharp, 1994, p. 2). In the United States, the "governing power" is distributed among three branches of govern-

Table 1.1

Ten Most Common Legal Issues in Training and Development

1. Failure to conform to training mandated by statute and enforced by a governmental agency.
   - Safety
   - Violence in the workplace
   - Preventing harassment and other forms of discrimination
2. Emotional distress and physical injury attributed to new-age training methods.
   - Adventure training
   - New-age-experiential training
   - Radical psychology in the classroom
3. Failure to comply with intellectual property rights.
   - Copyright infringement
   - Patent infringement
   - Trademark infringement
   - Trade secrets
4. Discrimination in facilitating an adult learning event.
   - Diversity training
   - Unorthodox training design methods
   - Facilitation of group exercises, role plays, and other exercises that invades privacy and religious freedoms
5. Death or injury to employees or the public caused by failure to train to standard.
   - Injuries with failure to perform a task correctly on the job.
   - Injuries arising during training
6. Equal opportunity and access to training and development programs.
   - Disparate treatment
   - Disparate Impact
7. Inadequate program evaluation
   - Failure to identify design features responsible for injury, discrimination.
   - Misstates program results and outcomes in violation of government or contractual obligations.
8. Failure of consultant to honor contractual commitment.
   - Professional malpractice
   - Overstating qualifications and experience as a consultant
9. Ineffective or nonexistent documentation.
   - Routine record keeping as documentation of performance.
   - If no documentation is maintained, training never occurred, even if it did occur
10. Ethical lapses before, during, and after services rendered.
    - Participating in fraudulent or criminal acts with or without consent of employer
    - Failure to report unethical or illegal activities

Source: Eyres, 1998; Mathiason and de Bernardo (1998); Sample (2007).

Table 1.2
Who May Recover Damages

Training Participants
EEOC/ADA Violations
- Privacy and freedom of religion issues (nontraditional training, new age)
- Discrimination in selection of trainees for advanced and specialized training
- Training that results in a disparate effect on federally protected class of employees
- Testing that unfairly discriminates against non-English or culturally diverse employees
- Failure to provide assistive devices or to reasonably accommodate disabled trainees

Injuries to Trainees
- Training facility
- Unsafe simulation/laboratory equipment
- Unsafe workplace (OSHA Legal Requirements)
- General duty to train to standard (required by OSHA as a general statement to enforce the importance of training)
- Workplace duty to warn of workplace hazards

Recovering Damages
The Government
Criminal prosecution
States
- Workplace health hazards
- Safety violations
- Criminal negligence

Federal
- OSHA
- Industry related (Nuclear Regulatory Commission)
- Environmental Resources Act

Loss of Benefits
- Anti-Drug Abuse Act of 1988
- Workers' Compensation

Third Parties
- personal Injuries
- training facility
- workplace

Property Damages
- Real or personal property in the vicinity

Source: Sample. *InfoLine* Issue #9309 (1993, p. 6). Copyright © 1993 ASTD. Reprinted with permission of American Society for Training and Development.

Table 1.3
Who May Be Liable?

Trainers
- Negligence: design of program, delivery and conduct of program, vendor selection, trainer selection, facility supervision

Owner/Employer
- Negligence: program design, supervision of training and facility, instructor selection, implement mandated training, vendor selection
- Course content that may be discriminatory
- Vicarious liability for the acts of the trainer or other supervisor involved in the training
- Invasion of privacy

The Employer
- Negligence: program design, selection of instructors/vendors, supervision of training activities
- Failure to implement statutorily mandated training
- Discriminatory course content
- Discriminatory selection of trainees
- Vicarious liability - intentional acts of supervisors or trainers
- Invasion of privacy

Outside Contractors/Vendors
- Negligence: program design, supervision of the training facility
- Misrepresentation: safety record, credentials, experience, bond or insurance requirements
- Contract agreement: failure to meet specification

Source: Sample. *InfoLine* Issue # 9309 (1993, p. 7).

ment—legislative, judicial, and executive. Statutes are the outcome of the legislative process in which elected representatives propose, debate, and vote laws into effect. Examples at the federal level include the Civil Rights Act of 1964, the Occupational Safety and Health Act of 1970, and the Americans with Disabilities Act of 1990. All three of these acts by the United States Congress have legal implications for the adult learning enterprise. States, counties, and municipalities have similar authority. Given the checks and balances mandated by the United States Constitution, all statutes are subject to review through the judicial system and are enforced through the executive branch of government. A summary of federal statutes that require or imply the importance of training will be found in Appendix B.

Most instances of litigation involving training and development personnel fall into the civil category. The examples cited earlier are instances of civil suits, either at the state or federal level. The most common civil action impacting the adult learning enterprise is negligence. These private rights of action are premised on nonintentional injuries or wrongs resulting in recoverable damages and injunctive relief to cease and desist. The example involving the injured telecommunications employee was not intentional or malicious on the part of the company, but it was an example of careless disregard for the safety of its employees. The example of discrimination against women and minorities in the mini-market case was in violation of the Civil Rights Act of 1964, and resulted in monetary damages and injunctive relief for the injured parties.

Statutes defining illegal behavior are criminal laws. Violations of criminal law are prosecuted by a representative of the state in the presence of a judge and jury. In *Wisconsin v. Shoreline Support Corporation* (1989), the owner of a construction business was prosecuted for criminal negligence when he allowed an adolescent boy to operate a bulldozer under unsafe conditions and without proper supervision or training. The death of the teenager was actionable in criminal court. Sustaining a conviction requires a finding of criminal intent and evidence that the elements of crimes are proved beyond a reasonable doubt. Incarceration, fines and community control are likely punishments in criminal cases.

The court system in the United States is based on two essential factors—jurisdiction and purpose. The federal court system has jurisdiction to hear and decide cases falling within the purview of statutes passed by Congress. State courts have various levels of jurisdiction based upon authority granted by each state legislature. State courts of limited jurisdiction include justices of the peace and municipal courts in many states. All states have courts with general jurisdiction in criminal and civil matters. The purpose of trial courts at state and federal levels is to hear testimony and evidence and to decide matters of fact and law, usually before a judge and jury. These courts of original jurisdiction (both federal and state) are subject to review by the appellate courts. Table 1.4 describes the hierarchical nature of the federal and state court system in the United States.

Table 1.4
Comparison of State and Federal Courts From Complaint Through Appeal.

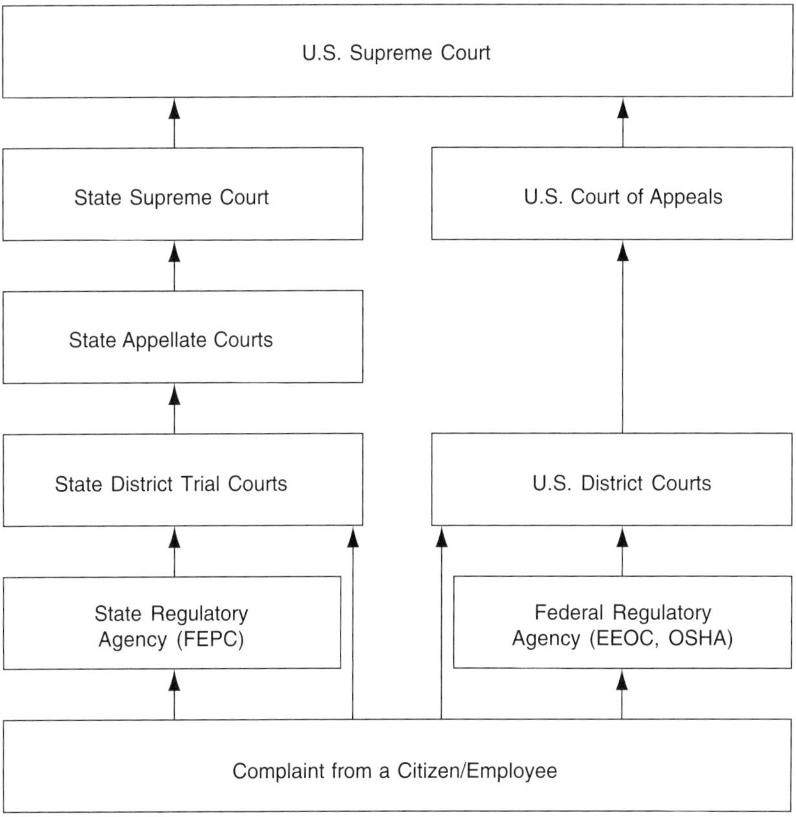

Under certain circumstances, someone making a complaint must initially notify an agency having jurisdiction to take such a complaint. Employees who believe they have a legitimate discrimination complaint are required to notify the Equal Employment Opportunity Commission through one of its many intake offices. Most states have Fair Employment Practice Commissions (FEPC) in which grievances against an employer are heard by staff employees These agencies are charged with the responsibility of resolving complaints by using mediation and conciliation techniques. Failure to resolve a dispute at this level may result in formal litigation through the state and federal courts.

Citizens may also originate certain types of complaints directly to a trial court of original jurisdiction. An attorney for the plaintiff may file a complaint in matters involving contractual disputes, property rights and tort actions (negligence). The defendant then must to answer the complaint, usually through an attorney. Failure to reach a settlement then requires a trial. Once a trial has been completed, either party to the suit may appeal the court's findings, and this applies in both civil and criminal cases. The state supreme courts and the U.S. Supreme Court decide what cases to hear on appeal.

Pretrial Discovery

Pleadings are the statements of opposing parties (plaintiffs and defendants) filed with the clerk of the trial court stating the nature of a civil wrong. The *plaintiff* starts the process by filing a *complaint* (also called a "petition" or "declaration" in some courts). The complaint states paragraph by paragraph the nature of the claims and the relief sought from the court. The defendant is notified of the complaint by *service of process* by an agent of the court (deputy sheriff, process server, or private business that serves legal documents). In many jurisdictions, a complaint and *summons* are used to notify the defendant. The summons demands that the defendant *answer* the allegations of the complaint within a specified period of time.

The defendant files an *answer* (a type of *motion*) denying most or all of the allegations in the complaint. The answer may state an affirmative defense or a counterclaim against the plaintiff. Other pretrial motions include the following:

- Motion to dismiss—filed by the attorney for the defendant stating that even if everything alleged in the complaint is true, the plaintiff is not entitled to a remedy from the court. If the motion to dismiss is granted, the plaintiff is not allowed to go forward with the suit. If the motion is denied, then the defendant must answer the complaint and the case goes forward for trial.
- Motion for summary judgment—at any time during the pretrial processes, or anytime prior to a verdict, either party to the lawsuit may request a *summary judgment*. A summary judgment is based upon information from *affidavits*, *depositions*, and *interrogatories* alleging that no material fact or issue exists for which a jury trial is necessary. If granted by the judge, the law-

suit ends; if material issues or facts remain, then the case continues.

The *pretrial discovery* process is designed to provide meaningful information to opposing counsel so that the case may move as expeditiously as possible to resolution. During the discovery process, factual information is gathered and agreed upon so that the judge and jury will hear only those facts and issues that are in dispute. Each side must disclose all relevant information, including the names of witnesses, experts, books, papers, and items relevant to the litigation. When properly utilized, the discovery process reduces the possibility of surprise and unfair advantage.

Two tools used by attorneys in the discovery process are *depositions* and *interrogatories*. *Interrogatories* are questions posed by the attorney for the plaintiff or defendant. *Depositions* are oral statements made by litigants, witnesses, and experts under oath and taken down by a court reporter prior to trial. The typical deposition includes the person to be deposed (witness or expert), the attorneys for the plaintiff and defendant, and a court reporter. Witnesses are examined by one of the attorneys and the court reporter takes down the responses.

The Seventh Amendment to the U.S. Constitution preserves the right of a trial by jury in civil matters, and most state constitutions provide for the right to trial by jury. Prior to trial, the plaintiff and defendant must decide whether the trial will be by judge or jury. A trial by jury can be waived (voluntary relinquishment of a known right) if the plaintiff and defendant agree and with permission of the judge.

The Civil Trial

Most states require a *pretrial conference* for all civil trials. The attorneys representing the *plaintiff* and *defendant* meet with the trial judge for two primary purposes: (1) to encourage a settlement and (2) to shorten the trial by further refining or narrowing the facts and issues. During the *pretrial conference*, guidelines with respect to the admissibility of evidence and qualification of expert witnesses may be determined. At the end of the conferences (there may be more than one), and if no settlement has been reached, the presiding judge sets a date for the trial.

Once the lawsuit has proceeded through discovery and survived any pretrial motions, and if there has been no settlement, the case is set for trial. The most basic function of a trial is to settle disputes without violence. The parties in the trial have their day in court to publicly present their evidence and legal theories. The judge ensures that only proper legal arguments and evidence are presented. The primary role of the judge is to maintain order in the adversarial process and to provide authoritative decisions on issues of law. The primary function of the jury is to hear evidence and to decide factual disputes.

If the trial is to be heard by a jury, then the first step is to select the jury. This process is called the *voir dire*, and it allows attorneys for the plaintiff and defendant to challenge a prospective juror's selection if it is believed that he or she cannot evaluate the evidence impartially. Each attorney has an unlimited number of challenges for cause and a limited number of peremptory challenges. Peremptory challenges are not related to a specific cause of suspected impartiality and are based on some factor other than race.

After the jury has been selected, each attorney makes an opening statement, and usually the plaintiff's attorney goes first. An opening statement provides the jury with an overview of the case and typically outlines the type of evidence to be produced. The attorney for the defendant has the option of making an opening statement following the plaintiff's statement, or deferring the opening statement until the plaintiff has finished presenting evidence.

Another issue discussed during the opening statement is the burden *of proof*. In civil trials, the plaintiff owns the initial burden of proof. If the plaintiff fails to meet the burden of proof during the presentation of evidence, the judge dismisses the case based upon a motion for a *directed verdict* by the defendant. If the judge agrees with the defendant, the case is over, and the defendant does not have to present any evidence. If the judge agrees with the plaintiff, the case moves forward.

Since the burden of proof is initially on the plaintiff, *evidence* is introduced to support the allegations set forth in the complaint. Oral *testimony* of witnesses and experts under oath and physical evidence are used to induce belief or refute some contention by the other party. Once the plaintiff meets the initial burden of proof, the burden automatically shifts to the defendant to refute the evidence presented by the plaintiff. Then the defendant has the burden of proof of proceeding with evidence from witnesses, experts, and physical evidence.

Examination of witnesses and experts by the plaintiff's attorney is called direct examination; examination of the same witness by the defendant's attorneys is called cross-examination. Cross-examination is limited to what was discussed during the direct examination by the plaintiff, and the plaintiff's attorney may conduct redirect examination on points raised by the defendant s attorney. Testimony of all witnesses and experts is subject to the criminal penalty for perjury. Perjury consists of making false statements while under oath.

After the presentation of all evidence by the plaintiff and the defendant, either party may move for a directed verdict at the close of the defendant's evidence. Such a motion is based upon the premise that the evidence is so clear that reasonable people would not differ as to the outcome of the case. If the judge directs the verdict, the case is taken away from the jury, and the judge enters a judgment for the party who made the motion.

After all of the evidence has been presented, and the judge has denied any motions for a *directed verdict*, the attorneys for the plaintiff and defendant are allowed to make closing arguments to the jury. During the closing arguments, each side reviews the strength of their evidence and the weaknesses of the opposing party. After the closing arguments, the judge instructs the jury of its responsibilities as finders of fact. The jury's duty is to determine the facts of the case, accept the law as stated by the judge, apply the law to the facts, and reach a decision for the plaintiff or defendant.

In a civil suit, the jury must determine if the plaintiff has met the burden of proof by the preponderance of the evidence. Essentially, the plaintiff's evidence must simply be more credible than the defendant's evidence. In contrast, in a criminal case, a defendant's evidence of guilt must be proven by facts beyond a reasonable doubt by the prosecutor.

The jury deliberates in private, and when it reaches a verdict, it returns to the courtroom, and in the presence of the judge and the parties, announces the decision for the plaintiff or the defendant. A general verdict states which party prevailed and does not include any special findings of fact. A special verdict consists of answers to specific factual questions posed by the judge to the jury. In this instance, the jury does not attempt to reach a decision in favor of either party. Instead, the judge applies the law to the facts determined by the jury.

The final step in the civil trial is the entering of a *judgment* and final motions. A judgment states the relief granted to the prevailing party. The relief may include costs and/or damages (monetary relief) and/or equitable relief in which the defendant would be ordered to act or refrain from acting in a way consistent with the judgment.

Two motions are likely to be made at the end of the trail. A motion for a new trial may be made by either party. This motion argues that a serious legal error was made by the judge during the trial. The losing party may also make a motion for judgment not withstanding the verdict. This motion is based on the belief by the losing party that he or she is entitled to a judgment under the law even though the jury rendered a contrary verdict.

Finally, either party may file an appeal. Reasons for an appeal may include errors in admitting or excluding testimony, rulings on motions, stating the law during jury instructions, or an excessive judgment. The party bringing the appeal is the *appellant*; the other party is the appellee or respondent. During the appeals process, the appellate court and may listen to oral arguments by attorneys for both parties, who also submit written briefs to support their arguments. The appellate court's decision in writing will affirm (agree with), modify (alter), or reverse (set aside) the trial court's decision. If the case is reversed and remanded, the case is sent back for a new trial or for a modification of some kind.

Each chapter will include one or more case studies designed to illustrate legal principles that impact the training and development function. The following case involving the previously mentioned Mr. Smith and a telecommunications company provides the reader with a step-by-step account of a civil trial that includes adventure training, a form of experiential learning.

CASE STUDY: FALLING OFF A LOG AND LANDING IN COURT!

This case begins on a clear, warm morning in August as the contract trainer greeted fourteen nervous corporate employees on the first morning of three days of adventure-based training. They were different from the usual young, energetic, ready for action corporate managers who had previously mastered the corporation's experiential teamwork training program. These employees were from two technical work groups of union employees, and they had never received the benefits of this type of training in the past. Their knowledge of the teamwork training was from the company grapevine. It was referred to as the "Rambo Course." Their supervisor had successfully completed the teamwork program about one year prior to this morning and he was now mandating that his work groups attend the company-sponsored adventure teamwork training class. An experienced contract trainer was conducting the program.

The company, a major telecommunications firm, had contracted with the trainer to deliver a series of experiential learning programs for senior and mid-level management personnel. Each program had between 9 and 15 participants. The trainer had previously conducted 12 of these teamwork programs.

The contract trainer had received instruction in the facilitation of the course materials by a business that specialized in adventure-based educational programs. Additionally, he had been supervised, coached, and certified by the corporate trainers of the company to which he was contracted.

Each teamwork program began with the same preparation. The first morning of each program consisted of group lectures concerning safety and the agenda for the three-day workshop. The instruction and exercises on the first day changed very little from program to program. After the first day, the trainer could make adjustment to the course parameters based upon group interactions and abilities observed by the trainer.

On the morning of the first day of this particular program, the trainer had explained the parameters of the program and the rules for participation. He explained that teamwork was directly linked to working together on the job and that each of these two work groups could improve their working relationship by successfully completing the program. The trainer explained to the participants the concepts of experiential training and the physical nature of the exercises, or initiatives, that he would be using. Many participants had heard about some of the more famous initiatives such as, "The Wall" or the "Tarzan and Jane Snake Pit," or "The Spider Web." Part of the first morning discussion was centered on debunking the myths that circulated about adventure-based initiatives.

The trainer explained carefully with posters, flip charts, and written materials the very crucial concepts of participant safety and the availability of a feature that was called "Challenge Out." The challenge out concept means that a participant could opt not to participate physically in any initiative without having to explain. A participant simply needed to indicate to the team that he or she desired to withdraw from the exercise. The participant would be fully involved with all phases of planning, implementation, discussion, celebration, spotting, and safety, but could not be required to participate physically.

After about two hours of classroom briefing and instructions, the team was then taken outside to the course to begin the program. The first of several initiatives is called the "Swinging Log" exercise. The swinging log is an exercise designed to induce failure because it cannot be mastered by most groups immediately. Because this initiative has simple instructions, is timed, and has no resources except the teammates, it immediately challenges the group to evaluate issues regarding planning, leadership, participation, and personal comfort levels of each participant. The purpose of this activity is to create a failure in the initiative and thus provide the opportunity for the introduction of a planning model that would be helpful back on the job. The remainder of the course would be spent using this work-planning model and relating the initiatives to real work situations.

The Swinging Log Challenge

The swinging log is a 20-foot pole about 12 inches in diameter suspended by a cable at each end. The top of the suspended log is approximately 18 inches from the ground. There is a tether cable at each end to minimize the swing of the log to approximately 3 feet from side to side. The group planning for the exercise requires the team to develop a strategy and activity sequence for all participating team members to balance themselves on the log. Once in the "balanced position, team members use inertia generated by the slight swaying movements with their bodies, which in turn enables the log "to swing gently to and fro" for a count of 10. Team participants define what is meant by the count of 10 and determine the level of success of the team. Safety spotters are arranged around the log whenever anyone is attempting to mount it. Other safety and comfort checks are routinely observed during the exercise. The time frame is limited to 25 minutes for planning and only three attempts at achieving the initiative can be made by the team.

Of the 14 team members, three challenged out of this exercise. Eleven attempted the implementation with the three who opted out and the trainer acting as safety spotters. The team had tried twice and failed to reach the desired goal. They had grouped for their third and final attempt. On this third attempt, one of the women fell over sideways while trying to maintain her balance. Part of the safety instructions had been the requirement of stepping down from the log rather than jumping if participants felt they were losing their balance. But rather than step down and cause her team to fail, this woman tried to hang on to the person in front of her as she lost her balance. As she fell she pulled the other person with her. The second person was not injured, but as the first woman struck the ground, the large bone in her left leg was fractured in several places. The accident happened about three hours into the teamwork training class. She later sued the corporation and the independent contract trainer.

The plaintiff was a 59-year-old employee of the defendant telecommunications corporation. She had more than 25 years of employment to her credit with the company. As a union employee, she received an hourly wage and was designated as a craft employee. Her attendance in the teamwork course was mandated by her supervisor. The company workers' compensation insurance paid all medical bills, and she qualified for retirement based upon her years of service and age.

The corporation experienced the usual high anxiety that results from a lawsuit. Fortunately, the trainer had taken several beneficial precautions when the accident occurred. First, on the day of the accident, he had written a four-page summary report of the events prior to and immediately after the accident. The events were described in detail, noteing times and names of persons involved. He had even noted the locations of the safety spotters and others in relationship to the swing log. Second, the trainer filed a copy of his report in the personnel files, as well as giving a copy to his supervisor. Several days after the accident, the trainer did a walk-through of the events leading up to the accident with the company safety inspector.

In the subsequent months, the meticulous notes and records of the current and previous teamwork programs proved to be most valuable for the defense of the trainer and the corporation. As a matter of fact, these notes were the key to the trainer's own defense against negligent training, and he became the key material defense witness as well.

In addition to the record of the accident that the trainer had written, he also kept all the team posters and flip charts that were used in the class for the morning of the first day of the teamwork program. As the corporation began to develop a defense to the multiple allegations of negligence, it was the trainer's notes and posters that provided the most detailed and vivid recollection of what had occurred. Other witnesses who were called to testify verified the recorded events as they had been described in the trainer's notes.

The Civil Court Trial

The case came to trial approximately one year and two months after the accident. During the trial which lasted for eight days, the woman who had broken her leg alleged that the swinging log had impacted her leg causing the fractures. It was not clear in the testimony if the other woman had stepped on her foot as she was dismounting the log, but this was never challenged by the attorneys.

As the trial progressed, an additional benefit was realized for the trainer because he had maintained a complete training manual in exactly the condition that he had received it from his certification course. Often professional trainers will discard or cannibalize training manuals once the material has been learned. His manual was complete along with other hand-written notes and instructions that he had received from the master trainers who had certified him for the course. During the trial, the plaintiff's attorney called the trainer to testify. The contract trainer spent six and one half hours on the witness stand giving testimony to defend himself and the corporation. The plaintiff's attorney grilled the trainer on every aspect of his certification, training, and the events of the accident. The responsibility of the attorney for the trainer and corporation was to intervene appropriately during the trial by rebutting claims by the plaintiff's attorney. During testimony, the plaintiff's attorney went page by page through the teamwork certification manual with the trainer. The plaintiff's attorney, with great passion and verve, attempted to portray the trainer as a "Rambo Trainer" who bullied little old ladies into performing physically dangerous stunts. The certification manual and the trainer's knowledge of the contents were crucial to demonstrating the integrity of the training process. The trainer had to demonstrate to the jury that he knew the purpose of each exercise, the conditions under which each could be conducted safely, and how to modify each exercise to meet various conditions. Since he and the corporation were on trial for negligence, it was crucial that the trainer demonstrate a thorough understanding of every aspect of the training manual.

Ironically, the skills that were ordinarily used in the classroom to train management personnel and participants were now being used to educate the jury concerning the facts of the case before the court. An additional two hours of cross-examination were required by the defense attorney. Using the trainer's flip charts and easel posters, which were brought into the courtroom, the trainer recreated the first morning of the teamwork class. As a witness for himself and the corporation, the contract trainer explained to the jury the content and process of the teamwork program in a factual and unemotional manner. The jury and the court became a classroom, and the years of training and facilitation were now being used to educate the jury and the judge.

The Verdict and the Appeal

In a case such as this with two defendants, the jury had to determine the percentage amount of negligence each defendant deserved—in this instance, the contract trainer and the corporation. When the verdict came in, the trainer was cleared of all negligence, and the corporation was found to be 100 percent negligent. A judgment of $875,000 was awarded the plaintiff against the defendant corporation by the jury. On appeal by the defendant corporation, it was determined that this judgment was excessive, and a subsequent settlement was agreed upon by the parties in excess of $300,000. Since settlements are not usually a matter of record, such amounts are usually hearsay, and that is the case in this instance (Sample & Hylton, 1996).

WHAT DO YOU DO WHEN THE PROCESS SERVER KNOCKS AT YOUR DOOR?

Having read this first chapter, you should be more knowledgeable about the civil court system in the United States, as well as your (or your employers) potential for future liability. What you may not be prepared for is what to do when the process server calls you to the door and hands you a copy of a complaint with an accompanying summons. Recall Mr. Smith who was served at his home at night. All businesses large and small should have a plan in place for the initial response to pending litigation (Cody, 1990).

A process server is an officer of the court whose sole responsibility is to formally notify the defendant of pending litigation. This person may be a deputy sheriff, someone from the clerk of the courts office, or someone from the attorney representing the plaintiff. For most people, service of process will be during the day and at the place of employment, and the first person in the chain of events will likely be the receptionist.

Whoever has first contact with the process server should immediately—and without fanfare—notify the company attorney (if on the premises), or a member of senior management, or the human resource manager (if there is one). The receptionist should not sign anything without the approval of senior management. It is very important to note the date, time, and circumstances under which the summons was served. This starts the legal clock for a timely response.

Upon satisfactory receipt of a summons, the employer should contact a representative of the company's insurer to determine if coverage exists. Coverage from an Employment Practice Liability Insurance (EPLI) policy typically includes paying for an attorney to defend the holder of the policy (Zinkewicz, 2006). It is not unusual for an employer to have independent counsel in addition to the insurer's attorney.

Management must also control all communication relevant to pending legal matters. Given that civil suits are a matter of public record, expect that the public and the press will be informed. The best reply to a member of the press or other media is "no comment," and if a public comment is deemed necessary, consult with the attorney. All employees and managers must adopt a policy of confidentiality prior to the first day in court. It is important to remember that all communications relevant to the allegations are "discoverable" prior to trial; casual comments and other gossip can undermine defense strategies.

Make sure that those involved in assisting the attorneys in the preparation of the employer's defense strategy understand the importance of "privileged communication." Reports, memos, emails and voice-mails requested at the direction of the employer's attorney are part of the "work product" used to build a defense, and therefore are privileged. Any investigation by management into the facts and circumstances surrounding the complaint should be under the direction of the attorney, otherwise the results may become discoverable by the opposing party.

Begin reviewing files and gathering documentation in anticipation of questions by the employer's attorney. Preparation includes responding in a timely manner to information requests from the plaintiffs' attorney; delaying responses will try the patience of the court. Provide only the information requested; do not volunteer any additional information. Opposing counsel will be requesting documents and asking a multitude of questions. Preparing employees for *interrogatories* and *depositions* is the responsibility of the employer's attorney. Employees knowledgeable about matters in the complaint will likely be deposed by opposing counsel.

Although a deposition is an informal affair, testimony is under oath and will be recorded by a court reporter. Be wary of overly friendly plaintiff's attorneys who will use the relaxed nature of the deposition to lull unsuspecting witnesses into saying more than they should. There is nothing improper in preparing a witness for a deposition or a trial. Witnesses may be rehearsed on how to testify as long as they are admonished to always tell the truth. According to Cody (1990), "Time spent on rehearsal and training is well spent. More cases are lost at the deposition stage than are lost after a full trial" (p. 59).

Knowing that the dreaded process server could someday knock on your door should encourage behavior that will prevent or reduce the likelihood of litigation where you work. The next section is a thumbnail summary of what employers and their training managers might do to avoid litigation. These essential steps will be expanded in subsequent chapters. The experienced instructional designer, trainer, or adult educator will already be familiar with many of the processes used to leverage learning to increase performance and productivity. What may not be appreciated at this point is the importance of leveraging how training is designed, implemented, and evaluated as a means of reducing the potential for litigation.

ESSENTIAL STEPS TO FOLLOW IN REDUCING LIABILITY

By no means comprehensive, these steps lay the foundation for current and emerging statutes and case law impacting the training and development function in organizations. These steps are consistent with best practices advocated by Eyres (1998), Mathiason & de Bernardo, (1998), (Sample, 2007b). Subsequent chapters in this text will add significant content to this general framework.

1. Conduct Needs Assessments and Performance Analysis
   - Use a systematic and structured process to assess needs and analyze performance problems by individuals, groups, teams and units within an organization.
   - Identify and systematically track internal trends that predict litigation (on the job accidents, insurance payouts, safety violations, complaints of harassment and violence, union grievances, complaints of differential treatment, etc.).
   - Instruction must be adequate to the task and for liability. The courts will use a test of reasonableness and foreseeability to determine need for and adequacy of training.
   - Participate in national forums, professional and business associations that track and report litigation trends. The recent accounting and business scandals should not have been a surprise to anyone.
   - Survey vendors and suppliers as to their continuing and developing liabilities.

2. Identify Training Goals of Strategic Importance
   - Continually review compliance and regulatory statutes for mandated training requirements.
   - Identify "implied" or "hidden" training requirements from statutes and case law; consider implications for disparate impact and differential treatment in selecting who attends training.
   - Provide training for those who must make decisions based on content of training, especially in the areas of safety, ethics, and federal compliance laws (EEO, ADA, etc.).
   - Do not rely on "one shot" training experiences to satisfy compliance requirements. Strategically integrate compliance into the culture and fabric of the organization.
   - The HRM (human resource management) and HRD (human resource development) partners must operate in tandem, not in opposition; they must operate as partners—not adversaries.
3. Design Effective Training
   - Use a proven approach to design training that systematically links each of the fundamental phases of the process—analysis, design, development, implementation, and evaluation.
   - Match the design of instruction to job-related requirements; insist that instructional goals and objectives drive the design process.
   - Evaluation begins with the design phase. Incorporate performance testing as well as knowledge-based assessments of learning. Consider the legal implications of pretesting participants.
   - Harassment prevention training should cover all types of illegal harassment, not just harassment based on race or sex.
   - Certain forms of training may invite litigation. Examples include nontraditional, new age, and adventure-based training. Accommodate the religious beliefs of participants when using "visualization" techniques which may impact personal beliefs and worldviews on work requirements.
   - Certain types of exercises, such as role play and simulation, if not expertly designed and facilitated may give rise to litigation.

- Consider the legal effects of using English language versions of instructional material with non-English-speaking employees, especially with safety-related and federal compliance laws.
- Be aware that training may create a higher standard (or duty) of care in the performance of tasks.
- Effective training may be a "trade secret" and/or appropriate for copyright registration.
- Establish a records retention and purging policy; decide to what extent flip charts, participant notes, reaction ("smile sheets") evaluations and test scores should be archived.

4. Select Qualified Instructors
   - Compliance-related training must have qualified instructors; examples include harassment prevention and safety-related training.
   - Review skills, formal qualifications (degrees, licenses, and certifications) for validity and instructional competency; require periodic updating of qualifications.
5. Monitor Training
   - Monitor training sessions on a periodic basis to ensure conformity to learning objectives, to lesson plans, and organizational legal requirements.
   - Inappropriate remarks during training by instructors or participants may form the basis of litigation; review instructional materials for evidence of bias.
   - Failure to intervene by the trainer may result in litigation (addressing discriminatory comments and behaviors, threats of violence).
   - Keep accurate records of attendance, location, and state of the physical training premises. Maintain copies of instructional objectives, lesson plans, and credentials of instructors.
   - Training that causes death or injury may result in criminal penalties, including fines and prison terms.
   - Ensure that records required by statute and administrative rules (i.e., OSHA, FEMA, Nuclear Regulatory Commission, etc.) are maintained, and that they are accurate and accessible.
   - Ensure that those who should have mandated training are not denied opportunities for it.

- Consider having an attorney conduct any training where participants may voice biases that could be interpreted as evidence of discrimination or where incidents of liability may be identified and discussed; maintain the attorney-client privilege.

6. Evaluation and Transfer of Learning
   - For compliance-related training, design evaluation processes that focus on expected job performance and the extent to which training resulted in compliant job performance job. Ensure that managers and supervisors regularly monitor employee performance, including records of performance.
   - Decide the extent to which reaction level evaluations are useful; discriminatory biases and allegations of liability could be expressed and these evaluations would be discoverable in litigation.
   - Consider alternative evaluation processes, such as having a trained instructor use a checklist of expected training behaviors to evaluate instructors.
   - Immediately remediate and document someone who fails a competency standard related to safety or other areas of possible liability.

NEEDS ASSESSMENT SURVEY OF TRAINING LIABILITY

Generating usable information that focuses attention on practical issues is one of the many reasons for conducting a needs assessment. Completing the survey below should heighten the awareness of those responsible for protecting the integrity of the human resource development program and its sponsoring organization. Interpreting the results and communicating to others within the organization can be challenging, if not unnerving. As a general admonition, do not discuss the results of the survey outside the walls of the organization. Such information can be considered proprietary (a trade secret) and may arouse the suspicions of plaintiffs' attorneys who might target the organization through disgruntled employees.

The questions below are designed to help you to better determine potential liability for your organization. Read each statement and note those statements which are true for your organization. If you are not sure, check with the appropriate people in your organization to decide if the statement applies. Each area potential of liability is discussed in this text, and a chapter reference is provided.

This organization . . .	If YES, see Chapter . . .
—— makes decisions about who will or will not attend training and development programs.	2
—— has had an EEO investigation that alleged unfair practices regarding methods used to select who will attend training programs.	2
—— uses qualifying tests as a predictor for successful completion of training and development programs.	2
—— uses evaluation of participant learning as a predictor to validate employee or promotional selection methods.	2
—— will likely have participants who have learning or physical disabilities apply for and attend HRD programs.	2
—— has a history of complaints from OSHA alleging unsafe business practices.	3
—— requires employees or contract personnel to perform tasks that are deemed hazardous by industry standards or government regulatory agencies.	3 & 4
—— requires employees or contract personnel to use equipment that could result in injury or death if not used properly.	3 & 4
—— requires employees to have contact with chemicals, hazardous materials, or bloodborne pathogens.	3 & 4
—— has a history of litigation alleging negligent selection, retention, training or supervision.	4
—— has a history of workers' compensation and other types of insurance claims.	4
—— pays a higher percentage rate for workers' compensation insurance compared to similar organizations.	4
—— mandates adventure-based training programs for developing employees and managers.	5
—— uses experiential exercises in a classroom setting in which participants may be expected to reveal and discuss personal beliefs and values.	5

— uses business practices or processes considered proprietary or secret. 6
— has subscriptions to magazines and technical, trade, or academic journals. 6
— produces training and development programs using print, computer-based instruction, multimedia applications, or elearning software applications. 6
— has employees who are required to follow strict ethical guidelines during the performance of job duties. 7
— employs officers, managers, or other employees who could engage in criminal activities, such as fraud, embezzlement, insider trading, money laundering, and crimes against the environment, and so forth. 7
— uses external auditors who have statutory and regulatory responsibility to report fraud and other illegal and unethical activities. 7

CONCLUSION

Chapter 1 is designed to heighten the awareness of human resource development professionals for liability associated with the assessment, design, development, implementation, and evaluation of programs. Note that italicized words are defined in the glossary of legal terms found in Appendix A.

This chapter provides a brief explanation of the workings of the civil courts, including an example of a civil trial from beginning to end. Although it is unlikely that anyone reading this text will be sued directly, it is likely that his or her organization will suffer the consequences of a variety of legal actions over time. Litigation in the training and development function is a reality.

The reader is encouraged to complete the brief liability Needs Assessment Survey of Training Liability at the end of the chapter. Areas of liability are associated with the chapters in this text. Since ignorance of the law is no excuse, we are better positioned to deal with the future by assessing our present strengths and limitations. A summary of federal laws that require or imply training will be found in Appendix B.

Chapter 2
Equal Employment Opportunity and Related Liability

Chapter Objectives

Having reviewed the information in this chapter, the reader will have

1. a practical knowledge of the Civil Rights Act of 1964 and 1991, and the Americans with Disabilities Act of 1990;
2. a practical understanding of the legal requirements and pitfalls associated with testing strategies used to select employees for training programs;
3. analyzed legal issues and problems associated with diversity training, including the potential for litigation;
4. a working knowledge of the special judicial requirements for using training as an affirmative defense by an employer in discrimination related litigation; and
5. reviewed recommendations for designing, implementing and evaluating harassment prevention training programs.

The following additional materials are located in Appendix C. Summary of Federal and State Requirements for Harassment Prevention Training.

INTRODUCTION

The passage of the Civil Rights Act of 1964 ushered a new era in how organizations would view the employer-employee relationships. The social policy underpinning this momentous legislation is steeped in making the employment playing field neutral for all applicants and employees. The Americans with Disabilities Act of 1990 was passed by Congress twenty-six years later. Not since the passage of the Fair Labor Standards Act in 1938 has federal and state legislation made such a significant impact on how business is conducted in the United States.

Included in this chapter is an extensive analysis of an employment law discrimination case. The $90 million judgment against a large convenience store chain for discrimination has direct implications for the practical side of designing training programs. This decision raises an important question regarding the retention of records that are subject to discovery. Should used flip charts and participant notes from previous diversity training programs be retained?

Title VII of the Civil Rights Act of 1964 (CRA 1964) prohibits employment discrimination based upon an individual's race, color, religion, sex, national origin. Any employer who employs 15 or more employees for 20 or more calendar weeks in the current or preceding calendar year is subjected to the provisions of Title VII. Provisions of this Act apply to all of the major functions and decision points in the management of human resources, including recruitment, selection, placement, orientation, supervision, training and development, and performance appraisal.

This Act is enforced by the Equal Employment Opportunity Commission (EEOC) which has the power to:

- advise employees on their rights and explain responsibilities to employers, employment agencies and unions,
- investigate complaints on behalf of employees and informally settle,
- dismiss a charge by issuing a right to sue letter, which allows the employee to file a suit in Federal District Court, or
- sue employers on behalf of employees who allege discrimination.

The Civil Rights Act of 1991 (CRA 1991) is a significant revision that clarified and extended the provisions of the CRA of 1964. The most important change allows for jury trials and punitive damages against employers. See table 2.1 for a summary of civil rights legislation.

According to Cascio & Aguinis (2005), discrimination is defined as "the giving of an unfair advantage (or disadvantage) to the members of a particular [protected class] group in comparison to the members of other groups" (pp. 18-19). A protected class includes applicants and employees who belong to certain groups, such as women and minorities. Two forms of discrimination are recognized by CRA 1964, Title VII:

Disparate Treatment. Disparate treatment is based on an intentional

Table 2.1

Summary of Civil Rights Legislation in the United States

Civil Rights Acts of 1866-1871

- A series of five acts established as part of Reconstruction after the Civil War. Section 1981 of the Civil Rights Act of 1866 forbids racial discrimination in employment relationships.
- Guarantees that all persons can make and enforce contracts and have equal protection under the laws (Civil Rights Act of 1866).
- Currently applied to governmental agencies, especially police and correctional programs since the mid-1980s (Civil Rights Act of 1871 §). 1983.

Civil Rights Act of 1964,
Title VII, and the U.S. Office of Contract Compliance

- Organizations that employ 15 or more employees more than 20 weeks a year fall under most of the provisions of the Civil Rights Act of 1964.
- Applies to private and public sector employers, state and local governments, and unions.
- Unlawful to discriminate in terms of "compensation, terms, conditions, or privileges of employment" and forbids employers to "limit, segregate, or classify employees" or deprive them of job opportunities or training due to of race, religion, color, sex, or national origin.
- EEOC has investigative and enforcement authority with respect to the Equal Pay Act of 1963, the Age Discrimination in Employment Act of 1967, Sections 501 and 505 of the Rehabilitation Act of 1973, Titles I and V of the Americans with Disabilities Act of 1990 and the Civil Rights Act of 1991.
- EEOC does not have jurisdiction over allegations of discrimination based on sexual orientation, status as a parent, marital status, or political affiliation; however, a state or municipality may pass legislation or ordinances that cover these forms of discrimination.
- Employees of the federal government are protected by the Civil Service Reform Act of 1978, the Merit Systems Protection Board, and several Presidential Executive Orders.
- Office of Federal Contract Compliance enforces Presidential Executive Order 11246 that requires affirmative action with any business or governmental agency receiving federal funds or contracts; powers include auditing affirmative action plans, compliance reviews, investigation of complaints, and instituting administrative and judicial proceedings.

Civil Rights Act of 1991

- Provides for jury trials in federal district court.
- Juries are allowed to award punitive and compensatory damages (with specific limitations).
- Extended CRA protections to employees of U.S. businesses in foreign countries unless Act conflicts with local laws.

- Prohibits separate cutoff scores or the readjustment of test scores for one group and not another group (race norming).
- Particularity requires that a specific employment practice be alleged as discriminatory.
- Motivating factors (e.g., female not promoted because of inadequate performance and also because her behavior does not fit stereotype of women).

act to discriminate by someone, including the intent to retaliate against someone who asserts his or her employment rights at work. This form of discrimination may be proven by direct evidence of bias (i.e., hatred directed at a person in a protected group), circumstantial evidence (i.e., relying on statistics to circumvent an employees legal rights), or evidence of mixed motives (using what appears to be a permissible argument as pretext for an illegal personnel action, such as promoting or condoning a hostile environment).

Adverse Impact. Adverse impact occurs when "any facially neutral trigger negatively affecting some more than others. For example, a street curb adversely impacts people in wheel chairs, a physical requirement adversely impacts females, and cognitive tests adversely impacts minorities" (Guttman, 2005, p. 20). Such neutral policies and business practices are unrelated to success on the job and unfairly and without intention impact a group of protected employees. The issue is not intent or motivation, but impact on groups of people. A height and strength requirement appears neutral or unintentional on its face, yet systematically discriminates based on race, ethnicity, and gender (Cascio and Aguinis, 2005).

Title VII of the Civil Rights Act of 1964 provides that when an employer "has intentionally engaged in . . . an unlawful employment practice . . . the court may enjoin the practice, and order such affirmative action as may be appropriate, which may include but is not limited to reinstatement or hiring of employees, with or without back pay . . . or any other equitable relief as the court deems appropriate." Amendments to the Civil Rights Act in 1991 provide that the charging party may recover punitive and compensatory damages for disparate treatment (intentional) discrimination, but not in instances of disparate impact (unintentional discrimination).

- *Compensatory damages.* Compensation for future losses, pain and suffering, inconvenience, mental anguish, injury to professional standing, character, and reputation.

- *Punitive damages.* Damages allowed against the employer who demonstrates malice or reckless indifference to the federally protected rights of employees. A successful argument by the employer that good faith efforts to adopt and communicate a policy of nondiscrimination coupled with education and training is an affirmative defense that may well reduce the likelihood of punitive damages.

Program designers and evaluators are well advised to become generally familiar with certain documents. The *Uniform Guidelines on Employee Selection Procedures*, (29 C.F.R. § 1607) have been interpreted by the U.S. Supreme Court as having a persuasive authority that guides the court in determining what constitutes the fairness of employment practices (*Griggs v. Duke Power*, 1971, and *Albemarle v. Moody*, 1975). A second document is the *Principles for the Validation and Use of Personnel Selection Procedure* (SIOP, 2003). A third document is the *Standards for Educational and Psychological Testing* (American Educational Research Association, 1999). All three of these documents inform the civil litigation system in the United States. Since judges and jurors are not trained in evaluation and measurement theory, they must rely heavily on professionally developed guidelines and expert testimony for their deliberations and findings (Landy, 2005).

The reader may be wondering at this point, what do guidelines for employee selection have to do with training and development? A general guideline to remember is that any significant personnel decision, including training, should conform to requirements for fairness and due process (Cascio & Aguinis, 2005; Ledvinka & Scarpello, 1991). More specifically, Title VII of the 1964 Civil Rights Act regulates testing of personnel, and the EEOC Guidelines define a test

> . . . as any paper-and-pencil of performance measure used as a basis for any employment decision. The guidelines in this part apply, for example, to ability tests which are designed to measure eligibility for hire, transfer, promotion, membership, training, referral, or retention. (29 CFR, 1607.2; emphasis added)

One may surmise that the following are within the purview of the above stated requirement:

- requirements for training prior to entry into a job,

- selecting employees to attend training and development, including their retention in a program,
- the use of measures in training as measures of performance, and
- making job assignments based upon performance in a training program.

A potential legal problem for trainers and their employer occurs whenever any measure used for a major employment decision is discriminatory, that is if it "adversely affects hiring, promotion, transfer or membership opportunity of classes protected by Title VII . . . unless the test has been validated and evidences a high degree of utility" (29 CFR, 1607.3). Such requirements for validity have been stringently applied in selection. In the landmark U.S. Supreme Court case of *Griggs v. Duke Power* (1971), it was held that an educational requirement of a high school degree was not job related, and, therefore, the effect of the educational requirement adversely impacted minorities.

If training and development programs are to be held to the rationale of the Griggs case, it would be necessary to demonstrate a relationship between training and actual job performance as defined by relevant criterion measures. *The Uniform Guidelines* requires that:

> Where a measure of success in a training program is used as a selection procedure and the content of a training program is justified on the basis of content validity, the use should be justified on the relationship between the content of the training program and the content of the job. (29 CFR, 1701.14)

According to Bartlett (1978, p. 181) "Unless training could be demonstrated empirically to make a difference in job performance, training requirements if showing adverse impact can be ruled discriminatory. Thus, training measures would be required to have a demonstrated relationship to later job performance before they could be used for any employment decisions."

The designers of training programs may have an occasion to use training as a criterion to validate their selection of trainees. The question to be addressed is to what extent should preemployment tests for entrance to training programs be based upon successful completion of the program, or should some other criterion, such as job performance, be required by test developers.

Case Examples: Using Tests to Select Employees for Training

This section reviews two court cases involving testing applicants for promotion to higher level positions. In the first example, a carpet manufacturing company developed a training program for employees that were a prerequisite for promotion into a higher salaried job of senior mechanic. A promotion to senior mechanic is highly valued because of the additional pay and benefits. Employees who have been with the company as entry level mechanics for at least three years are eligible to apply for admission into the program. Applicants must pass two tests before they are admitted to the senior mechanic training program—a mathematics test and a verbal fluency test. Cutoff scores had been determined and used for some time. The reasoning for the testing is that understanding classroom instruction requires verbal fluency and math skills.

Several Hispanic males with over five years as mechanics with the company expressed a desire to attend the senior mechanics training program. They failed to meet the required cutoff score on the two tests. They alleged that the verbal fluency and math examinations are not related to performing the actual job of senior mechanic. The course manager argues that a certain level of proficiency in verbal skills and math is required for successful completion of the course.

This situation poses an interesting dilemma. The course manager is correct when he says that proficiency is necessary for predicting successful completion of the course. Those who score high on the proficiency tests are more likely to successfully complete the course, and those who score lower on the tests, in fact, do not successfully complete the course.

An evaluation of the relationship between end-of-course performances with actual job performance demonstrates no or low correlation between these two important factors for the Hispanic employees. If successful completion of the course is not related to actual job performance, then the use of the two proficiency tests would be an example of adverse impact (*Stallworth v. Monsanto Co.*, 1974).

The second case example involving an apprenticeship training program demonstrates the power of court enforced remedies. In two class action suits brought by attorneys and the EEOC for 13 Ford employees, allegations were made that the auto manufacturer demonstrated disparate impact in the use of the Apprenticeship Training Selection System (ATSS). These suits allege that, since 1997, Ford discriminated against African Americans on the basis of race in selecting apprentices. Also included in the suit as defendants along with Ford are the United Automobile, Aerospace, and Agricultural Implement Workers of America. The two cases were consolidated and heard by a federal district court judge in Ohio.

The settlement agreement requires that Ford, without admitting to any wrongdoing, must immediately cease using the ATSS system for applicant selection for the apprenticeship program. Parties to the settlement must select a board-certified industrial psychologist to conduct a complete task analysis and develop a selection system for the apprenticeship program. The defendants, Ford Motor Company and the union, will pay for this service. Ford will select 276 members of the settlement class as well as three of the plaintiffs for inclusion in the revised apprenticeship eligibility list. Each of the members of the settlement class will receive $2,400 and each of the 13 charging parties received $30,000. The total amount of the recovery to the class of employees is approximated at $8.55 million, which does not include $1.5 million for attorneys and settlement monitoring (*EEOC v. Ford Motor Company, Inc.* 2005).

Case Example: Training and Constructive Supervisory Feedback

According to the revised EEOC Compliance Manual, training includes both formal training and informal training through feedback from supervisors (EEOC, 2006; Carroll & Miller, 2006). The following case illustrates the importance of supervisory feedback as part of the training process.

Roberta, a brown-skinned woman of Cuban descent, was a new filing clerk for an insurance business. Her primary duties were to sort and file medical insurance forms for payment. It was clear within a month's time that Roberta was processing her paperwork too slowly due to her mistakes. The business terminated her, and she then filed an allegation of race discrimination. The investigation determined that although white employees who perform at a substandard level are coached with feedback, and therefore do not repeat mistakes and make feweer new ones when given supervisory coaching. Roberta and other employees of color received less feedback and understandably would repeat mistakes and take longer to reach a satisfactory level of performance. The evidence in this case is consistent with *Vaughn v. Edel* (1990) which was sufficient to establish a discriminatory work environment.

THE AMERICANS WITH DISABILITIES ACT (ADA)

The most recent federal legislation to significantly impact employers is the Americans with Disabilities Act (ADA) of 1990. This act prohibits discrimination against persons with disabilities in employment, public services, transportation, public accommodations, and telecommunications services. The ADA became effective July 26, 1992 for employers with 25 or more employees. Employers with 15 or more workers must comply beginning July 26, 1994. All aspects of employment are covered, including the application process and hiring, on-the-job-training, advancement in wages, benefits, and employer-sponsored social activities. In essence, the ADA protects qualified disabled persons from job discrimination (Papinchock, 2005). To be considered a qualified disabled person, a job applicant or employee must be able to perform the essential functions of the job. Employers must accommodate the employees known mental or physical disabilities unless that would impose an "undue hardship."

A qualified individual with a disability is a person who has a physical or mental impairment substantially limiting a major life activity, has a record of such impairment or is regarded as having an impairment. A disability can include a physiological disorder or condition, cosmetic disfigurement, anatomical loss, emotional disorder or condition, or medical obesity (Papinchock, 2005).

It is important to note that the ADA does not guarantee an individual with a disability the right to the job for which he or she is applying. The employer remains free to make decisions based on the particular skills or knowledge necessary for the job. The decision made by the employer regarding who to hire must be based on reasons unrelated to the existence of a covered disability. Nor is the employer required to give preference to an applicant with a disability over another applicant without a disability.

The first step an employer should take is to determine the essential functions of a job. Human resource development specialists may be required to perform a job analysis that would meet ADA requirements for "essential functions" analysis. Second, employers must provide disabled employees with reasonable accommodations necessary to perform the essential functions of the job. Examples of accommodations include modifying work schedules, reassigning job duties, removing architectural barriers, and offering auxiliary aids, interpreters or taped text. According to one source, nearly 60 percent of employers surveyed spent less than $100 for each instance of an accommodation, and another 25 percent resulted in spending from $100 to $500 for each accommodation (Reid, 1992).

There are several implications for training and development in organizations covered by the Americans with Disabilities Act:

- *Interviewer Training.* Many interviewers and recruiters will require "disability etiquette" training in order to feel comfortable interviewing applicants with disabilities. Illegal questions, such as, "Do you have any medical condition that would preclude you from performing your job?" or "Have you ever had workers compensation?" are prohibited. Instead, ask "Are you able to perform all of the essential functions listed in the job description?"
- *Recruiting and selecting disabled trainers.* Although affirmative action is not required by the ADA, managers of training programs and centers are encouraged to address the recruitment and selection of disabled trainers. This is important from a role-modeling perspective (Navran, 1992).
- *Supervisory Training.* Several aspects of the supervisor's job should be updated with training:

    1. Current employees returning to work from disability leave may require a reasonable accommodation. Special issues arise where the return to work involves workers' compensation.
    2. Watch words used to describe employee behavior. Statements such as "crazy in the head," and "nut case" and other expressions describing peculiar behavior may imply the legal status of "regarded as disabled" which is actionable under the ADA (McDonald, 2004). Be careful when taking notes during a selection interview. Instruct supervisors to only use job-related terminology. Avoid behavioral descriptors such as "she seems a bit batty" or "a little loopy, but otherwise qualified."
    3. Fear of managing the qualified disabled worker must be ad-

dressed in supervisory training. All employees, including disabled ones, are expected to perform the essential job functions to standard. Reasonable accommodation does not mean special (unfair) consideration at performance appraisal or for promotional opportunities.

4. Supervisors should understand the implications of alcohol and drug use on job performance. The Act specifically provides that an individual currently using illegal drugs is not a "qualified individual with a disability." The ADA does protect alcoholics and past drug users who have successfully completed treatment, or who are in a legitimate treatment program, such as an Employee Assistance Program. Employers may hold legal drug users and alcoholics to the same performance standards as other employees, even if poor performance or other unsatisfactory behavior is due to drug or alcohol use.
5. Prepare to make reasonable accommodations for the disabled learner. Many accommodations are relatively inexpensive. Examples include magnifying glasses to aid reading, taped text for those who are visually impaired and instructional materials with large lettering. Training seminars, offsite conferences and meetings must also be accessible.

THE COMPELLING ARGUMENT FOR MANDATORY HARASSMENT PREVENTION TRAINING

Title VII of the Civil Rights Act of 1964 has always included prevention along with investigation, enforcement and compliance as a responsibility of the Equal Employment Opportunity Commission. Over time, the notion of prevention has become equated with education and training. In 1980, EEOC promulgated *Guidelines on Discrimination Because of Sex* (EEOC, 1980). Harassment prevention is accorded the status of "the best tool for the elimination of sexual harassment" including "developing methods to sensitize all concerned."

Three landmark U.S. Supreme Court decisions have clarified the importance of establishing and communicating policies, training all employees—including managers and supervisors—and providing discipline when necessary.

Faragher v. City of Boca Raton (1998). After resigning as a lifeguard,

Beth Ann Faragher brought an action against the City of Boca Raton and her immediate supervisors, alleging that the supervisors had created a sexually hostile atmosphere by touching and sexually explicit language. Faragher asserted that this conduct constituted discrimination in violation of Title VII of the Civil Rights Act of 1964. The District Court concluded that Faragher's supervisors' conduct was sufficiently serious to alter the conditions of her employment and constitute an abusive working environment. The court then held that the city could be held liable.

In a 7-2 opinion delivered by Justice David H. Souter, the Court held that an employer is *vicariously liable* under the CRA for actionable discrimination caused by a supervisor. The Court also held that such liability is subject to an *affirmative defense* looking to the reasonableness of the employer's conduct as well as that of the plaintiff (victim). The City had entirely "failed to disseminate its policy against sexual harassment among the beach employees and that its officials made no attempt to keep track of the conduct of supervisors like [Faragher's]." Justice Souter, stated that "under such circumstances, we hold as a matter of law that the City could not be found to have exercised reasonable care to prevent the supervisors' harassing conduct".

*Burlington Industries, Inc. v. Ellerth (*1998). After working for Burlington Industries for 15 months, Kimberly B. Ellerth quit because she allegedly suffered sexual harassment by her supervisor. Despite her refusals of the supervisor's advances Ellerth did not suffer any tangible retaliation and was, in fact, promoted once. Moreover, while she remained silent about her supervisor's conduct despite her knowledge of Burlington's policy against sexual harassment, Ellerth challenged Burlington, claiming that the company forced her *constructive discharge.*

In a 7-2 opinion, the Court held that employers are vicariously liable for supervisors who create hostile working conditions for those over whom they have authority. In cases where a harassed employee suffers no job-related consequences, employers may raise an *affirmative defense* by proving two elements: "(1) that [the employer] took reasonable care to promptly prevent or correct any sexually harassing behavior, and (2) that the employee unreasonably failed to take advantage of corrective or preventative opportunities or otherwise failed to avoid harm" (Gutek and Stockdale, 2005, p. 236).

Kolstad v. American Dental Association (1999). Carole Kolstad sued the American Dental Association for gender discrimination, under Title II of the 1964 Civil Rights Act, when it promoted a man instead of her. At trial, the district court denied Kolstad's request for punitive damages based on a showing that the ADA acted with "malice" and "reckless indifference" to her federally protected rights. When the court of appeals affirmed this decision, Kolstad appealed and the Supreme Court granted her *certiorari*. The question for the U.S. Supreme Court to decide is whether the employer's conduct has to be "egregious" or "outrageous," independent of its state of mind, in order to sustain an award of punitive damages under Title VII of the 1964 Civil Rights Act?

In a complicated split opinion, the Court held that if an employee can show his or her employer knowingly acted in violation of federal law, then *punitive damages* may be sustained. The Court explained that the "malice" or "reckless indifference" standard applied to the relationship between employers and federal law, and is not a characterization of the severity threshold that the discrimination itself must meet. In other words, if employers maliciously or recklessly violate a federal antidiscrimination law, regardless of the severity of their discriminatory acts, then *punitive damages* may be imposed. The Court remanded Kolstad's case for renewed consideration of her employer's state of mind during the alleged violations (*Kolstad v. American Dental Association,* 1999).

After the Supreme Court handed down its landmark decisions in 1998 and 1999 in the *Farahger, Ellerth*, and *Kolstad* cases, the EEOC published new guidelines that explicitly informed employers of the necessity of harassment prevention training. According to the EEOC guidelines, if feasible, every employer

> should provide training to all employees to ensure they understand their rights and responsibilities [relating to workplace harassment] An employer should ensure that its supervisors and managers understand their responsibilities under the organization's anti-harassment policy and complaint procedures. Periodic training can help achieve that result. (EEOC, 1999)

The continuing importance of clearly stated and communicated antidiscrimination policies and procedures was affirmed by the Supreme Court in *Pennsylvania State Police v. Suder* (2004). Suder alleged *constructive discharge* after being sexually harassed by male supervisors. She informed the agency's EEO officer that she was being harassed and failed to file a complaint prior to her resignation. The Supreme Court clarified the nature of constructive discharge and reiterated the importance of effective procedures for reporting allegations of harassment and the importance of ensuring that supervisors are abiding by policies that prohibit harassment.

Two states, California and Connecticut, have statutes that require mandatory harassment prevention training. The New Jersey Supreme Court has established a "bright-line rule" that requires harassment prevention training for managers and supervisors (*Gaines v. Belino*, 2002; DeMaria & Gardiner, 2002). Others states have strongly recommend harassment prevention training. The NO FEAR Act required that all employees of the federal government receive harassment prevention training by September 30, 2005, that all new employees receive similar training within 60 days of employment, and thereafter receive harassment prevention training every two years (Johnson, 2005). Appendix C provides a summary of federal and state requirements for harassment prevention training.

Costs Estimates for Litigating Harassment and Discrimination Claims

A recent survey by Cannon, Kruse, Owen, Simkin, and Wood (2006) determined that employment law litigation in the United States increased from 26 percent in 2005 to 48 percent in 2006. This increase is of significant concern to businesses, shareholders, and consumers. According to this survey, "The average litigation expenditure for United States companies surveyed has increased by 50 percent from last year to $12 million—a figure that does not include ultimate case settlement or judgment payments" (p. 13).

The financial impact on business is significant. Judgments for damages during 2005 were $380 million, down slightly from the previous year. Table 2.2 shows the statistics for 2005 and identifies the type of harassment litigation and the amount awarded to complainants. One study found that large corporations average $6.7 million per year dealing with harassment claims in addition to the costs of litigation (Hicks, 2001).

Based on an empirical analysis of the impact of employment discrimination litigation, Donohue and Seligman (1993) predicted that provisions of the Civil Rights Act of 1991 will

- cause a 17 to 25 percent increase in the average size of damage awards,
- result in an increase in the volume of cases by 9 to 12 percent,
- result in roughly "10,000 more complaints filed with the EEOC

Table 2.2
Equal Employment Opportunity Commission Charge and Awards Statistics for 2005.

Type Complaint	No. of Complaints	Judgments
Gender	23,094	$91.3 million
Age	16,585	$77 million
Sex harassment	12,697	$47.89 million
Disability	14,893	$44.8 million
National origin	8,035	$19.4 million
Religion	2,340	$6.1 million
Retaliation	22,740	$90 million

Source: U.S. Equal Employment Opportunity Commission Charge Statistics, FY 1992 through 2005 (www.eeoc.gov.ststs/charges.html)

and 800 to 1000 more case filed in federal district court each year" (p. 765).

The average cost of a jury verdict or settlement in a civil rights case ranges from $153,000 (Zink and Gutman, 2005) to $250,000 (Employment Law Learning Technologies (2002), depending on the quoted source. These figures do not cover attorneys' fees and business costs associated with investigating such claims. Table 2.3 summarizes hard and soft costs associated with these types of cases.

Several large businesses have suffered extreme monetary judgments in past years (not to mention international bad press) for discrimination related cases. These include such large organizations as Mitsubishi ($34 million), Texaco ($176 million), Coca-Cola ($192.5 million) and U.S. Information Agency, Voice of America ($508 million). Note that the availability of jury trials, class action suits and punitive damages increases the likelihood of extreme financial penalties.

Forward thinking businesses may consider the purchase of Employment Practices Liability (EPL) insurance which typically provides coverage for employment litigation in the following areas:

- wrongful employment practices (negligent hiring, retention, supervision; wrongful termination),
- sexual harassment, and
- discrimination.

Table 2.3
Estimate for Defending One Harassment/Discrimination Claim

Hard Costs (average)	
• Fees for attorney if the case goes to trial	$150,000 to $250,000
• Fees for attorney if case is settled prior to trial	$95,000 to 120,000
• Estimate of settlement costs or jury awards	$150,000 to $250,000
• Number of hours expended by manager	30 to 40 hours
• Number of hours expended by employee	30 to 40 hours
• Number of hours spent by employee investigating claim	40 to 60 hours
• Number of hours spent by employee trial preparation	40 to 60 hours

Soft Costs
- Impact on the work group in terms of distraction and reduced morale.
- Impact on the cost of insurance if company is covered and experiences losses.
- Impact on stock price and reputation if there is publicity around the claim.
- Potential of copycat lawsuits or other claims due to internal and external publicity.
- Impact on attracting the best employees given potential negative publicity of a claim.

These "specialty lines" insurance policies cover the cost of defending against employment-related claims and pay for settlements and judgments for damages, although coverage varies across insurers (Hightower, 2004). According to Johnson (2004), insurance carriers are predisposed to provide discounts on premiums for businesses that provide harassment prevention training. Given the significant increase in claims against businesses for these types of cases, EPL insurance costs increased by 50 percent in 2002 with even higher increases predicted in the future (Abelson, 2002). Only directors, officers, and senior management, including the top ranking HR manager, should know that EPL insurance has been purchased by a business. To broadcast this information to employees, and eventually to plaintiffs' attorneys, is to open a Pandora's Box of potential litigation (Sunoo, 1998).

Return on Investment for Harassment Prevention Training

Training focused on reducing claims and litigation associated with harassment-related incidents has demonstrated a clear return on investment (ROI) to the business. Chapman (2003) argued the point forcefully by comparing the benefits, detriments, and costs associated with proactive training and reactive approaches to resolving harassment-related litigation. She compares costs between two examples: company A with 500 employees using costs associated with taking a claim to trial, and company B with 20,000 employees using costs to settle a claim prior to trial. Costs are estimated based current jury verdict and settlement amounts.

Harassment prevention training places the employer in a position to argue a "good faith" attempt to protect its employees from discrimination and harassment, to reduce the potential for extended defense costs, and to avoid punitive damages. Chapman (2003) also states that there are "other priceless benefits associated with creating a respectful environment, including greater productivity, better understanding of and adherence to company policies, less risk of future complaints, improved morals and reduced EPLI premiums" (p. 36).

Effective training has the potential of negating or reducing the initiation of claims, as well as providing good faith effort that may result in the avoidance of punitive damages. The following examples demonstrate several ways to formulate a return on investment argument.

A nationally known law firm specializing in harassment prevention training was retained by a large organization that was averaging 110 employment-related claims annually between 1995 and 1998. Since instituting a prevention training program in 1998, the organization has experienced a 42 percent reduction in the number of claims per year, down from an average of 110 claims per year to 64. An independent study not commissioned by the law firm confirmed that, excluding settlement and award costs, the organization had a hard cost saving of $2.2 million dollars per year (Employment Law Learning Technologies, 2002). In a return on investment case study published by Hill and Phillips (1997), the client healthcare company found that sexual harassment prevention training resulted in a reduction of internal complaints by 36 percent and the number of claims litigated dropped by 41 percent. Expenses attributed to legal fees and settlement expenses fell by 49 percent, saving the company over $800,000 in one year. Additional benefits included a reduction in turnovers attributed to harassment from 11 percent to 3 percent in the year of implementing the prevention training.

The return on investment argument for harassment prevention training is a powerful one that makes good business sense for the employer, employees, and shareholders (Sample, 2007c). Recent Supreme Court cases, *Farragher, Burlington* and *Kolstad*, and Title VII mandates for training, set the stage for an employer arguing a good faith effort, which is key for an affirmative defense.

But, Is the Training Really Effective?

Managing cultural diversity in our organizations involves more than just reducing or preventing the likelihood of litigation for employers. Sanchez & Medkik (2004) also included as primary objectives: (1) to capitalize on the nation's diverse workforce, (2) to remedy the effects of past discrimination, and (2) and to reduce interpersonal conflict and stress. Bisom-Rapp (2001) stated that sexual harassment training typically addresses (1) increasing knowledge about harassment, (2) eliminating inappropriate behavior, and (3) changing the attitudes of potential harassers. The extent to which these objectives are being met is clouded with controversy. According to Forbes magazine, U.S. corporations in 1997 with over 100 employees implemented diversity related training programs at a an estimated cost of $10 billion (Lubove, 1997). During this same time period claims and litigation based on discrimination has dramatically increased overall (Roberson, Kulik, & Pepper, 2003).

Diversity training initiatives continue to receive mixed and controversial reviews resulting in confusion for human resource management, training, and development professionals (Grace, 1994; Hemphill & Haines, 1997; Hite & McDonald, 2006; Sanchez & Medkik, 2004; Von Bergen, Soper & Foster, 2002). Bisom-Rapp (2001) raised a very provocative question regarding judicially condoned diversity training and its intended purpose. Her argument stems from an observed incremental movement by the appellate courts to position training as an affirmative defense on behalf of a business. If the business establishes a proactive policy, implements training and communicates and trains to the policy and disciplines as necessary, then the organization will reduce or prevent potential liability. The final linchpin in her argument is that diversity training initiatives have not been shown empirically to have long term effects in reducing discrimination in the workplace (see also Sanchez & Medik, 2004 and Hayles & Russell, 1997).

Several studies conclude that training focusing on sexual harassment sensitizes participants to instances of sexual harassment (Blakely,

Blakely & Moorman, 1998; Moyer & Nath, 1998). Limited evidence of effectiveness was reported by Rynes & Rosen (1995). They concluded that only 33 percent stated that their efforts were either "quite (30 percent) or extremely (3 percent) successful" whereas a full 50 percent reported "neutral or mixed" outcomes, while a significant proportion described their results as either "largely (13 percent) or extremely (5 percent) unsuccessful." Carrell, Mann, & Sigler (2006) conducted a longitudinal study to determine the effects of diversity programs and practices in organizations. Differences from 1992 to 2004 showed "desirable change in the effects of workforce diversity for ten of the twelve effects" (p. 11).

Hemphill and Hines (1997) in their book, *Discrimination, Harassment, and the Failure of Diversity Training*, argued that these types of programs have failed due to several factors. These conclusions are drawn from interviews with over 600 organization executives, managers, directors, and consultants who specialize in diversity related issues. Note their conclusions:

- Participants found many training programs divisive, disturbing, and counter-productive;
- Diversity trainers were often inexperienced and/or ineffective;
- Minority groups had expectations raised and were then disappointed;
- White males were stereotyped and blamed;
- There was reverse discrimination and reverse stereotyping;
- A nationwide backlash occurred against diversity training programs;
- Sensitive and personal issues were brought out in hostile public settings;
- Employees experienced unnecessary anxiety and emotional upheaval; increased distrust was engendered;
- Many workers were resistant to attending further diversity training programs; and
- Little or no transfer of learning took place about differences to changing discriminatory and harassing behaviors.

Poorly designed diversity training programs have the potential to demoralize participants and to reinforce stereotypes (Von Bergen, Soper, & Foster, 2002; Wildermuth & Gray, 2005). Several such incidents have made headlines in the national media.

- A male air traffic controller employed by the Federal Aviation Administration was required to attend a three-day cultural diversity workshop. One of the exercises for the workshop used a role reversal technique designed to simulate the work area in the Chicago Control Center. Two rows of chairs were arranged so that the men would walk between the chairs while female participants adopted the role of harassers. Men "walking the gauntlet" were subjected to cat calls, butt slapping, and other uninvited touching. According to Judge Norgle, "Following the gauntlet, the directors conducted a discussion at which time Hartman [the complainant] and the other men were numerically rated with their names on a chart subscribed to drawings of male genitalia. The chart illustrated human penises in various states of arousal. The participants rated Hartman the lowest" (*Hartman v. Penna*, 1995). Testimony of record indicated that the men were embarrassed and uncomfortable participating in the exercise. Hartman at first declined to participate, but finally acquiesced because of group pressure.
- A bloody shooting spree at a Lockheed Martin in July 2003 left four dead (all black) and eight seriously wounded (majority white). The assailant, a white employee at the plant, left a diversity training program, only to return with a shotgun and a semiautomatic rifle; after the rampage, this employee took his own life. He was known by his employer to have hatred for minorities, especially blacks, and he was required to attend an anger management class, as well as the diversity training program. Lockheed Martin is being sued by survivors of the incident for civil rights claims (Anonymous, 2003).
- Employees of R. R. Donnelley & Sons Co. were forced to sit through multiple showings of a movie portraying lynching in the Old South. This diversity training program was intended to confront alleged racism by white employees at Donnelley. These employees were also forced to complete a questionnaire that asked for responses to statements such as "It is a fairly well-established fact that blacks have a less pleasant body odor than white people" and "One of the main characteristics of Puerto Ricans in the U.S. is their sexual looseness and immorality" (Lebove, 1997).
- A telecommunications company was providing train-the-trainer experiences for the purpose of selecting diversity trainers. Can-

> didates were asked to share an experience that led to their involvement in diversity training. One white woman shared a story about a long-term relationship that she had been having with a black man. They had planned to marry, but she said several of his black female friends put pressure on him not to marry a white woman. The relationship ended. Someone in the group asked the woman if she was angry with black women. She said no, only those who couldn't seem to accept the idea of interracial marriage. When the white woman finished talking, she looked up at one of the leaders of the train-the-trainer program—a black female—who took offense and began belittling the woman by saying, "You white bitches are always taking up air time, and I'm sick of it." The white woman was not selected as a diversity trainer. She claimed she saw hate and anger in the black trainer's eyes. She was awarded damages as a result of her experience with the experiential training (*Fitzgerald v. Mountain States Tel. & Tel. Co.*, 1995).

Employers are left with a dilemma: should the employer train for the sake of establishing a safe harbor that shields the business from litigation, or should the business invoke training and development as a means to make real differences in the way diverse populations work together? The following case study may be helpful in answering that question.

CASE STUDY: DISCOVERY, FLIP CHARTS AND A $90 MILLION JUDGMENT

A settlement of a massive sex discrimination class action suit against Lucky Stores in California for more than $90 million clearly demonstrates the importance of strategic cooperation between training programs and human resource management. The settlement was based upon a 1992 decision rendered in the U.S. District Court for the Northern District of California (*Stender v. Lucky Stores Inc.*, 1992).

Case Facts

In August of 1988, the plaintiffs, Nancy Stender and five other women, filed a complaint on behalf of themselves and of a class of female, black and Hispanic past, present and future employees of Lucky Stores. They alleged discrimination based upon sex, race and national origin. The lawsuit was brought under Title VII of the 1964 Civil Rights Act and the California Fair Employment and Housing Act. The suit was heard by a judge in a bench trial without a jury.

The *Lucky Stores* lawsuit is best described as a three-stage process. The first stage consisted of extensive pretrial discovery and more than 10 weeks of fact and expert testimony during the trial. The second stage was a series of hearings regarding the liability for back pay and the consideration of alternative methods for calculating such damages. The third stage consisted of arguments and negotiations by opposing counsel and the agreement to a settlement approved by the federal district court.

The key finding by the court was that Lucky Stores decisions on hiring, initial placement, training and promotion were not based on objective standards, and that training and promotion were based on nonexistent criteria, and were left to the sole discretion of individual store managers. The following circumstances are also noteworthy:

- The store managers and assistant store managers were not instructed about standards applicable to hiring or for making promotional decisions. There was no documentation of decisions about who to hire, train or promote, or about why certain people were selected and not others.
- There was no documentation showing which employees received training or requested additional hours of training.
- There were no job descriptions to provide guidance in evaluating whom to hire, promote and train.
- Management consistently failed to follow its own established posting policies.

The federal district court found that the absence of personnel policies requiring decision makers to collect accurate information about applicants and employees, apply written selection criteria, and be accountable for their decisions, increases the likelihood that gender stereotypes will influence their decision. The court also found a lack of clear and objective guidelines on placement, promotion, and training elevated the potential for abuse by discrimination to a level sufficient to deduce the intent necessary for a finding of direct and intentional discrimination, i.e., *disparate treatment.*

Further intent of disparate treatment was concluded from two previous class action settlements by Lucky Stores for sex discrimination in the early 1980s. An *affirmative action* policy established in 1983 required the human resources manager to make recommendations for the lawful recruitment and selection of employees, the preparation of formal job descriptions, and the need for more equal representation of women in departments that offered employees better opportunities for advancement. Information from the corporate office determined an awareness of the low percentage of women in management, and that based upon the *affirmative action* policy, the company needed to re-emphasize the importance of compliance.

In addition to evidence of discriminatory intent, the plaintiffs' attorneys established, through expert testimony, statistical evidence sufficient to establish an inference of intentional discrimination. Expert testimony established gross statistical disparities in the initial placement of men and women, and statistically significant shortfalls in the promotion of women, the movement of women from part-time to full-time positions and the allocation of additional hours to women.

The plaintiffs also established *disparate impact* which is different from *disparate treatment.* In disparate impact, proof of intent is not required because personnel practices may be neutral or appear fair on their face, but are discriminatory in practice. In *Lucky Stores*, the District Court cited court precedent that leaving decision-making power to the sole discretion of lower level supervisors whose conscious and unconscious prejudices are unchecked by objective, published criteria can satisfy the causal requirement of a disparate impact claim. The plaintiffs established conclusively that management at Lucky Stores did not consistently follow the policies.

One of the most important facets of this case involves punitive damages. The district court ruled that the plaintiffs had sufficiently established their claim for *punitive damages*, as provided for in the Civil Rights Act of 1991. The court based its conclusion on *Lucky Stores*' prior knowledge of the significant problems with the under-representation of women in managerial positions and its repeated failure to implement appropriate recommendations. The court also relied on evidence of the discriminatory attitudes of some of the store managers and the company's abandonment of two affirmative action programs, despite continued evidence of gross gender imbalance. This finding of reckless indifference by the court allowed the plaintiffs to pursue *punitive damages* pursuant to the Civil Rights Act of 1991.

Instructional Materials as Evidence

During the trial, evidence was submitted that included instructional materials from an in-house diversity training program for all store managers. One of the exercises required the managers to list various stereotypes that they had heard about women and minorities in the workplace. As is typical in the pretrial discovery process, participant notes, instructional materials, including flip charts, were made available to attorneys representing the plaintiffs. Lucky Stores strongly objected to providing these documents to the plaintiff. Included in these materials were notes and flip charts that explicitly illustrated the flagrant stereotypical comments.

Attorneys representing Lucky Stores claimed that these materials were privileged as part of the work product developed under the scope of services provided by Lucky Store attorneys. The court disagreed holding that attorney-client privilege did not apply as the meetings were held "not for the purpose of 'facilitating the provision of professional services to a client,' but rather for training managers" (Eyers, 1998, p. 113). Eyers (1998) commented further that

> The court relied on the notes as evidence that Lucky's managers harbored discriminatory attitudes toward women. The judge found that the comments were not just portrayals of social stereotypes, but reflections of what many Lucky managers firmly believed. Thus the court concluded that the notes constituted evidence of discriminatory attitudes and stereotyping of women by Lucky's managers. (p.113)

The financial settlement was the third stage of the *Lucky Stores* lawsuit. The settlement agreement, which was approved in January 1994, provided monetary relief and attorneys' fees to the plaintiffs and to the class, and establishes detailed guidelines and procedures to correct prior violations of the antidiscrimination laws and to ensure equal employment opportunities for women in the future.

A summary of the settlement is outlined below:

- Payment of $1,205,000 damages to each individual plaintiff.
- The establishment of three separate funds totaling $59,145,000 for allocation among three separately defined groups of class members by Lucky Stores.

- The establishment of a $20,000,000 pool to implement the terms for injunctive relief that included new personnel policies and procedures, training, and affirmative action goals.
- Assessment of $13,750,000 in attorneys' fees and litigation costs against Lucky Stores.
- Lucky Stores will contribute up to an additional $13,000,000 if specific goals and targets for hiring and promotion are not met.

Implications for Instructional Designers and HRD Specialists

The critical lessons to be learned from *Lucky Stores* experience is that senior management in all organizational contexts must be accountable for compliance with the antidiscrimination laws and that this responsibility involves a series of distinct responsibilities and obligations. The special case for training supervisors and managers in EEO and other regulatory requirements must not be ignored (Sample, 1995a).

Given the context of the *Lucky Stores* lawsuit, the following obligations of management are minimally required:

- Formulating and disseminating clear, concrete and comprehensive personnel policies and procedures.
- Ensuring through appropriate training and education that business owners, senior managers, supervisors, and employees understand their responsibilities with respect to EEO laws.
- Monitoring these personnel policies and procedures to guarantee that they are being consistently and properly followed.
- Establish policies regarding the development and retention of flip charts, notes, and any other documentation of participants' comments.

The problems of Lucky Stores appeared to derive precisely from the failure by management to articulate and circulate distinct standards and guidelines, and from the freedom of local store managers and assistant managers to make discretionary and subjective decisions, often with disastrous consequences. Consequences not only include negative publicity in the media, but also loss of customers and market share. One of the worst consequences could be court ordered supervision and monitoring of the human resource management function.

In the *Lucky Stores* context, there were indications of potentially deep-seated employment problems. It is insufficient for a company to deal with personnel issues on a superficial basis. Grievances and complaints may appear to be dealt with, and yet the infrastructure of the human resource system may in fact be symptomatic of broader improprieties. Senior management, corporate counsel, human resource managers, risk management specialists, and trainers must continue to forge strong internal strategic partnerships as a preventative tool against the threat of employee litigation (Sample, 1995a).

RECOMMENDATION FOR DEVELOPING HARASSMENT PREVENTION TRAINING

This section consists of eight recommendations specific to harassment prevention training. Note that the requirements from relevant court decisions—especially *Faragher*, *Ellereth*, and *Kolstad*—are fundamental to the recommendations (Sample, 2007c).

1. Harassment prevention begins with selection and promotion. Effective employee selection remains the most cost-effective solution for ensuring competence and reducing the likelihood of long-term conduct and discipline problems. Effective selection also reduces long-term training and development costs associated with core job skills and attitudes. Note the "implied" requirement for training managers and others to comply with EEOC, ADA and other employment law statutes related to recruitment, selection, and placement.

Human resource specialists charged with the responsibility of hiring employees, or approving the hiring practices by managers should be aware of three legal landmines—negligent hiring, negligent retention, and negligent referral (Risser, 1993, Soverign, 1999).

- Under a legal theory of *negligent hiring*, an employer may be-liable where an employee or other third party is harmed by another employee. The cause of action arises when the employer knew or should have known through reasonable investigation prior to hiring that the applicant was unsuitable. Examples include former employees who were violent at work, evidenced harassing behaviors and attitudes, stalked or demonstrated signs of hatred toward members protected by state or federal law. Hiring an employee who later harms or harasses a third party puts the employer at risk for negligent hiring if the harm was foreseeable. Promoting a suspected or known harasser to higher level positions of authority as a way of avoiding a confrontation or discipline is contrary to Title VII of the Civil Rights Act. Such personnel actions undermine a commitment and culture that abhors such illegal behavior, and sends the wrong message to employees and other third parties. At the least, this would be an example of *negligent hiring*, and other theories of negligence, such as *negligent retention*, may apply as well.

- An employer who knows, or should have known of an employee's errant performance, and who continues to retain the employee, who later injures or harasses someone, is open toa cause of action known as negligent retention. Maintaining the employment of someone who continues to harass employees or other third parties, such as customers and vendors is an example of *negligent retention.*
- Former employers are often concerned that providing a negative job reference may result in litigation against the business alleging defamation. However, the current employer prospecting for new employees has a desperate need for job related information that will minimize the risk of a negligent hiring. Employers who are seeking job-related information on applicants are advised to be more assertive in ferreting out those who are violent, who harass third parties, or who have serious safety and job-related driving records.
- Previous employers who lie and otherwise conceal such information, presuming the hiring employer will be diligent in search of job-related information, may be setting up a cause for their company's liability. If the newly hired employee harasses or injures another employee, then the hiring employer may have a cause of action against the referring employer under a theory of *negligent referral.* Certain organizations, such as Homeland Security and business security, social services, law enforcement and corrections, medical and allied health professions may have higher duties to investigate applicants. Several states, such as Florida (FS 768.095) and Oregon (ORS 30.178) provide limited immunity against allegations of defamation for the inquiring employer as long as questions are job related and the information is used in good faith and without malice.

2. Harassment prevention training should be predicated upon a credible and disseminated nonharassment policy. Given the *Farragher* and

Ellerth decisions, Jenero & Galligano (2003) strongly advocate that every "employer should prepare, implement and disseminate comprehensive policies against discrimination in any form, including harassment, retaliation and whistle-blowing. If the policies are not communicated to the employees, they will be viewed as ineffective, or worse, as evidence of employer knowledge of its discrimination obligations, which the company elected not to enforce" (p. 120). Given that harassment is a foreseeable possibility, not having a policy is as bad as failing to communicate an existing policy to employees (Stokes, Stewart-Belle, & Barnes, 2000).

Harassment prevention programs should not only specify applicable statutes, but also must include a copy of relevant HR policies from the employer that (1) prohibit illegal employment practices; (2) state the organization's method for communicating policies (posting policies, mandatory training for employees and managers, etc.); (3) provide several avenues for making complaints of harassment (other than the employees direct supervisor); (4) establishe sanctions for behavior inconsistent with policies, including progressive discipline and possible termination, (5) state guidelines for investigating complaints; and (6) provide for internal review and an appeal mechanism for ensuring due diligence, compliance and fairness. Simply restating a statute as the organization's policy will be insufficient! Large organizations, especially those that consist of merged businesses with varying sets of HR policies, should consider (1) streamlining HR policies, including antiharassment policies, for conformity across the business, or (2) customize training to include relevant HR policies for the different business units.

Businesses from the United States operating overseas are reminded that the Civil Rights Act of 1991 extends those protections to employees of U.S. companies in foreign countries, unless the Act conflicts with local laws. Given varying customs worldwide, it may be necessary to customize harassment prevention training to meet host country's legal requirements.

3. Harassment prevention training should be based on needs assessment and performance analysis tailored to the industry and organization's workplace environment. According to Paskoff (2006), "it is vital that participants view training as one element of an overarching initiative. For it to be truly effective and credible, training cannot be delivered in a vacuum with no connection to the broader goals of the organization" (p. 228). Needs assessment is an integral element in the design, development, implementation and evaluation of training programs. Roberson, Kulik & Pepper (2003) explored five controversies involved in conducting needs assessments within a diversity training context: (1) whether an employer should focus on awareness training, skill training, or both; (2) broad versus narrow definition of diversity; (3) whether to confront or not; (4) homogeneous versus heterogeneous training groups; and (5) analysis of trainer demographics.

Littler & Mendelson (2005) suggested an audit approach that includes the following:

- Identify applicable laws that require training set forth in federal, state and local statutes, regulations and ordinances including laws that are specific to the particular industry, and applicable case law.
- Identify the level of training needed by executives, HR professionals, managers, and nonsupervisory employees.
- Identify "hidden or implied" training requirements, such as skills training, workplace-harassment training, workplace-violence training,and occupational safety and health training.
- Identify industry practices regarding the provision of additional training.
- Audit claims and litigation experience in the areas of workers' compensation, EEO, OSHA, all forms of harassment, wrongful discipline, wrongful discharge, negligent hiring, training and supervision, and workplace violence.
- Survey supervisors and employees to determine areas in which they believe training is required (p.912).

If at all possible, require that "diversity culture audits" conducted by consultants and needs assessment information conducted internally by HR professionals or externally by consultants be completed at the direction and under the supervision of an attorney. Reports generated by consultants will typically be viewed as a part of the normal course of business rather than privileged communication. The objective is to protect such information from the pretrial discovery process by shielding such reports under the "attorney-client" privilege. Recall that in the *Stender v. Lucky Stores*, the employer argued that notes and flip charts from the managers training program were privileged information. The court disagreed stating that the "managers' meetings were held, not for the purpose of 'facilitating the provision of professional legal services to a client,' but rather for training managers" (Eyers, 1998, p. 113).

4. Harassment training meets the "good faith effort" test promul-

gated in Kolstad *and as required by Title VII.* Compensatory and punitive damages may be recovered under the Civil Rights Act of 1991 if the complaining party establishes that the employer "engaged in a discriminatory practice . . . with malice or with reckless indifference to the federally protected rights" of an employee (Title VII, 42 USC § 1981a (b) (1). Under the Supreme Court's ruling in *Kolstad v. American Dental Association* (1998), an employer may raise and *affirmative defense* to avoid or limit punitive damages by demonstrating a good faith effort. Proof of such an effort consists of adopting antidiscrimination policies, and communicating these policies to managers and employees, including progressive discipline when necessary.

Subsequent case law has clarified the adequacy of the employer's "good faith" effort to avoid punitive damages. In *Greene v. Coach, Inc.*, (2002), an employer provided an antidiscrimination policy in the employee handbook, along with supplemental literature to employees regarding the importance of nondiscrimination, and an affidavit from the HR director "attesting to its good faith efforts to comply with antidiscrimination laws" (p. 414). This employer provided four training programs over the four-year period and maintained records of attendance. Lacking in evidence was proof that the alleged harassing managers were aware of the policy or that they attended any training during the time is which the harassment had occurred. The court concluded that the "dearth of antidiscrimination training at the time period in issue" (p. 415) could lead to a conclusion that no "good faith efforts" had been made at the time of the alleged harassment.

The outcome was different for the employer in *Dobrich v. General Dynamics Corp.*, (2000). In a fact situation similar to Greene, the employer was shielded from punitive damages for the following reasons: [1]

- General Dynamics' antidiscrimination policies included written employee complaint procedures.
- The work site in question was staffed by an HR office with EEO specialists.
- New employees underwent an orientation program, part of which included a review of antidiscrimination policies and outlining complaint procedures.
- Memoranda were posted on bulletin boards and sent to employees on a regular basis.
- All supervisors received four hours of training related to General Dynamics' antidiscrimination policies.

5. Harassment prevention training should be designed, implemented, and evaluated systematically. Select a standard instructional systems design (ISD) model to design the training program (Dick, Carey & Carey, 2004; Piskurich, 2000; Rothwell & Kazanas, 2003). Use task analysis information to focus the design, development, implementation and evaluation of the training program to the specific context and needs of the organization. The structural rigor of a well-executed ISD approach ensures logical linkages across the phases of the instructional design process.

Avoid a "one-size-fits all" or "cookie-cutter" approach to designing training. Design training to fit the context of the employer and the industry. Give serious thought to the goals, scope and approach in designing training. The choice of goals will influence the scope and approach of the program. Goals decide the direction of the training effort, scope determines the breadth of the effort, and approach represents the type of program selected.

Goals may focus on one or more of the following: (1) prevention of litigation, including knowledge about laws and policies impacting employees; (2) awareness of the impact of discrimination on productivity and interpersonal relationships; and (3) changing behaviors, values, and beliefs of those most likely to harass others.

The purpose of harassment prevention training is to shield the employer from the ravages of discrimination related litigation, especially from punitive damages. This singular purpose narrows the scope and approach. Such programs need not necessarily be time consuming (half-day and one day designs are common) to meet minimum requirements as defined by EEOC (1999), *Faragher*, *Ellereth* and *Kolstad*. These programs must meet strict guidelines for program content, accuracy of information, instructor expertise, and documentation of attendance by employees (McLaughlin & Merchasin, 2001).

Program designs that focus on more than employer liability prevention necessarily require additional goals, a larger scope and deliberate attention to approach. Employers such as Procter and Gamble (Blackburn, 1999), Chevron (Stuller, 1995) and Corestates Financial Corporation (Lunt, 1994) exemplify broad scale attention to diversity issues, not just liability prevention. Holmes (2005) outlines a systemic approach to plan and connect diversity to business performance.

The approach by Holmes is based on five essential steps:

1. Clarify the benefits of the diversity program.

2. Identify SMART goals (Specific, Measurable, Achievable, Relevant, Time bound).
3. Develop action plans.
4. Define performance expectations.
5. Evaluate impact on performance.

Approaches vary and should conform to the likelihood of acceptance by those who will attend the diversity program. Analysis of needs assessment data is useful in this regard. Five approaches, all very different, are summarized below.

- Griggs & Louw (1995) described an African philosophy for developing a diversity training program. "Ubuntu" is a Naguni word meaning "the quality of a human being," and is an acronym for the change process associated with diversity training: U means to uncover, B is to build and bridge, U also means to understand, N refers to neutral space, new input, and negotiation, T equals transformation, and U also means utilization. Each letter of the word represents a step in the process that is characterized in practical terms. The facilitator will use a chart explaining the "why, how, when, where and who" chart with trigger questions to initiate learning for the participants.
- Tower Records has a one-week training program on legal issues. Given that its employees come from artistic backgrounds, the HR unit wanted to capitalize on the creative talents of its employees. A mixed training strategy uses roles-plays, traditional lecture, small group discussion, as well as board games. Not any board game, but a board game in which participants dress up as life-sized game pieces and work with props, such as huge dice. According to Wallstein (1998), using this approach has resulted in a decrease from 129 complaints in 1996 to only 47 two years later.
- The ING Group, a global financial services group, believes that an inclusive culture contributes to long-term profitability. This approach extends beyond employer liability prevention and utilizes a drama-based training specialist working with an attorney to help raise awareness of the business benefits of diversity. All 1,000 personnel in the UK wholesale banking operation participated in this unique approach. Role-plays and instructor-led in-

formation sessions made this a memorable experience for ING employees (Dawson, 2005). Another UK based business, Phillips Petroleum, uses drama as part of a two-day workshop that covers several business objectives, including diversity and coaching. A drama specialist acts out typical "scenes that mangers may face during the day-to-day roles . . . [the actor] makes mistakes and they get the audience to help and coach them" (Anonymous, 2002, p. 239).

- Is it Diversity or Conversity? Wildersmuth & Gray (2005) advocated an educational intervention that focuses on commonalities rather than differences. "Diversity" focuses on differences, can be interpreted as divisive, comes with historical baggage, and starts from a defensive position. "Conversity,"a term coined by Wildersmuth & Gray (2005), focused "on commonalities leading to attitudes and behaviors that capitalize on human differences for organizational success" (p. 3). The authors provide a facilitators' workbook that includes a CD-ROM of ready-to-use instructional materials. An approach such as this, when coupled with a harassment prevention educational program, provides both employer and employees with a much broader scope than mere litigation prevention.
- Distance-learning approaches are showing a lot of promise for a number of management topics, including harassment prevention and safety training. Well designed elearning programs will leverage multimedia (streaming, audio, video and animation), provide users with opportunities to collaborate interactively with the course material, each other and the instructor. Quizzes and testing can be designed for mastery learning, meaning that users recycle through difficult content until they demonstrate competence. Well-designed elearning is as effective as face-to-face teaching, becomes very cost effective when economies of scale are considered, and provides "any-time, any-place" opportunities for learning. Travel costs are reduced for the leaner at a distance compared to participants who travel to off-site training locations. Managers and account executives maximize billable hours by scheduling learning around clients' needs and expectations.

Consider these questions when evaluating an elearning vendor and its products and services (Grollman & Cannon, 2003):

1. Who hosts the courseware, the vendor or the corporation—behind whose firewall?
2. How well does the elearning program align with the corporation's business objectives?
3. Does the pricing from the vendor fit the needs and expectations of the business?
4. How accurate is the content and how often does the vendor update the courseware?
5. Is the vendor financially solvent and stable or have a history of litigation that challenges its products and services?

Be sure to always take a test drive of the elearning program to see if it meets the needs of the business. Brightline Compliance, a Washington consulting firm, provides an opportunity for human resource personnel to evaluate an actual learning module from their online "Preventing Workplace Harassment" program.[2] Designing an evaluation process for any type of harassment prevention program must be carefully considered. Information from program evaluations is subject to pretrial discovery. If true-false or multiple choice tests are used to assess knowledge and if a pass-fail score is established, then be prepared to remediate and document anyone who fails the end-of-course test (Johnson, 2004). Opportunities for open-ended comments on evaluation forms are problematic, especially if highly negative comments are made about the instructor, the training program or conflicts with other participants. Such comments are subject to legal discovery and could be interpreted out of context.

6. Harassment prevention training should be provided to all employees that covers all forms of legally defined harassment—race, religion, ethnicity, national origin, disability, age, sex (gender and sexual orientation), as well as retaliation, whistle blowing, and hate and stalking crimes. It is a mistake to design a harassment prevention program around a single legal issue, such as sexual harassment. According to Johnson (2004) "of the 109,472 harassment lawsuits that were filed with the EEOC during the 1990s, 33 percent were sex-based, 14 percent were national-origin based, and 43 percent were race based" (p. 125). There is consensus among federal appellate courts since *Farragher* and *Ellereth* that the liability standards developed for sexual harassment cases applies to all types of harassment.

Be sure to check current state and municipal ordinances for each state for where the employer has resident employees. For example, the

Florida Human Relations Act (FS 760) includes marital status as a protected category and there is no upper or lower age limit on age discrimination.

According to EEOC guidelines, employers should "provide training to all employees to ensure they understand their rights and responsibilities" (EEOC, 1999). Mixing managers and employees in the same training program is ill-advised. The challenge for instructional designers and trainers is to ensure that the program content informs both groups without encouraging employees to initiate lawsuits (Littler & Mendelson, 2005). Each group requires a separate and distinct focus.

It is important for supervisors and managers to receive a thorough understanding of legal requirements and the consequences for misconduct by employees of the employer, including the manager's risks and liabilities.

Instruction for employees should avoid emotionally charged terminology such as "lawsuits," "claimants," "suing," "litigation," and "damages," all of which provide the wrong focus for the employee and may unnecessarily encourage lawsuits. According to Littler & Mendelson (2005), focusing the attention of the employee on conduct expectations, the duty to report harassment and the mechanism by which the reporting should occur should be the essence of instruction. Avoid opportunities for employees to use the content of the training as a means of encouraging or instigating litigation!

Several states and agencies of the federal government now require harassment prevention training. See Appendix C for a complete listing of requirements for the various states and agencies of the federal government. Under provisions of the NO FEAR ACT, all federal agencies in the United States must train all employees on their rights and remedies under the various discrimination statutes, as well as whistle-blowing and retaliation. Future requirements include training all new employees as part of the agencies orientation program (but not less than 60 days after the employee's appointment), with refresher training every two years (EEOC, 1999; Johnson, 2004).

7. Harassment prevention training should be documented with follow-up audits. Document harassment prevention training by following these simple guidelines. Maintain a complete master copy of all training materials and handouts, including instructional objectives, a transfer-of-learning plan, and resumes of instructors that that list areas of expertise and credentials, and master copies of any materials used to evaluate the effectiveness of the training (Sample, 2007c).

For each training session, require participants to sign an attendance form that includes the name of the instructor, dates, times and location of instruction; if training occurs on multiple days, have participants sign for each day. of instruction. The instructor should note in writing the names of participants who miss any part of the training. Archive these attendance forms in a safe and secure location, being mindful that original signatures, not copies of attendance forms with signatures, are preferred as evidence of attendance. "Keeping inadequate training records could turn out to be substantially more expensive than the cost of good training" (Littler & Mendelson, 2005, p. 919), and some jurisdictions will presume that undocumented training never occurred, even if it did.

Consider having each participant sign a form at the end of the training certifying that (1) he or she understands the content of the harassment prevention training program, (2) agrees to abide by the principles set forth in the program, and (3) acknowledges receipt and acceptance of any workplace policies that are part of the program.

As part of the audit process, ensure that participants remember the core knowledge from the training program. Devise ways of keeping the message alive with managers and employees. Use newsletters, employer websites, brown-bag lunches, and periodic refresher training to "do the right thing" by focusing on fairness and equity in the workplace. "More and more frequently, employees are being deposed and asked about a company's [harassment prevention] training program. Often, even though they attended, they did not remember anything about the training' (McLaughlin & Merchasin, 2001, p. 5).

8. Harassment prevention training should rely on qualified instructors with expertise in facilitation. Competent human resource professionals, trainers with special expertise in harassment prevention training, and employment law attorneys are all possibilities as trainers. A team approach is recommended in which an attorney explains the statutory rights and obligations of employees and the employer's HR representative explains and answers questions regarding the organizations antiharassment policies (Jenero & Galligano, 2003). Depending on the design of the program, a third member of the team could be someone with training in adult education, psychology, anthropology, or sociology who could facilitate role-plays and discussion groups.

Do not make promises of "What is said here stays here." Such promises are unenforceable as many managers are (or should be) under a policy obligation to report any instances of known harassment. Comments during training are not only reportable under many HR policies, but are discoverable as part of the pretrial process (McLaughlin & Merchasin, 2001; Wildermuth & Gray, 2005).

Trainers in harassment prevention programs should be very knowledgeable about the law of discrimination. In *Cadena v. Pacesetter* (2000), the defendant argued that training provided by the employer should be considered "a good faith effort" that would preclude any finding to support punitive damages. The manager responsible for sexual harassment training testified that she discussed the topic of harassment at meetings with her co-workers on a monthly basis. This manager stated in her pretrial deposition that a "male supervisor would not commit sexual harassment if he either exposed his genitalia to a female subordinate or grabbed her breasts, so long as he apologized after the incident." Based on [the manager's] admitted ignorance about sexual harassment, a jury could reasonably infer that [the defendant employer] failed to make a good faith effort to adequately educate its managers and employees about its nondiscrimination policy and Title VII" (pp. 13-14).

Trainers should avoid the use of "legalese" and references to outdated Latin maxims such as "quid pro quo." Language of this nature only serves to confuse the employees. According to McLaughlin and Merchasin (2001), "Employers should focus on what employees most need to know: what is and isn't harassment, how to report it and how to maintain a retaliation-free workplace" (p. 4)

Trainers and participants are cautioned against drawing legal conclusions during the program. Littler & Mendelson (2005) argued that "If the trainer says, 'This conduct is sexual harassment'—he or she is drawing a legal conclusion that could compromise future legal defenses" (p. 917). It is better to describe such conduct as "inappropriate and not consistent with HR policy" rather than label a hypothetical example as harassment. Employees who pose such questions could be the employer's next plaintiff. Finally, trainers who are not attorneys must avoid giving legal advice, lest they be accused of practicing law without a license.

The training program itself should not constitute evidence of harassment or discrimination. Verbal or written remarks regarding racial, ethnic or sex-based issues during a diversity training program have been used as evidence of discrimination, and may be the basis for claims alleging extreme emotional distress (Eyres, 1998). Recall from the *Stender v. Lucky Stores* case study that notes and flip charts from a diversity training program proved invaluable to the plaintiffs' attorneys. Other cases (see *Moller v. Department of Social Services*, 1995; *Caggiano v. Fontoura*, 2002; *Fitzgerald v. Mountain States Tel. & Tel. Co.*, 1995) provide examples of inappropriate conduct during training.

CONCLUSION

Litigation associated with state and federal civil rights laws are of significant concern to employers. The costs to defend allegations of harassment, including the costs of settlements and judgments, may pale in comparison to adverse media. The U.S. Supreme Court has provided an affirmative opportunity for employers through case law to develop antiharassment policies, communicate and train to those policies, and provide progressive discipline as necessary. Employers that provide "good faith" training and supervision position themselves to avoid or reduce the impact of civil rights related litigation. See Appendix C for a summary of federal and state requirements for harassment prevention training

Employers should continue to monitor testing strategies used in training programs, such as apprenticeship training, to make sure that no adverse impact occurs. Entry level selection criteria to attend training and any end-of-course testing results that may impact employability or promotability must be justified as job related.

Harassment prevention training when conducted competently will reduce costs associated with litigation, including reduced turnover and higher retention of talented employees. The return-on-investment (ROI) for this type of training is easier to calculate than similar savings and benefits associated with "diversity" training.

Endnotes

1 An extensive review of cases that clarify "good faith efforts" by employers is beyond the scope of this reference. For additional review of cases on this subject, see Johnson (2004), Jenero & Galligano (2003), and Tuttle & Winokur (2003).

2 Access Brightline Compliance at http://www.bright linecom pliance.com/ Note that the author is not endorsing this product or Brightline Compliance, but merely providing an example of an online harassment prevention learning module for preview.

Chapter 3
Occupational Safety and Health Related Liability

Chapter Objectives

Having reviewed the information in this chapter, the reader will have

1. a working knowledge of the Occupational Safety and Health Act (OSHA) of 1970;
2. a practical understanding of the importance of the OSHA general duty clause, specific industry standards, and health and safety training requirements;
3. analyzed legal cases and issues associated with safety and violence in the workplace;
4. reviewed issues associated with safety multilingual and learning disabled employees; and
5. reviewed recommendations for designing, implementing and evaluating health and safety programs governed by OSHA and other regulatory agencies.

The following additional information will be found in Appendix D. Summary of OSHA General Industry Training Requirements, and Appendix E. Summary of Safety Related Training Resources.

INTRODUCTION

The impact of accidents at work runs the gamut from hammered thumbs to serious injury, death and destruction of property. Accidents are typically associated with not following procedures or an engineering defect in design or materials, or some combination of the two (Langewiesche, 1998). It is likely that examining the investigation of tragic accidents involves a combination of these two elements. A third causal factor is what Perrow (1999) callded "systemic" accidents. These "new age" accidents will occur in unforeseeable ways and are predicted to be the "normal" accident of the future. Technologically advanced organizations are steeped in tightly coupled and interactive complexity. Nuclear power plants, chemical processing plants, airlines—and many others—fall into this category. Operational parts of these organizations are connected in multiple and often unpredictable ways in which the speed and inflexibility of the operating system prevent recovery from a misstep. The result is an accelerating cascade of interactive failures that no engineer could foresee or imagine or that a well-trained employee could reverse in the heat of the moment.

This chapter will focus on a review of requirements mandated by OSHA for safety and health in organizations in the United States, including implications for the training function. Issues and problems associated with violence in the workplace will also be explored.

Regulating safety and health in organizations was historically a responsibility of the states. It was not until 1877 that Massachusetts passed the first factory inspection law. Rarely enforced safety laws were enacted in 22 other states by 1890. During the 1960s, sufficient concern was raised about safety in the workplace. There was a 29 percent increase in injury and death rates between 1961 and 1970, and the National Safety Council "estimated 14,000 deaths due to accidents on the job and 2.2 million disabling injuries annually (with the latter statistic probably underestimated by a factor of five)" (Ashford, 1976, p. 3). Congress passed the Occupational Safety and Health Act (OSHA) in 1970 in response to a public outcry for safer workplaces.

Subsequent to the passage of OSHA in the United States, there were several high profile industrial accidents that caused worldwide concern:

- The accident at the Three Mile Island nuclear power plant in 1979 was the most serious in U.S. commercial nuclear power plant operating history. Although there were no deaths or injuries, the incident caused sweeping changes in how nuclear power plants operated.
- The Bhopal chemical accident of 1984 was the worst industrial accident in the history of the world. It was caused by the accidental release of 40 metric tons of methyl isocyanate into the air from a Union Carbide pesticide plant located in the heart of Bhopal, India. The leak killed thousands and injured as many as 600,000 others, at least 15,000 who later died from their injuries.

- The world's worst nuclear power accident occurred in 1986 at Chernobyl in the former USSR (now Ukraine). Numerous safety procedures were disregarded while testing one of the reactors. The chain reaction in the reactor went out of control creating explosions and a fireball which blew off the reactor's heavy steel and concrete lid. The Chernobyl accident killed more than 30 people immediately, and 135,000 people had to be evacuated because of high levels of radiation.
- The *Challenger* space shuttle disaster in 1986, followed by a similar occurrence in 2003 with the *Columbia* shuttle, is a grim reminder that highly complex and interactive technologies can fail because of faulty communication and decision making by educated and technically competent people. The ABC television movie *Challenger* includes a reenactment of the conference leading to the ill-fated decision to launch the space shuttle. Behaviours and attitudes exhibited by engineers and managers from NASA and government agencies are consistent with the groupthink phenomenon popularized by Irvin Janis (1972).

These types of major industrial accidents have serious concerns beyond any fines that OSHA or other regulatory agencies may levy on an employer. "These concerns can include material personnel injury litigation, adverse publicity, damage to labor-management relations, and an incredible strain on the time and resources of facility and supporting corporate personnel" (Zimmerman, 2005, p. 42).

Although the focus of this chapter is on OSHA and its responsibilities, it is important to recognize that other agencies at the federal and state level also regulate health and safety. Each of these agencies has promulgated specific education and training requirements. Additional federal agencies that currently regulate health and safety include the following:

- Mine Safety and Health Agency (MSHA). This U.S. Department of Labor agency develops and enforces safety and health rules applying to all U.S. mines, helps mine operators who have special compliance problems, and makes available technical, educational and other types of assistance.
- Department of Energy (DOE) regulates safety and health in nuclear power facilities, as well as construction, and medical

uses of nuclear material in medical facilities.

- Environmental Protection Agency (EPA) requires hazard warnings on pesticides that may injure farm workers and the public.
- Federal Aviation Administration (FAA) provides oversight and establishes and enforces safety policies for aviation and airlines industries.
- National Transportation Safety Board (NTSB) investigates safety related accidents, determines probable causes of accidents, issues safety recommendations, researches transportation safety issues, and evaluates safety effectiveness of governmental agencies involved in transportation in the following settings: railroad, maritime, highway, aviation, and pipelines.
- Drug Free Workplace Act of 1988 applies to employers who seek or have contracts with the federal government of $25,000 or more, as well as recipients of federal grants (municipalities and not-for-profit organizations). Training requirements include publishing a drug free workplace policy and promoting a "drug-free awareness" program. The U.S. Department of Labor enforces and provides technical assistance for this federal law.

The above list is not intended to be exhaustive. Be sure to check for other federal and state health and safety regulations.

OCCUPATIONAL SAFETY, HEALTH & WORKPLACE SAFETY

Statutory directives that mandate safety and health compliance training are variously viewed as an irritating nuisance providing vague and confusing direction (Stape, 2005) to a divisive system that results in two training structures within an organization (Erickson, 1996). Both Stape and Erickson bemoaned the lack of central unifying theme from senior management that makes the clear business argument for health and safety training.

The traditional training structure includes all types of training, such as employee orientation, job and soft skills training, management and organization development. The second structure includes compliance training in response to mandated federal and state health and safety regulations. Given these two types of structures, employers are likely to have two sets of safety rules. The formal rules are supported by safety policies which are signed by employees stating that safety is a priority

Table 3.1

Potential Losses Associated with the Failure to Integrate Organizational Training With Mandatory Compliance and Regulatory Training.

- Increased direct health care costs for employers (insurance premiums), employees (out-of-pocket expenses).
- Regulatory fines and other legal costs associated with facility audit, civil and criminal proceedings related to environmental, health, and safety incidents.
- Costs associated with pre-trial preparation (time and effort of managers and employees).
- Facility rehabilitation costs associated with damage and clean up of site contamination.
- Adverse publicity impacting market share, business reputation as well as recruitment and training of replacement personnel for reported health and safety incidents or conditions.

Source: Reprinted from *Practical Guide for Occupational Health*, p. 242, Copyright© 1996 with permission of Elsevier.

for the employer. However, as Paap (2006) pointed out from her research in the construction industry, "the company's actual focus seemed to be on maintaining an appearance of safety . . . while getting the job done quickly and cheaply as possible" (p. 159).

Compliance programs typically receive *de minimus* funding, time, and attention to rigor and detail. Erickson explained that, "Regrettably health and safety training objectives become confused with regulatory compliance objectives—a confusion that too often reflects a misguided corporate preoccupation with doing as little as possible to comply with specific regulations, which in turn, is an attitude that typically reflects an hierarchical isolation of upper management from the realities of the modern workplace" (1996, p. 244). Table 3.1 describes problems associated with the failure to integrate organizational training with mandatory compliance and regulatory training.

Overview of OSHA Structure and Responsibilities

The Occupational Safety Health Act of 1970 applies to all employers with one or more employees, except state and local governments. Challenges to OSHA citations, penalties and abatement deadlines are resolved by the Occupational Safety and Health Review Commission (OSHRC). This independent and quasi-adjudicatory agency takes appeals from businesses that object to OSHA citations. The National Institute for Occupational Safety and Health (NIOSH) is a division of the Centers for Disease Control within the U.S. Department of Health and Human Services. NIOSH is the U.S. government's occupational safety and health compliance and research agency (29 U.S.C. § 669).

The various states are precluded from regulating workplace safety unless OSHA authorizes a federally approved state plan. Any approved state plan must have standards that are at least equivalent to OSHA standards. States plans must also protect local government employees. OSHA will pay up to 50 percent of the funding for an approved state plan (29 U.S.C. § 667) and 21 states and two territories operate approved plans that include both the public and private sectors.[1] States are free to regulate any hazard not covered by an OSHA standard, and where an OSHA standard applies, state law is not allowed. The only exception is if the state standard covered is under an approved OSHA plan. The states retain jurisdiction over workers' compensation laws and programs.

The Occupational Safety and Health Administration (OSHA) is housed within the U.S. Department of Labor. OSHA is responsible for policy making and enforcement responsibility that includes the following (Clarke, 2006; Zimmerman, 2005):

Occupational Safety and Health Administration

- setting safety and health standards,
- conducting workplace inspections,
- issuing citations and proposed penalties for violations,
- funds education, training, and state consultation programs,
- monitors state OSHA performance, and
- coordinating voluntary compliance programs.

Employees have the right to

- a place of employment free from recognized hazards,
- notification by the employer regarding exposure to toxic materials and harmful physical agents,
- file a confidential complaint with OSHA regarding unsafe work conditions,
- receive education, training, and information from NIOSH.

Employers have the right to

- an opening conference to accompany an inspector on an inspection,
- seek a variance from a standard is another equal or better method or control is available,
- appeal any citations and fines.

Fines

- OSHA fines run the gamut from $7,000 for a “serious” violation to $70,000 for a “willful” violation.

OSHA citations have implications beyond fines that may be levied against employers. Employers in the construction industry with an extensive citation history may find themselves struggling for new business if the request for proposal (RFP) asks for safety violation history. Submitting the “lowest qualifying” bid is no guarantee of a contract if the work includes high work and the bidder has an extensive OSHA citation history. OSHA citations are a matter of public record, so the media and insurance underwriters have access to OSHA citations, all of which may impact business reputation and costs for insurance (Clarke, 2006).

The General Duty Clause

OSHA covered employers have a general duty to “furnish to each of his employees employment and a place of employment which are free from recognized hazards that are causing or are likely to cause death or serious physical harm to his employees” (OSHA 29 U.S.C. 654). A 1977 U.S. Appeals Court decision determined that the general duty clause also “includes training of employees as to the dangers and supervision of the work site” (*General Dynamics v. OSHARC*, 1977). Hazards not covered by existing standards require training on procedures to ensure safe work practices. Examples of such methods include apprenticeship training, job-instruction training (JIT), vestibule training, and coaching.

Instruction of general work safety practices includes knowledge of exits and evacuation procedures, ergonomic practices specific to jobs (such as lifting or carpal tunnel syndrome prevention), use of protective equipment, fire protection and handling flammable or corrosive chemicals, and general first-aid procedures. Specific instruction is required for hazards associated with specific job assignments (avoiding electrical shock, safety glasses, etc).

Table 3.2
Most Frequently Cited OSHA Standards

Citation	Industry
Scaffolding	Construction
Hazard communication	General industry
Fall protection	Construction
Respiratory protection	General industry
Control of hazardous energy (lockout/tagout)	General industry
Powered industrial trucks	General industry
Machines	General industry
Electrical wiring, equipment	General industry
Ladders	Construction
Electrical systems design	General industry

Source: OSHA Frequently Cited Standards. Retrieved from http://www.osha.gov/pls/imis/citedstandard.html on October 30, 2006

General and Specific Industry Standards

General industry standards apply to all employers unless exempted by OSHA. Categories include personal protective equipment, hazardous materials handling and storage, first aid, fire protection, and occupational health and environmental controls. OSHA has also promulgated specific training standards that apply to the three largest industries under its jurisdiction—general industrial, maritime and construction. The general industry training requirements are summarized in Appendix E. Maritime and construction training requirements are available at www.osha.gov. Table 3.2 displays the 10 most frequently cited OSHA standards for the years 2004-2005.

Several of the general industry standards have significant implications for training for many employers:

- Bloodborne pathogens—law enforcement and corrections; emergency medical technicians, hospital and human services medical care; medical research facilities and laboratories. The most prevalent diseases include HIV and hepatitis B virus. The OSHA Bloodborne Pathogens Standard (29 CFR 1910.1030) states that "all employees with occupational exposure" to such pathogens are required to attend a training program offered by their employer (Weissman, 2006).

- Guidelines for workplace violence prevention program. OHSA has recommended (not mandated) that certain businesses adopt policies and training to prevent and respond to violence in the workplace. Health care and social service workers, late night retail establishments and taxi drivers are included in this group (OSHA, 1998b). In addition to recommended training requirements by OSHA for employers, Rosen (2000) advocates that "it is critically important to teach them how to advocate for change within the political structure of an organization" (p. 459).
- Hazard communication and hazardous waste. The "employee right to know" requirement established by Congress mandates that employers train employees who may be exposed to hazardous chemicals under normal working conditions. Employers are required to post material safety data sheets (MSDS) along with warning labels for hazardous chemicals. OSHA provides several technical resources for developing HazCom training, including OSHA's *Draft Model Training Program for Hazard Communication Training* (Klane, 2005).

EXAMPLE OF SAFETY RELATED TRAINING CASES

A search for examples investigated by OSHA and other safety regulatory agencies determined that most reported cases involve failing to perform a training responsibility on which the trainee depends. The following three case examples illustrate this kind of failure, and point out the care that must be taken by employers and training managers.

- Stacker Conveyor Safety. A construction company was operating an 80-foot stacker-conveyor at a gravel pit within ten feet of an energized 12,000-volt power line. An employee was electrocuted when the stacker operator equipment moved the equipment which came into contact with a high voltage electrical line. Utility representatives had warned the stacker operator before the accident that the clearance was dangerous. No designated supervisor was at the worksite when the conveyor was moved. The victim, employed for only two months, as well as other employees, had received no training, and there was no record of discipline to prevent violations. Five days after this tragic incident, this same stacker operator was found to be running a feeder-conveyor within eight feet of a power line and had expressed an intention of completing a few more weeks of work before moving the machinery. The president of the construction company was deemed individually liable. The argument that he was not present at the mine at the time of the electrocution was deemed no defense as he knowingly authorized the moving of the machinery without ensuring that adequate precautionary measures had been taken. The operator received a $16,000 civil fine and the president was fined $5,000 (*Steen Construction Co.*, 1992).

- Fall Protection in a Utility. An electric utility company was charged by OSHA for failure to provide fall protection to its utility workers. They were required to traverse high steel bridge structures during a training program designed to inoculate them against a fear of heights when working on electrical substations at a height of 110 feet. The training program was usually provided for apprentice workers, but in this instance, the workers were installers with three years experience. The installers had cross walked at 33 feet unprotected with safety belts or nets, but refused to free walk at 55 feet. They testified that the instructor was intimidating them into traversing steel beams and structures in an unsafe manner. They testified that during their previous three years they had never had a problem coping with heights, and that they never were required to free walk the top of a substation structure. OSHA determined that if the purpose of the training was to reduce height anxiety, it should have been given to apprentice workers with such anxiety instead of to experienced installers who had no previous height anxiety, but who were needlessly exposed to serious fall hazards (*Cleveland Electric Illuminating Company*, 1994).
- Tower Crane Safety. The Tampa Shipyards, Inc. facility was found to have willfully violated the general duty clause by using an 80-foot tower crane to hoist a 33-ton load when the crane was set to lift no more than 21 tons. The crane collapsed when the load was being swung horizontally. The load exceeded the manufacturers recommended load limit, and the "leaderman" (a first-line supervisor according to a collective bargaining agreement) was aware of the potential for an "overlift" safety problem. OSHA determined that instead of operating the crane under written

> safety instructions, Tampa Shipyards crane operators were subject only to a "use your best judgment" policy. There was no level of supervision between the lead workers and the superintendent, and the lead workers were responsible for informing the superintendents of potential safety problems reported to them. The shipyard could have made numerous feasible and useful improvements to its crane safety program that would have materially reduced the risk of operators attempting overlifts on the cranes. It was recommended that a written apprenticeship program and safety instructions be distributed to all crane operators, and that implementation of the program for monitoring compliance be instituted (*Tampa Shipyards, Inc.* 15 OSHC 1533, 1992).

One must keep in mind the importance of supervisors as first-line trainers in any organization. This point is important because supervisors can be held liable for failure to supervise and to train to standard. Sage (1990) emphasized the importance of supervisors in changing workplace behaviors and attitudes. Sage stated that the standard of care owed by trainers and supervisors to their adult learners is the duty of supervision:

> If there is a failure to exercise reasonable care in performing this duty, either in the commission or omission of an instructional act or training activity, and that failure results in an injured trainee, the [supervisor as] trainer is assumed liable. (Sage 1990, p. 10)

Safety Training and the Multilingual Employee

The workplace has become culturally diverse, and in some geographic locations and businesses, the number of Spanish-speaking entry-level employees may exceed the number of English-speaking employees. Languages and dialects other than English are not unusual at every level of a business, from the shop floor to the boardroom. This magnitude of linguistic and cultural diversity poses special challenges for safety and health training. The problem is compounded by varying levels of literacy in the workplace by English-speaking employees.

Employees, regardless of ethnic origin and facility with written and spoken English language, have a right to know of hazards in the workplace. Training for employees must be "effective" and "readily understandable" covering "categories of hazards . . . or specific chemicals" including specific procedures, work practices, emergency procedures personal protective equipment to be used as well as explanation of labeling systems and material safety data sheets (MSDS) (OSHA § 1910.1200). According to Eyers (1998), "Federal standards recommend, but do not require, bilingual safety information and training. OSHA inspectors are generally told, however, that if employees must receive their job instruction in a language other than English, then safety training and information will probably also need to be conducted in that foreign language . . . The more extreme the safety or health risk, the higher the duty to overcome language barriers (p. 54).

Employers are well advised to consider state and federal civil rights law and court decisions before adopting recruitment and selection practices that restrict employment of non-English speaking employees. National origin discrimination is against federal and state statutes, and is enforced at the federal level by EEOC. Employers are encouraged to provide incentives for those workers to improve their English skills, such as English classes for non-native English speaking employees. Such specialized training will help workers with limited English skills acquire skills necessary for advancement, thus minimizing the potential for adverse impact.

English-only rules in the workplace are highly suspect because of their relationship to issues of national origin. Employers should weigh the possible discriminatory effects against legitimate "business necessity" requirements. A business necessity argument that meets the following guidelines may be allowed under EEOC (Bennett-Alexander & Hartman, 2001):

- job safety justifications for the rule,
- requirements for supervision or effective communication with employees and customers,
- potential effectiveness of the rule in carrying out business objectives,
- English proficiency of workers affected by the rule.

For example, an English-only rule based on safety requirements could be allowed in a safety sensitive organization, such as a refinery. All employees could be expected to speak only English in the event of an emergency, and that English be spoken in any work area where there was potential for explosions, fires, injuries and causalities. Note that such a rule probably would not apply to casual conversations when employees were not performing a work task.

Safety Training for the Learning Disabled

Employers must not assume that employees who evidence learning disabilities are automatically exempt from performing safety sensitive work tasks or from safety and health training. Job applicants and employees with a qualified disability who can perform the essential functions of a job with a reasonable accommodation must not be discriminated against because of a covered disability. Learning disabilities in adults include hype- and hypoactivity, attention deficits, impulsivity, and social interaction problems (McCalman, Bates, Morris, & Wilder, 1996). The dilemma faced by the employer is a two edged sword. "Trainees with disabilities have dual rights: the right to know and understand hazards they may face on the job, and the right to equal job opportunities. People with disabilities cannot be automatically excluded from the opportunity to attend training, to successfully compete the post training evaluation, and to be placed on the job. Yet the OSHA mandates that employees not be placed on jobs for which they are ill prepared to work safely" (Eyres, 1998, p. 58).

CASE STUDY: THE VALUJET 592 AIRCRAFT TRAGEDY—PROBLEMS WITH MAINTENANCE, SUPERVISION AND TRAINING

The expanded case study for this chapter chronicles the events leading up to and following the tragic ValuJet 592 airlines crash in 1996. This particular accident is consistent with Perrow's (1999) prophecy of an accident attributed to systemic failures in supervision, regulatory oversight, and human carelessness. The airline's maintenance contractor and an additional three employees, were prosecuted at the federal and state level. The lynchpin issue for the federal prosecution was failure to adequately train maintenance employees.

The Accident

Flight 592 departed Miami International Airport on May 11, 1997 at 2:04 EST heading south towards the Florida Everglades. The pilot planned to eventually turn north over the Gulf of Mexico. The destination is Atlanta, Georgia and the weather was balmy and sunny, and by all accounts the weather was optimal for flying.

Here is a transcript of the pilots' voices eight minutes before the crash:

> 2:09:02 [sound of click]
> 2:10:07 "what was that"
> 2:10:08 "I don't know"
> 2:10:12 ** ("bout to lose a bus?")
> 2:10:15 "we got some electrical problem"
> 2:10:17 yeah
> 2:10:18 "that battery charger's kicking in. ooh, we gotta"
> 2:10:20 "we're losing everything"
> 2:10:22 "we need to go back to Miami"
> 2:10:23 [sounds like shouting from the passenger cabin]
> 2:10:25 "fire, fire, fire, fire" [from a female voice in the cabin]
> 2:10:27 "we're on fire, we're on fire"
> 2:10:28 [sound of tone similar to landing gear warning horn for three seconds]
> 2:10:30 ** to Miami [calling Miami control tower requesting immediate return to airport]
> 2:10:36 [sounds of shouting from passenger cabin subsides]
> 2:10:42 [sound of horn]
> 2:10:44 "fire"
> 2:10:46 [contacting Miami control tower] uh, smoke in the cockpit . . . smoke in the cabin
> 2:10:52 [sound similar to cockpit door moving]
> 2:10:58 "OK, we need oxygen, we can't get oxygen back here"
> 2:11:10 [sounds of shouting from passenger cabin]
> 2:11:11 "completely on fire"
> 2:11:14 [sounds of shouting from passenger cabin subsides]
> 2:11:21 [sound similar to loud rushing air]

About eight minutes from takeoff, Flight 592 made a vertical right bank and nosedived into a watery grave 17 miles south of the airport. Two pilots, three attendants and 105 passengers perished instantly. What could have precipitated such a tragedy?

Events Leading Up to the Accident

The culminating event of this tragic occurrence begins with ordinary people doing their job at the SabreTech maintenance facility located in Miami. ValuJet had a contract with SabreTech to refurbish and provide ongoing maintenance. One of the tasks required mechanics to remove "expired" oxygen generating canisters from the aircraft. These canisters used a small explosive device to trigger the generation of oxygen. When detonated, the shell of the canister will heat to as much as 450-500 °F. A heat shield protects the canister from coming into contact with the aircraft. Face masks attached to the canister would drop from the ceiling in the event of sudden decompression in the aircraft.

According to policy directive provided by ValuJet to SabreTech, the shipping of unexpended canisters requires the attachment of a shipping cap on the firing pin. Failure to attach the cap could result in a fire risk. According to National Transportation and Safety Board (NTSB, 1997), 72 SabreTech employees, many who were contract employees, logged over 1910 hours replacing canisters on three ValuJet aircraft. Langewieche (1998) described the working culture at SabreTech at this time as a "world of boss men and sudden firings, with few restrictions or guarantees for the future [employment]" (p. 86). These mechanics, working on a tight timeline, placed canisters without the plastic safety caps in five cardboard boxes. Some of the heat shields had been removed along with the lanyard used to pull the firing pin. Many of the canisters still contained oxygen and could be "fired," even though they were "expired" due to age. Routine records noted that two mechanics signed off on the work for one or more supervisors, indicating that safety caps had been attached. Green tags were affixed to the boxes indicating that the contents were "repairable," which was not the case due to an automatic expiration date on the oxygen canisters.

The cardboard boxes remained for several weeks on a SabreTech rack designated for ValuJet parts. The boxes were then moved to the shipping and receiving department and left on the floor in an area assigned to ValuJet property. An inspection by a potential vendor (Continental Airlines) resulted in a cleaning up of the work area. A shipping clerk decided to ship the boxes of canisters to ValuJet in Atlanta, and did so without authorization, believing the green tags meant "unserviceable" or "repairable." Given no information to the contrary, the clerk presumed that the canisters were empty. A shipping load was made up that included the boxes of canisters and three aircraft tires. The shipping ticket read "Oxy Canisters" followed by "Empty" in quotation marks. These canisters are considered "hazardous materials" and shipment by air is prohibited unless prior authorization is obtained from OSHA.

A few days later, the boxes and tires were delivered to the ValuJet ramp agent for acceptance and boarding on ValuJet 592. The ramp agent and the pilot both failed to catch the tragic mistake of loading the boxes of canisters along with the inflated tires. The boxes were stacked around one of the larger tires that were lying on the cargo floor, with the other tire leaning against the bulkhead.

The Investigation

The investigation into the cause of this accident included the National Transportation Safety Board (NTSB), the Federal Aviation Administration (FAA), the Federal Bureau of Investigation (FBI), the Dade County State Attorney's office, the Metro-Dade Police Department, the office of the United States Attorney, and the Environmental Protection Agency (EPA). Criminal indictments were filed at state and federal levels, as well as civil suits by family members of those who perished in the crash.

The investigation by the NTSB (1997) concluded that the probable cause of the accident was a fire in the forward cargo hold by the "actuation of one or more oxygen generators being improperly carried as cargo" (p. x). This conclusion is supported, in part, by several FAA tests in which oxygen canisters and tires placed together in a simulated cargo space caught fire when detonated. Temperatures were measured as high as 2000 °F, about 13 minutes after the canister was detonated, with peak temperatures at 3,000 after 16 minutes (NTSB, 1997, p. 54)

Fault finding was extensive and broad in scope (NTSB, 1997):

- The failure of SabreTech to properly prepare, package, and identify unexpended chemical oxygen generators before presenting them to ValuJet for carriage.
- The failure of ValuJet to properly oversee its contract maintenance program to insure compliance with maintenance training, and hazardous materials requirements and practices.
- The failure of the Federal Aviation Administration (FAA) to require smoke detection and fire suppression systems in cargo compartments, to monitor ValuJet's oversight of SabreTech

maintenance operation, to develop programs that would address potential known hazards with oxygen canisters, and the provision of hazardous materials training.

Training at ValuJet and SabreTech

According to the NTSB (1997) final report, ValuJet employed six full-time instructors in maintenance at the time of the accident. New employees in maintenance are required to complete a 4-hour orientation for deicing and personal safety and a 32-hour technical training program for each type of aircraft they will encounter. Additional training may occur and probationary employees are assigned to lead mechanics for on-the-job training. Recurrent training is required for all ValuJet employees who are authorized to make inspections. Training for contract employees was conducted by a ValuJet employee. Documentation is maintained in the employees personnel file.

The manager of maintenance training was trained by a ValuJet employee on ValuJet policies and procedures, who then trained SabreTech employees. The NTSB (1997) accident report briefly outlines the general maintenance training that SabreTech personnel received. The report emphasizes the fact that ValuJet "did not provide a hazardous materials training program to its employees regarding the shipping of hazardous materials, or was such a program provided by ValuJet" (NTSB, 1997, p. 65). The hazmat training at SabreTech was limited to disposal of hazardous wastes, but not the shipping of aircraft parts such as oxygen canisters. The shipping clerk had received minimal hazardous material training, but nothing regarding the shipment of aircraft parts. Lead mechanics and higher at SabreTech were "required to verify that they had read the SabreTech FAA-approved repair station inspection procedures manual. A statement that the person having done so was entered into their personnel file" (NTSD, 1997, p. 66).

With the exception of the shipping clerk, nothing in the NTSB (1997) accident report concludes that any of the employees in the chain of events, including the ramp agent and pilots, received any of the required training. Supervisors "pencil whipped" their signatures to forms signed by maintenance workers attesting that tasks associated with the tragedy had been completed according to documented specification on work order 0069. Maintenance workers bowed to managerial and supervisory pressure to falsify and prematurely certify the performance and completion of work, a practice known as "pencil whipping."

Criminal and Civil Proceedings

On July 13, 1999 the U.S. Attorney in Miami announced a twenty-four-count federal indictment charging four defendants with various crimes. The indictment charged SabreTech and three employees, Daniel Gonzalez, Eugene Florence, and Mauro Valenzuela with conspiracy to make false statements to the FAA, an offense punishable by up to five years in prison and a $250,000 fine. The indictment alleges that the defendants and others known and unknown to the grand jury, entered into a conspiracy, the goal of which was to place the short-term business and monetary interests of SabreTech ahead of public safety concerns in the conduct of the aircraft repair station. The federal indictment further states that Gonzalez, who was SabreTech's Vice President and Director of Maintenance, supervised maintenance and repair work, including its documentation, so as to rush and compress the work, even if it meant skipping prescribed work steps and falsely asserting that work has been completed.

The federal indictment further specified that SabreTech removed oxygen generators from two ValuJet Airlines aircraft and handled them with gross disregard for their hazardous nature, and that Florence and Valenzuela signed off on work cards falsely indicating that the installation of shipping caps, which could have prevented the oxygen generators from igniting, had been accomplished, when, in fact, the shipping caps had not been installed. SabreTech employees delivered some of the unexpended oxygen generators contained in five boxes for loading on ValuJet 592.

On the same date of the federal indictment, the state attorney in Miami announced the filing of a 221 criminal counts against SabreTech. The company was charged with one count of illegal transportation of hazardous waste, a third-degree felony; 110 counts of third degree felony murder, a second-degree felony and 110 counts of manslaughter, a second degree felony. It is the first time in the history of aviation that an airline in the United States was prosecuted for a crime. The criminal charges are based on the actions of SabreTech and its employees in the handling and transportation of hazardous waste in the form of oxygen generators that it loaded onto ValuJet flight 592. In its handling of the oxygen generators, the organization and its employees violated Florida State criminal law governing the lawful transportation and disposal of hazardous waste. The felony murder charges were filed because the deaths of all 110 people aboard ValuJet flight 592 came as the direct result of that criminal act. The manslaughter charges were the result of the criminal and negligent actions of SabreTech and its employees in loading the full oxygen generators onto ValuJet flight 592 which directly resulted in the crash and deaths on flight 592.

At the conclusion of the of the federal district court trial, SabreTech was found guilty on nine of the 24 indictments, including "willfully failing to train its employees in accordance with hazardous materials regulations" (*U.S. v. SabreTech*, 2001). All three of the indicted employees were acquitted. The district court sentenced SabreTech to pay a fine of $2,000,000 and restitution of $9,060,400. SabreTech appealed on several grounds, including the finding of failure to train its employees, to the U.S. Court of Appeals.

The appeals court concluded "there was sufficient evidence presented at trial to support SabreTech's conviction [for failure to train]. The evidence demonstrates that SabreTech had a manual instructing personnel with regard to the handling and packaging of hazardous material and knew that it should inform its employees of these regulations. Moreover, several SaberTech employees testified that they received no hazard materials training while employed at SabreTech" (*US v. SabreTech*, 2001). Other matters on appeal were remanded to the trial court for review. Final resolution of this federal case required SabreTech to a probationary period of three years and a $500,000 fine on the sole remaining count (Cordle, 2002). As for the 221 count criminal indictment against SabreTech, a Florida circuit judge reduced the charges to one charge, transporting hazardous materials, and required SabreTech to pay a $500,000 fine (Cordle, 2001).

In addition to the criminal proceedings stated above, ValuJet (now Air Tran) and SabreTech continue to endure the resolution of civil suits from families of those that perished in the accident. According to one source, families of the victims have received settlements averaging $1 million, for an aggregate sum of $262 million (Cordle, 2000).

Culture of the Work Environment and Training

Spector (2006) stated that training in organizations such as SaberTech and ValuJet take place in the "context of a complex work environment. Whether or not the skills learned in training are used on the job is dependent in large part on the environment of the job. Just because management provides training does not mean that employees or their direct supervisors will support its use on the job "(p. 175). Stimson (1998) in his review of the ValuJet 592 tragedy explored how "continuous learning and improvement and constant questioning of accepted practices and thinking about what you are doing are cultivated" (p. 5).

Using a modern aircraft carrier as an example, Stimson explained how bureaucracies can exist in tandem with collaborative work processes. When a carrier is active with tandem takeoffs and landings, "Cooperation and communication largely override hierarchical position. There is no time for instructions to move up and down the chain of command. Team play, constant communication (telephone, radio, hand signals, writing), watching colleagues' actions, and the oversight of more experienced personnel, who monitor activities, mean that mistakes are rare and can be corrected before harm is done. . . . The steady turnover of officers and crew also means that the aircraft carrier is a floating school, with little chance for operations to become routine" (p. 4). What other organization with 5,000 employees, most who are in their late teens, can boast of such a safe working environment?

VIOLENCE IN THE WORKPLACE

Violence in the workplace is a major concern that impacts all facets of contemporary organizations. In 1993, homicide accounted for more than 1000 deaths in the workplace, and in the same year, 2.2 million people were attacked at work. In the intervening years, workplace homicides have steadily decreased by 49 percent to a low of 561 in 2004 (excluding the 2,886 work-related homicides resulting from terrorist attacks of September 11) (Bureau of Labor Statistics, 2005a, p 1). One source estimated that "there is an average of 5,500 incidents per day, an average of 17 workplace violence homicides per week, and 13,000 women being assaulted, stalked, or murdered at work each year by a significant other" (Viollis, Roper, & Decker, 2005, p. 71).

It is estimated that costs associated with workplace violence in 2002 were $121 billion, and that costs continue to rise (Viollis, et al., 2005). Each incident of workplace violence may result in one or more of the following: business interruption, increased costs for insurance, inappropriate use of sick leave (stress avoidance), psychological services for victims and observers of workplace violence, pre-litigation costs, civil damages beyond workers' compensation coverage (wrongful death actions), and threat to business reputation due to negative media attention. Reducing the impact of this serious problem requires a strategic effort from those responsible with managing and training employees.

Given these statistics related to incidents and costs of workplace violence, it must be noted that the majority of fatalities are not related to violence. According to the U.S. Bureau of Labor Statistics, the top four ranked causes of workplace fatalities in 2005 were transportation related accidents (43 percent), contact with objects and equipment (18 percent), assaults and homicides (14 percent), and falls (13 percent). Exposure to harmful substances and environments (9 percent) and fires and explosions (3 percent) accounted the remaining causes of work related fatalities (Bureau of Labor Statistics, 2005).

Few workplaces are immune from violence. There is an upsurge of violence in places where the public has access to employees and others, such as retail and service businesses that serve customers all hours of the day; schools and public libraries; caregivers in medical facilities, emergency rooms, social services anterooms and offices of personnel (Bowie, Fisher, & Cooper,2005; Waddington, Badger & Bull, 2006). Public sector offices at the municipal, state, and federal level have experienced increased incidents of violence. In this regard, the U.S. Postal Service may not deserve its reputation for employees "going postal," at least in more recent times (Perline & Goldschmidt, 2001).

Violence in certain occupational categories, primarily late night retail businesses, resulted in OSHA (1998b) publishing strategies for employers. These recommendations do not represent a new OSHA standard as the employer's responsibility to address workplace violence is governed by the General Duty Clause. Given that these are recommendations, failure to adopt "is not evidence of a violation of the General Duty Clause (OSHA, 1998b, p. 2). Table 3.3 describes the recommended actions for employers and managers to take that demonstrates commitment and involvement in reducing workplace violence.

Risk factors that predict violence in the workplace may be categorized as behavioral, psychological, and situational. Behavioral indicators (those used to establish "profiles") include learned violence and acting out behaviors, interest and fascination with weapons (guns and knives), excessive alcohol and substance abuse and psychotropic medicines, and bullying tendencies (Harvey, Heames, Richey, & Leonard, 2006; Perline & Goldschmidt, 2005).

Social and situational predictors include the hiring process, layoffs and job security, disputes with supervisors and others, arbitrary

Table 3.3

Strategies for Ensuring Management and Employment Commitment to Reducing Violence in the Workplace

Managers Commitments

- Create and disseminate a policy to managers and employees that expressly disapproves of workplace violence, verbal and nonverbal threats, and related actions.
- Take all violent and threatening incidents seriously, investigate them, and take appropriate corrective action.
- Outline the comprehensive plan for maintaining security in the workplace.
- Assign responsibility and authority for the program to individuals or teams with appropriate training and skills. This means ensuring that all managers and employees understand their obligations.
- Provide necessary authority and resources for staff to carry out violence prevention responsibilities.
- Hold managers and employees accountable for their performance. Stating expectations means little if management does not track performance, reward performance, and when standards are not met, provide corrective actions.
- Take appropriate action to ensure that managers and employees follow the administrative controls or work practices.
- Institute procedures for prompt reporting and tracking of violent incidents that occur in and near the establishment.
- Ensure that employees who report or experience workplace violence are not punished or otherwise suffer discrimination.
- Work constructively with other parties such as landlords, lessees, local police, and other public safety agencies to improve the security of the premises.

Employee Involvement

- Participate in surveys and offer suggestions about safety and security issues.
- Participate in developing and revising procedures to minimize risk of violence in daily business operations.
- Assist in the security analysis of the establishment.
- Participate in performing routine security inspections of the establishment.
- Participate in the evaluation of prevention and control measures.
- Participate in training new or current employees.
- Share on-the-job experiences to help other employees recognize and respond to escalating agitation, assualtive behavior, or criminal intent, and discuss appropriate responses.

Source: OSHA. (1998b). Recommendations for workplace violence prevention programs in late-night retail establishments. Washington, D.C.: U.S. Department of Labor, pp. 2-3.

job changes, disciplinary actions and perceived distributive or procedural justice. Psychological predictors include entitlement beliefs and perceived injustice, impulse control and coping skills, stress from multiple sources, identity and self-esteem (Perline & Goldschmidt, 2004).

Domestic Violence and the Workplace

Incidents of assaults and homicides of employees by spouses are a serious problem that employers cannot afford to ignore. Assaults and threats include harassing phone calls and emails to spouses while at work, stalking to and from work, and within the employer's premises. One source estimates that over 50,000 attacks related to domestic abuse occur where the spouse works (Ceausu, 2005). Homicide was the second leading cause of death for women at work in 2000 (Census of Fatal Occupational Injuries, 2001). Employers who fail to act responsibly will suffer potential litigation and financial repercussions. Research conducted by the Family Violence Prevention Fund concluded that lost productivity attributed to domestic violence on an annual basis is estimated at $727.8 million, and that 7.9 million paid workdays are lost each year by employers (cited by Gurchiek, 2006).

Employers who act affirmatively to develop zero-tolerance workplace violence policies and who and train managers and supervisors regarding that policy, are in a better position to avoid or limit potential for litigation. This includes provisions of the Americans with Disabilities Act and the Family Medical leave Act that require reasonable accommodation and medical leave when necessary (Johnson & Gardner,1999; Tebo, 2005).

The assistance of mental health professionals is encouraged if an employee is demonstrating signs of violent behavior. Analysis of verbal statements, reported observations by third parties, or written correspondence that threatens violence will demonstrate a reasonable standard of care by the business. Preemptive counseling may reduce violent behavior in an employee. An Employee Assistance Program (EAP) will demonstrate a willingness on the part of both the employee and employer to resolve violent behavior at work. It is possible that the employee will be helped, and the employer will reduce potential negligence through timely intervention. An EAP will provide a defense against ADA claims for failure to provide a reasonable accommodation.

Employer Liability For Workplace Violence

Employers may be liable for violence in the workplace under various theories of law. Here are the most relevant theories (Perline & Goldschmidt, 2004; Voillis, et al., 2005; Whitten, & Mosley, 2000):

- Employees who are stalked and assaulted at work by a spouse (or anyone for that matter) may seek *tort* relief, and the homicide of an employee may result in wrongful death litigation. *Negligence* is the breach of a legal duty to use reasonable care to prevent a foreseeable risk of injury to others. Issues involving negligence include providing a safe working environment, warning of dangerous working conditions, hiring responsible personnel, and providing security.
- Within the scope of negligence actions are the following: *negligent referral, selection, supervision, retention, and training.* See Chapter 4 for additional information regarding the importance of training supervisors and managers.
- Criminal charges may be brought against the attacker, and both the employee and employer may seek restraining orders barring the spouse from the employer's premises.
- *Vicarious liability* requires that under certain circumstances, employers will be responsible for the actions of their employees if harmful acts are committed within the scope of employment.
- Under federal *Occupational Safety and Health Act* and state legislation, employers have a duty to provide a safe working environment. Substantial civil and criminal penalties may be levied against employers who violate these laws.
- Under The *Americans with Disabilities Act,* an employer may defend personnel actions against an employee who otherwise has a qualified disability if the employee creates a direct threat to the safety to self or others. This action assumes that no reasonable accommodation exists that would remove or reduce the danger (see Chapter 2).

RECCOMENDTION FOR DEVELOPING SAFETY-RELATED TRAINING

The following recommendations for developing safety-related training is divided into two sections. The first section focuses on issues associated with safety training in general, and the second section focuses of training related to violence in the workplace. These recommendations are consistent with OSHA (1999a, 1999b) and several other sources (Awadalla & Roughton, 1998; Daniel & Farb, 2005; Erickson, 1996; Klane, 2004; Perline & Goldschmidt, 2004; Waddington, Badger & Bull, 2006).

Note that regulatory standards change quite frequently, so be sure to update instructional programs by continually reviewing those regulatory agencies that impact your organization.

Developing Safety-Related Training

1. Selection. Recall that selection is the first line of defense in reducing all forms of harassment and illegal discrimination in an organization (see Chapter 2). The same rationale applies to safety and violence in the workplace. Selecting competent employees includes attitudes toward safety. Driving arrests and convictions for alcohol and substance abuse-related crimes, previous histories of assaults and convictions of serious crimes against persons and property, and violations of spousal restraining orders may be predictive of unsafe and potentially violent employees. Whitten & Mosley (2000) recommended executing releases from applicants that explain the scope of background and reference checks, with special emphasis on previous disciplinary and performance actions.

Attitudes and behaviors toward safety may be assessed and predicted through valid pre-employment testing. One such predictor is impulse control (a preference to think before acting). Research using the "Job Candidate Profile," which measures various aspects of impulse control at work, determined that those applicants with "higher scores tended to have fewer on-the-job injuries, committed fewer safety infractions and were rated by supervisors as safer workers" (Kamp and Krause, 1997, p. 27). Be sure to consider the implications for potential discrimination if psychological tests are used as part of a selection strategy. EEOC guidelines require that such tests predict job success (must be valid and job related), and ADA allows pre-employment psychological testing of normal personality traits (but not psychological disorders potentially requiring medical treatment).

To ignore such predictors is to invite discrimination-related complaints (see Chapter 2), as well as potential litigation for negligent training, negligent selection, negligent retention and negligent referral (Perline & Goldschmidt, 2004; Viollis, et al., 2005; also see Chapter 4).

Make it a standard policy to train managers and supervisors in the selection of safety conscious employee.

2. Comply with all safety and health laws and regulations. Employers are responsible through the general duty clause of OSHA, as well as specific standards, to ensure the safety of employees. Specific training requirements are embedded in specific industry, maritime and construction industries. A listing of specific training standards for industries is provided in Appendix D. Note that some states have stricter health and safety requirements than OSHA, and that OSHA is not the only agency that regulates health and safety.

Instructional designers should be aware of their employers' responsibility to ensure that chemicals and hazardous wastes used or brought into a worksite provide the dissemination of materials safety data sheets (MSDS), container labeling, as well as supervisory and employee training. OSHA (n.d.) has developed a Model Training Program for Hazard Communication that conforms to OSHA § 1200.

Risk management and training personnel should collaborate on the identification of applicable statutes, relying on consultants and other technical experts as necessary. Compliance must be based on specific work sites and equipment.

3. Conduct a Hazard and Risk Assessment Survey. The hazard and risk assessment is divided into the following key elements (Erickson, 1996; Manuele, 2000):

a. Physical elements determine "geographical areas of potential risk" including buildings, sheds, transmission lines, roadways and any other structural element.
b. Material elements include the "identification of any physical, chemical or biological substance or agent" that poses a threat to health or safety, including products and by-products of the manufacturing process.
c. Operational elements include jobs, skills, and processes in coordinated efforts designed to realize the goals of the employer (products or services), and also include job analysis (Carlisle, 1986) and procedure development (Ward, 1988).
d. Procedural elements "constrain workplace behaviors to defined limits, provide management a rational basis for exerting quality control and oversight of the health and safety program, as well as provide regulatory agencies with evidence of good faith efforts toward compliance." Ward added that "written procedures

give specific directions to the training staff on how to perform work." (1988, p. 75).

e. Human elements are not only employees, but also anyone who becomes at risk to known hazards, including visitors, members of the public, vendors making deliveries, contract employees, etc.
f. Informational elements include gathering, storage, and retrieval of pertinent information necessary to support decision making, and these are critical for an effective safety management.
g. Actual incident history, including OSHA recordable and lost work day cases and workers' compensation history;
h. Incidents that under slightly different circumstances could have resulted in serious injury or damage;
i. Input from workers on tasks they perceive to be hazardous; and
j. Hazardous, nonroutine tasks (e.g., maintenance and trouble shooting) and other known high hazard tasks; new tasks with which workers may not be familiar.

4. Complete a job analysis and high risk task analysis. Job analysis is the foundation from which a multitude of personnel decisions are derived, and include recruitment, selection, placement, training and development, supervision, performance appraisal, promotions, transfers, terminations, and layoffs. The outcome of a well-documented job analysis is a job description that identifies essential functions, specific tasks associated with each function, and the knowledge, skills and attitudes (KSAs) that support each task. Jobs were previously codified into the DOT (Dictionary of Occupational Titles) which has now been replaced by O*NET (Occupational Information Network) (Jenneret & Strong, 2003). O*NET is a comprehensive and easily accessible source of information for job analysts and instructional designers.[2]

The results of the hazard and risk assessment combined with the applicable OSHA and other laws and regulations require a careful analysis of discrete tasks within a job. Identifying tasks for high-risk training differs from normal task analysis because the stakes are higher (Sample, 1996; Schultz, 2004; Ward, 1988).

A well-executed task analysis and written task procedures serve multiple masters. Trainers should incorporate task information and work procedures into the design and delivery of the training. Supervisors will use the same information for instruction, on-the-job training, coaching, performance appraisal, and qualification purposes. Human resource managers will use this information to evaluate jobs for compensation and safety personnel are on notice regarding high risk work.

Tasks are analyzed using a variety of techniques (Fine & Cronshaw, 1999). An ergonomic approach to tasks analysis is described by Montante (1994). This process uses a chart that identifies, among other things, triggers, purpose, and actions which help identify any limiting subsystems impacting overall performance of a task. Schultz (2004) described a task analysis process that identifies risks associated with conveyor machines in a variety of manufacturing settings. Specialized software applications are available for conducting ergonomic related analysis. Craven (1998) reports the use of TaskAnalyst which uses the NIOSH ergonomic lifting equation to assess the physical stress on two-handed lifting tasks.

Occupational tasks are typically procedure driven. DACUM, which stands for *"Developing A CurriculUM"* is a structured approach for identifying duties and tasks for occupational education and technical training curriculums. This approach has been used successfully by educational institutions, business and industry since the 1980s to identify duties and tasks (Kosidlak, 1987). DACUM was developed in Canada and was subsequently popularized in the Unites States at the Center on Education and Training for Employment (CETE) at Ohio State University. DACUM is used primarily for identification of instructional needs, instructional program planning, curriculum development, training materials development, creation and revision job descriptions and standards, employee recruitment, ISO 9000/14000 performance, and career guidance. Institutions such as community colleges and vocational technical schools and manufacturing businesses that collaborate using DACUM will have developed a seamless process that facilitates educational institutions in the preparation of skilled workers at the community and regional levels.

DACUM involves seven steps:

1. committee orientation to DACUM;
2. job review to arrive at a mutually acceptable working title(s) for jobs and specialization areas;
3. identification of duties or general functionl areas of responsibility under which tasks will fit;
4. identification of specific tasks performed in each duty area (each statement including an action verb, object, and one or more qualifying words);
5. review and refinement of task and duty statements;

6. identification of related requirements such as general knowledge and skills, tools and equipment, supplies and materials used, worker traits and attitudes, and future occupational trends/concerns; and
7. task analysis to determine specific steps, performance standards and related requirements. Information from the task analysis is incorporated into modules, learning guides, and other instructional materials as a final dimension of the process (Norton, 1993).

DACUM is implemented primarily by educators or trained facilitators and was developed as a way of bringing business and industry into the development of educational programs. Robert Norton (1993), who developed the technique, states that DACUM is a "significant technique for initiating needed cooperation (between business and education) in tech prep . . ." (p. 1). The process, in effect, functions as an "abbreviated version" of the widely known Functional Job Analysis (FJA).

Expert performers and supervisors are brought together for a two-day focus group to interact, describe their jobs, and rate activities according to their frequency and importance. Workshop participants in the original DACUM structure are "not hampered or constrained by a literature base or any instructor-created document" (Norton, 1993, p. 1), but, rather, are given a blank slate on which to define and describe their occupations. From these focus group sessions, a profile chart is created which details and graphically displays the duties and tasks involved in a particular occupation. The results are submitted to a larger group of employees and immediate supervisors for verification. Task-specific instructions are then developed based on the component tasks that have been determined and verified.

The Center on Education and Training for Employment at Ohio State University maintains a bank of over 400 examples of completed charts which are available for a reasonable fee (www.dacumohiostate.com). These charts are useful as a starting point for a fully validated DACUM chart conducted at the local level by an expert facilitator and a panel of qualified subject matter experts.[3]

5. Write comprehensive policies, procedures, and rules for high-risk tasks. It is not enough to identify tasks that are reasonably associated with the potential for harm to employees and third parties. Given the nature of work in a high risk occupation, such as police officers, crane operators, or fork-lift operators, it will be necessary for employers to develop policies, procedures, and rules that direct and control work of employees. Policies are most often found in employee handbooks and state in general terms what is expected of employees. Procedures and rules are often found in operational manuals. Procedures typically specify a step-by-step process for accomplishing a specific task or for operating equipment, whereas rules define specific boundaries of conduct for which a consequence could be applied for infractions. According to Ward (1988), "The central reason for procedures is to control work. Control is required to create and maintain consistency in the operation of training" (p. 75-76) and the operation of work at job sites.

It is critical that whatever is instructed in a class room (or through other media such as computer-assisted-learning or on-the-job training) is exactly what is expected by line managers and supervisors at a workplace. Hence, it is important to have of an accurate and complete job description that is supported by relevant and accurate policies, procedures, and rules. Human resource job analysts, risk managers, safety specialists, instructional designers, and line managers must all literally be on the same page, otherwise employees in training are likely learning the wrong skills. Training units should certify employees as competent at the task level, whereas line managers and supervisors should qualify employees after they have been trained and are performing on the job (Sample, 1995). A feedback loop from line managers to the training unit is critical to ensure that skills learned in training are the ones required at the work site.

6. Design and develop instruction for high-risk tasks. Instructional designers and others charged with the responsibility for designing and developing instruction for high-risk tasks must be prepared to engage employees and managers in ways that promote safety in the workplace. Select a standard instructional systems design (ISD) model to produce the training program (Dick, Carey & Carey, 2004; Piskurich, 2000; Rothwell & Kazanas, 2003). Use task analysis information to focus the design, development, implementation, and evaluation of the training program to the specific context and needs of the organization. The structural rigor of a well-executed instructional systems approach ensures logical linkages across the phases of the instructional design. Given the potential liability associated with safety-related instruction, it is very important to document with approval signatures as each step is completed.

The decision to "make-or-buy" instruction is one that has implications for time, resources, and contextual fit. Given a complete understanding of the contextual and task requirements for instruction, the designer may elect to purchase or otherwise obtain instructional "off-the shelf modules." If no such modules are available or they are too costly, then the designer may have to be develop an "in-house" version. Appendix E provides a summary of training-related safety resources that are available to all organizations. Most of these resources are available directly from the Internet and include the following topics: workplace safety, drug-free workplace, and violence in the workplace. Media include streaming videos, slide presentations, and paper-based learning products.

A key component in the design and development process concerns planning for the transfer of learning from the classroom (or elearning, job-instruction training, or other learning event) to the work site. In order to visualize the effectiveness of the transfer, staple "yourself [as the instructional designer] to the learner [employee]" (Wick, et al. 2006, p. 68). Imagine the journey of the participant from the beginning of the safety training program into the future by six months or a year. Consider the following questions that employees might ponder:

1. Am I clear about my responsibilities to my employer regarding my attitudes and behaviors for my own safety and the safety of others?
2. Will I be punished or ostracized for reporting unsafe work procedures with equipment that may cause injury to me or others?
3. What is my support system for clarifying possible unsafe or violent behaviors by others?
4. Where does my manager stand on the importance of the compliance with safety and health policies?
5. Is this stuff really important to higher-ups in the organization? How will I know that my safety-conscious work behavior and attitudes are valued?

Finally, consider the remote possibility that these same questions, and many others, will be asked by federal and state inspectors if there is a serious workplace accident or occurrence of workplace violence. Under those circumstances, inspectors will become "stapled" to employees! Given these circumstances, how would your employees respond to questions regarding the "effectiveness" of the safety training program?

The politically astute manager of the instructional design and development unit must be able to consistently negotiate the divergent concerns and expectations of various stakeholder groups. Examples include union and management, employers and external regulatory personnel, engineers, technicians, and support personnel, security and risk-management personnel, and corporate legal staff. Signatures affirming the accuracy of instructional content from subject matter experts, safety technicians and engineers, and other knowledgeable personnel should be required through each phase of the design process.

7. Provide training for employees. According to Eyres (1998, p. 50), employees should be provided the following safety training:

- Training for all when the program is first established.
- Training in general workplace safety and job-specific health and safety instruction whenever employees are given new job assignments for which they have not previously been trained.
- Job-specific instruction and any new general workplace safety information whenever employees are given new job assignments for which they have not previously been trained.
- Specific training and instruction whenever new substances, processes, procedures, or equipment presenting a new or different hazard is introduced to the workplace.
- Specific training and instruction whenever the employer becomes aware of a new or previously unrecognized hazard.

8. Evaluate and document training. Establish a system by which the training unit certifies performance as a condition of program completion, followed by on-the-job qualification requiring supervisors to assess job performance through observation of the trained employee. This process will assist in the transfer of learning to the job, especially if a feedback loop to the training unit is part of the evaluation.

Maintain a complete master copy of all training materials and handouts, including instructional objectives, a transfer-of-learning plan, and resumes of instructors that list areas of expertise and credentials, and master copies of any materials used to evaluate the effectiveness of the training. For each training session, require participants to sign an attendance form that includes the name of the instructor, dates, times, and location of instruction; if training occurs on multiple days, participants sign for each day. The instructor should note in writing the names of participants who miss any part of the training. Archive these attendance forms in a safe location, being mindful that original signatures, not copies, on attendance forms are preferred as evidence of attendance.

Erickson (1996) suggests that monitors be assigned to evaluate high-risk-training programs. Monitors can provide helpful feedback to new instructors, make sure that contract trainers follow the instructional plan, and to certify the number of clock hours required for mandated training.

Maintain all documentation required by OSHA and any other safety compliance agency, such as the U.S. Nuclear Regulatory Agency or the Environmental Protection Agency. Under certain circumstances, federal or state inspectors may demand immediate access to documentation.

Program Elements for Preventing Workplace Violence

1. Management Commitment and Employee Involvement. The development of a joint management/employee workplace violence committee responsible for overseeing assessment, development, and evaluation of prevention programs. Other responsibilities are 1) establishing a joint committee that includes managers, union representatives and employees, safety and security personnel, risk management specialists, and attorneys; 2) providing a contextual definition of workplace violence; 3) developing and communicating a "zero-tolerance for violence" strategy and policy; 4) communicating these policies through various media (posted warnings, company newsletters, etc.) within the organization; 5) explaining these policies in employee and operations manuals (including the necessity for progressive discipline, when appropriate); and 6) and forming the basis for required periodic training of supervisors and managers (Awadalla and Roughton, 1998).

2. Hazard Assessment and Worksite Analysis. OSHA (1998b) recommended the completion of a work-site hazard analysis for existing and potential hazards for workplace violence. If necessary, require that a team of knowledgeable employees conduct the analysis. Larger businesses may want to identify representatives from senior management, operations personnel, security, employee assistance, occupational safety and health, legal and human resources staff. Eemployees and union representation should collaborate on the study. External consultants may be useful for both large and small organizations.

A workplace hazard analysis consists of three essential steps: 1) analyze records and past incidents of violence, 2) conduct an initial work site inspection and analysis, and 3) conduct regularly scheduled audits and evaluations of the program. Employers must be able to identify and respond swiftly and effectively to violent conduct at work. Although no single warning profile will always predict such behavior, experience informs us that certain characteristics, in combination with others, may be predictive of violence at work (Perline & Goldschmidt, 2004:

- History of violent behavior (previous work settings, family his tory);
- Unusual and consistent discussion and fascination with weapons, guns, and explosives at work;
- Direct and veiled threats of violence;
- Serious personal, family, or financial problems with no outlet for anger and frustration;
- Significant changes in behavior (mood swings, outbursts, insubordination, paranoia);
- Deterioration of work performance;
- Substance, alcohol, or prescribed medicine abuse; and/or
- Withdrawn behavior in employees for whom work is their only source of people contact and life satisfaction.

None of the characteristics listed above are perfect predictors. Employers must use common sense and intuition when evaluating preexisting and current situations involving violent conduct at work. Liability reduction and prevention require a focused, coordinated, and cooperative effort between line management and supervisors, and those responsible for personnel policies and training.

3. Hazard Prevention and Control. The development of effective policies and training are not the only options that an employer must consider in preventing workplace violence. Engineered controls, although potentially expensive, may be necessary for a variety of organizations. The following recommendations may apply to health and human services, industrial and retail service businesses.

- Make physical changes in the workplace with new construction, if necessary, that reduces the potential for violence in the workplace, including safe rooms. Provide separate restrooms for employees and customers that are secure and can be locked from the inside.
- Create physical barriers between customers, clients, and em-

ployees, including pass-thorough drawers to exchange money and reduce contact with others.

- Consider the installation of sophisticated lighting arrangements (sound and motion detectors), sophisticated mirrors, and video cameras, and detectors for knives, guns, and explosives.
- Enclose certain areas within an office (such as a nurse's station, a place for money handlers and lottery ticket sales in convenience stores, and a place for bank tellers) with bullet proof pass-through windows or drop-down security gates or panels, and secured entrance and exits.
- Install silent alarms or panic buttons that can be activated quickly and without detection.
- In common areas for health care facilities and social service organizations, provide light weight furniture with rounded edges, and bolt it to the floor or wall if feasible.

4. Employee Assistance Programs. The assistance of mental health professionals is encouraged if an employee is demonstrating signs of violent behavior. Analysis of verbal statements, reported observations by third parties, or written correspondence that threatens violence will demonstrate a reasonable standard of care by the business. Preemptive counseling may reduce violent behavior in an employee. An Employee Assistance Program (EAP) will demonstrate a willingness on the part of both the employee and employer to resolve violent behavior at work. It is possible that the employee will be helped, and the employer will reduce the potential for negligence through timely intervention. An EAP will provide a defense against ADA claims for failure to provide a reasonable accommodation.

CONCLUSION

Employers of large and small companies are well advised to develop, communicate, and train employees regarding safety and health issues in the workplace. OSHA and several other federal regulatory agencies have legal authority to inspect, investigate, fine, and enjoin organizations from unsafe work practices. Especially difficult for all organizations, particularly those that serve the public, is that they are susceptible to violence in the workplace. A summary of OSHA general industry training requirements will be found in Appendix D.

Organizations with extensive OSHA citation histories pay more for insurance, have reduced opportunities to compete for new business, and serious industrial accidents result in negative media attention worldwide. Citation histories from most, if not all, regulatory agencies are open to the public, including attorneys for injured employees who are seeking justice beyond their potential workers' compensation awards.

Instructional designers must work closely with a myriad of disparate stakeholders, each of whom may have different goals and issues to promote. Employers and owners of businesses may seek simple solutions to complex safety and health issues believing that safety is a cost, not an investment. Safety managers and technicians are concerned that polices, procedures, rules, and training are not sufficient to prevent accidents and risk-management staff wants to reduce the cost of insurance premiums. Corporate attorneys are concerned that lapses in any of the above will put the employer at risk of serious litigation.

The design of effective safety and health-related instruction is facilitated by available materials and media developed by regulatory agencies and vendors. A partial list of these resources will be found in Appendix E. Effective safety training that is expertly designed, implemented and documented will result in safer workplaces and reduced opportunities for litigation associated with high risk work tasks.

Endnotes

1 States and territories operating federally approved occupational health and safety plans include Alaska, Arizona, California, Hawaii, Indiana, Iowa, Kentucky, Maryland, Michigan, Minnesota, Nevada, New Mexico, North Carolina, Oregon, South Carolina, Tennessee, Utah, Vermont, Virginia, Washington, Wyoming, Virgin Islands, Puerto Rico (29 C.F.R. 1952, 90-394).

2 O*NET can be accessed on the Internet at http://www.onetcenter.org/whatsnew.html

3 The Center on Education and Training for Employment, Ohio State University, 1900 Kenny, Ohio 43210-1090. Telephone: 1-800-848-4815, ext. 2-8481. Internet: www.dacumohiostate.com

Chapter 4
Negligent Training and Related Liability

Chapter Objectives

Having reviewed the information in this chapter, the reader will

1. define negligence and summarize the elements that constitute negligent training;
2. explain how workers' compensation is a no-fault remedy for injuries that occur on the job;
3. analyze examples of negligent training cases from various business and governmental contexts;
4. define negligent selection, supervision, and retention and explain why they are often combined with negligent training in lawsuits;
5. review the importance of supervisors as first-line trainers in organizations;
6. explain how governmental agencies may be sued in federal district court for a civil rights violation based on instances of negligence; and
7. summarize recommendations for identifying high liability tasks.

The following additional materials are located in Appendix F. Supervisory Audit of Training Related Liability.

INTRODUCTION

A *tort* is a legal classification for a "civil wrong" for which a court may provide a remedy for damages. Tort law addresses wrongs from breaches of duties that arise between people, businesses, associations, corporations and governmental units acting in their private capacities. Torts may be intentional (such as a trespass on property, a battery on a person, or intentional infliction of mental distress) or nonintentional (automobile accident, slip and fall in a store) (Schwartz, Kelly, & Partlett, 2000).

Actions arising out of nonintentional torts are litigated as instances of *negligence*. In these cases, carelessness not associated with intentional behavior that causes injury to people or property, resulting in damages, allows the complainant recovery against the defendant. Such damages may include recovery for costs associated with actual injuries: compensation for lost wages, medical expenses, pain, suffering, humiliation, and emotional distress (Bennett-Alexander & Hartman, 2001). Since torts are civil matters, they are heard by courts having civil jurisdiction, although there are instances where criminal conduct may arise from a malicious intentional tort. Recall that O. J. Simpson was acquitted of murdering two people (a criminal act); however, he lost in a civil suit alleging an intentional tort (wrongful death) by the families of the two victims.

The same set of facts that give rise to a complaint in negligence may also result in one or more of the following:

- state and federal civil rights claims arising out of instances of negligent training (see Chapter 2 and the section later in this chapter on municipal liability);
- OSHA-related safety inspections and fines (see Chapter 3);
- criminal prosecution of the employer (or owner) for intentional, malicious or aggravated negligence (see discussion later in this chapter); and
- workers' compensation payments for injuries to employees.

WORKERS' COMPENSATION

Prior to *workers' compensation* statutes, it was not unusual for an employer to be sued by an employee for injuries sustained on the job. Each case would be settled or litigated at great cost to both the injured employee and the business owner or employer. The advent of the workers' compensation alternative system provides a no-fault procedure for indemnifying the injured employee. Injuries are compensable if they occur "in the course of and arising out of employment" and the system is funded through insurance paid for by the employer (Soverign, 1999). The employee does not have to prove an unsafe workplace, nor will the employee be held accountable for carelessness or contributing to the injury. By law, workers' compensation is liberally interpreted in favor of the employee because the injury would not have occurred but for the job (Hood, Hardy & Lewis, 1999).

Under the "exclusive remedy rule," the employee receives payments according to a schedule of benefits that establish a dollar amount based on the loss of bodily functions. Level of disability is typically determined as follows (Jasper, 2005; McConnaughhay & Collier, 2000).

- Temporary total disability—employee cannot work for a short period of time.
- Temporary partial disability—employee cannot perform all work activities for a short period of time.
- Permanent partial total disability—employee has limited work capabilities for the remainder of his or her work life.
- Permanent total disability—employee cannot work for the remainder of his or her work life (loss of eyesight, limb, and paralysis.
- Death benefits—limited to cover burial expenses.

Employees are not eligible for pain and suffering or mental anguish under the workers' compensation system, and are precluded from suing their employer except when gross or intentional negligence is the basis for the complaint (Schwartz, Kelly, & Partlett, 2000). Cases are decided on a case-by-case basis in the trial courts. A case management system has been inaugurated in recent years to combat and reduce fraud. Figure 4.1 provides a summary of the typical types of injuries covered by state no-fault workers' compensation laws.

There are a few exceptions that bar workers' compensation for injuries to employees. Typically excluded are employees who become intoxicated or who use drugs while at work (unless the employer provides the liquor). Self-inflicted injuries are not covered by workers' compensation. Injuries to an innocent bystander from the horseplay of others are covered; however, an instigator of horseplay that results in injury may not be covered unless such activity is tolerated by the employer. Finally, an "employee who is the victim in a fight *about* work is covered by workers' comp" (Risser, 1993, 218).

ELEMENTS OF A NEGLIGENCE COMPLAINT

Negligence is generally defined as unintentional conduct that falls below the standard of care that is necessary to protect others against

Table 4.1
Workers' Compensation

Types of Injuries Covered

Coming and going rule – Employees usually are not covered going to and coming from work. Exceptions may include making a detour for the business (dropping a package off at the post office) or riding in an employer-provided vehicle or through a transportation plan (van pools, ride sharing, etc).

Parking lot injuries – If the employer provides, pays for, or recommends using a particular lot, employees are covered from the time they turn into the driveway until they drive out, and they are covered for injuries to and from the lot, even if the lot is two blocks away.

Employer-related business travel – Business trips, including overnight stays and weekends, for reasonably foreseeable accidents (like slipping on a wet bathroom floor or falling down an escalator). Injuries related to personal venturing, such as shopping or hiking, are not covered.

Off-site business-related injuries - Employees are covered if they were on employer-related business when they were injured. Employees who have car accidents while driving on company business are covered, unless personal "business" is conducted, such as dropping off clothes at the dry cleaners.

Exceptions to the No-Fault Requirement

Intoxication – Employees who abuse drugs or who drink on the job and hurt themselves are not allowed to claim workers' compensation; however, the rule is different if the employer provides liquor.

Self-inflicted injuries – Employees who deliberately injure themselves are not entitled to workers' compensation. The employer is generally not held responsible for suicide of an employee.

Recreational activities – Injuries sustained in off-duty and voluntary events are generally not covered by workers' compensation.

Horseplay and fights – Innocent employee bystanders who are injured by horseplay and fights are covered, but not the employee who initiates horseplay or fight (varies by state). Whether or not the employer tolerates horseplay or fights may determine coverage (also varies by state).

Holiday and social activities – Injuries occurring during voluntary holiday and social activities are not covered by workers' compensation. Participation in athletic programs, such as tag football, softball and basketball, should be voluntary; employers should obtain signed consent forms indicating that participation is voluntary.

Source: Modified and adapted from Hood, Hardy, & Lewis (1999). McConnaughhay & Collier (2000) and Soverign, (1999).

exposure to an unreasonable risk of a foreseeable injury. A cause of action for negligence consists of three essential elements: (1) a legal duty owed by one party to another; (2) a breach of that duty; and (3) damages proximately caused by the breach (Schwartz, Kelly, & Partlett, 2000). In *strict liability,* the injury or damage is so severe that the law dispenses with the need to prove intent or mental state if it is reasonably certain that the harm could have been foreseen. Examples include reckless operation of dangerous equipment causing death or injury, deliberate indifference by retail store security in using a lethal chokehold to restrain a suspected shoplifter.

Negligence suits are initiated and resolved primarily in the states' civil courts on a case-by-case basis. If a claim of this nature is not settled, the plaintiff will present the case before a judge and jury. If the plaintiff prevails, the jury will award damages; if the defendant prevails, the plaintiff receives no relief. Both parties have the option of appealing to a higher court for review.

The elements of a negligence complaint are described more specifically as follows:

1. A legal duty or standard of care: May be specified in a statute or part of the "common law" from judicial precedents; a hypothetical "reasonable person" is used by the courts to establish to which a duty or standard has been breached. What constitutes a "reasonable person" will vary with education, training, professional obligations to society and the potential for harm. For examples, physicians are held to a higher standard than are nurses, who are held to a higher standard than are lay people.
2. Breach of duty: A person (or employer) should exercise the care expected of an average, normal person under like circumstances; a breach occurs when the standard of care falls below that expected of a reasonable person and was foreseeable, and is referred to as the "reasonable care" standard.
3. Proximate cause: The breach of duty was the legal cause of damage or injury; to what extent was the negligence a substantial factor in bringing about harm to someone. If the harm would have resulted even if the defendant had not been negligent, then the defendant is not the causal agent; therefore, no proximate cause or negligence would be found. The closer the connection between the act and the harm, the more likely that legal causation exists.

4. Injuries/damages: There must be actual harm resulting in actual physical injury or property damage (Schwartz, et al., 2000).

NEGLIGENT TRAINING

Negligent training as a cause of action became more popular in the state courts during the 1980s and 1990s (Fenton, Ruud, & Kimbell, 1991; Mathiason & De Bernardo, 1998). According to Eyres (1997), "Employees and training participants litigate when they are injured during training, or when they make a mistake on the job that they assert wouldn't have happened if they had been properly trained" (p. 67). All of the states except Minnesota recognize negligent training as a viable tort action. Minnesota does recognize negligent supervision and negligent retention.

Negligent training may occur in such environments as classrooms, laboratories, simulators, as well as work sites where on-the-job training and coaching occur. Assaults and batteries occurring on the classroom or work site, false imprisonment, trespasses, and conversion of personal property are examples of intentional torts for which civil liability is a remedy. Training in the use of dangerous equipment or training in handling noxious chemicals and working in unsafe environments for which there are safety compliance issues, may give rise to actions resulting in negligence (Ward, 1988; Eyres, 1998).

Case Example: Negligent Training in a Hospital

The following facts in a wrongful death allegation demonstrate the legal elements necessary to sustain a negligent training case in a state civil court. The context is fire in a hospital room. On the day of the fire a sister was visiting her brother, one of two people to die as a result of the fire. The brother who was suffering from a head injury was not ambulatory. He was sitting in a chair smoking a cigarette. He had the permission of one of the nurses to smoke. No one told the sister to not let her brother smoke. No ash tray was visible so the sister used a juice cup and a plastic soup tray for disposing of the ashes. A nurse came in and restrained the brother in his chair with ties to prevent him from sliding out of the chair. The sister held the cigarette to the brother's mouth and she disposed of the ashes in the soup container. She testified that there was one or more used cigarettes in the soup container; she does not remember throwing the soup container into the trash can, but could have.

Shortly after the sister left the hospital room, a fire started in a trashcan next to brother's bed. A second male patient was in the same room in a bed next to some windows. The nurse who first discovered the fire did not believe the second patient in the room to be in immediate danger. She first unsuccessfully tried to untie the patient who was restrained in his chair. She then tried to smother the fire with bed linens. When this did not subdue the flames, she ran out of the room and called for help; two other nurses responded immediately. The nurses attempted to pull the legs of the patient in the chair across the floor into the hallway; he slid out of the chair when these restraints burned through. One of the nurses tried to reenter the room for the second patient but was prevented by smoke, fire and heat.

Two nurses sounded an alarm and called for security and neither nurse attempted to remove the second patient from the room. Both ran by a fire extinguisher but neither grabbed it before returning to the room. One of the nurses eventually tried to enter the room with a fire extinguisher to rescue the second patient but could not do so because of the fire. The second patient died of smoke inhalation and the first patient died later due to infections from burn wounds.

The hospital had a "no smoking" policy except in designated areas, and the hospital room of the deceased was not designated for smoking. Those violating the no smoking ban were to be admonished from continuing any smoking and the policy was to be enforced by all employees and especially all supervisory and security personnel. The hospital also had a policy regarding fire emergencies in which patient removal was to be accomplished immediately. The policy used the acronym "RACE"—"R" meant to rescue or remove the patient first, "A" meant that the alarm should be sounded second. "C" meant that that the fire should be contained, followed by "E" for extinguishing the fire. The hospital had a training movie depicting a trash can fire that demonstrated how to pull a patient out of bed by using bed sheets to drag the patient across the floor.

All of the above-mentioned elements of negligence can be found in these facts. The hospital had a legal duty to instruct their nurses in the correct performance of their work. Although the hospital had a policy on fire evacuation procedures, the nurse in this instance was not trained on the policy. The breach of the duty resulted from failing to remove the patient from a room on fire. A proximate causal link between the death of the patient (injury/damage) and the legal duty to adequately train the nurse on fire evacuation policy was argued successfully before the court (*Stacy v. Truman Medical Center*, 1992).

SOURCES OF LEGAL DUTIES AND STANDARDS OF CARE

Legal duties and standards of care in terms of negligence have their origins in common law, statutes and administrative rules, and case law. Statutes provide criminal penalties and civil remedies beyond what is available from common law precedents. Common law is used whenever statutes and case law fail to provide adequate remedies. Most of the compliance required training has origins in federal and state statutes which are further expanded by administrative rules and regulations. For example, the U.S. Code of Federal Regulations (CFR) provides enforcement guidelines and administrative procedures for OSHA, EEOC and ADA, and many other federal statutes. California passed the California Corporate Criminal Liability Act (California Penal Code § 387) which makes corporations and their managers criminally responsible when they fail to warn their employees and report "serious concealed dangers of which the corporation and its managers have actual knowledge . . ." Prison sentences up to three years and fines of $25,000 can be imposed on individuals, and fines of up to $1,000,000 can be imposed on corporations.

Criminal Negligence—Negligent Training and Wrongful Death.

There are instances in which employers may be criminally responsible for failure to adequately train their employees. In these types of cases, higher levels of proof and state and federal constitutional guarantees for prosecuting and defending criminal cases will apply.

ValuJet Flight 592 crashed on May 11, 1996 in the Everglades south of Miami, Florida. In addition to the civil action, SabreTech received a 24-count federal criminal indictment that charged three employees with, among other things, failing to properly train employees. This case is discussed in depth in Chapter 3.

In *State v. Shoreline Support Corporation* (1989), a Wisconsin employer was found guilty of reckless homicide of one of its bulldozer operators. The deceased bulldozer operator was a recent high school graduate and had been dating the daughter of one of the owners of the reclamation business. He was also an epileptic who was under the care of a physician and whose seizures were controlled with medication. Although the deceased had a driver's license, his physician had warned the patient's father that the son should not drive. Medication was altered when seizures reoccurred in March and May of 1986. The deceased began working for Shoreline after graduation from high school. The training provided to the deceased consisted of observing one of the owners operate the bulldozer. Between June 6 and June 17, the deceased logged 49 hours working for Shoreline, 43 of which were logged on the bulldozer. One of the owners testified that he trained the deceased in the operation of the bulldozer from one to seven hours a day during his first week on the job.

In the Shoreline case, uncontested testimony established that the work site was inherently dangerous, and was no place for an inexperienced bulldozer operator to be working unsupervised. The operator was required to maneuver an 8- by 20-foot bulldozer along a strip of land which measured between 16 and 75 feet in width. The operator scooped rubble in the bulldozer shovel, made a 180 degree turn, and dumped the rubble over the edge of a cliff. At the time of the fatal accident, the operator had approximately 43 hours of experience with the bulldozer. Since the accident was not witnessed, it was reasonable to assume that the operator was not being supervised at the time of the accident. Testimony by an expert witness established that bulldozer operators are normally provided 1500 hours of training and supervision before working under the conditions described above. The appeals court noted that a jury could have reasonably found that the lack of training and supervision of the employee were causally related to his death and that the employer acted recklessly in its failure to train and supervise the young bulldozer operator.

REPRESENTATIVE NEGLIGENT TRAINING CASES

Examples of negligent training from a variety of business contexts include construction, private security, retail, restaurant and entertainment establishments, personal fitness and athletic programs. The following case summaries illustrate negligent training from a variety of business contexts. Each case demonstrates the elements necessary to sustain an allegation of negligence based on negligent training.

One of the earliest cases involving negligent training involved a black powder blasting contractor and a brick manufacturer. The brick company contracted with the blasting company to discharge shale type rock in its quarry. A 13-year veteran employee from the defendant blasting company calculated the blasting requirements, set the charges, and detonated the blast. The miscalculation of the charges caused a devastating blast that resulted in substantial physical damage to the brick company and an in interruption and loss of business. In court testimony, the employee who set the charge admitted that he had no prior training or experience in calculating, setting, and detonating dynamite charges in shale rock. The blasting contractor admitted that he had no knowledge of the blaster's shale experience and in fact had never inquired as to his background in such work. No training had been provided by the defendant employer for blasting in shale rock.

This case was tried by a Pennsylvania jury which found in favor of the plaintiff brick company and recovery was significant. This case was also retried in a federal district court with similar results—the blasting contractor was held liable for all damages for inadequate training that resulted in harm and damage (*Waterston Brick Co. v. Hercules Powder Co.*, 1967).

The second case example concerns a fire that started when fumes from a truck that had just been sprayed inside a building were ignited by an exhaust fan. This particular business sprays plastic liners on beds of pick-up trucks. The sales-manager, the plaintiff, drove the truck out of the building, but went back into the building in an attempt to help his coworkers, whom he believed were trapped inside. He suffered first-, second-, and third-degree burns over 20 percent of his body, including his head, arms, and back. He needed several skin graft surgeries. His medical expenses were $558,000, and his future medical expenses are estimated at $178,000. As a sales manager, he was earning $36,000 annually. His lost wages were $36,000, and following rehabilitation, he returned to work.

The plaintiff sued his employer, Rhino Linings, which did not have workers' compensation coverage, and its parent company, alleging negligent training and negligent supervision. He also alleged that Rhino ignored orders from the local fire department to get a spray booth to contain the fumes, and failed to obtain a permit. A business adjoining the Rhino Linings business suffered property damage. The owner of the adjoining business joined plaintiff's suit.

The parent company contended it had no responsibility for the conduct of the plaintiff's employer. It denied knowledge that the employer had operated without a permit. Defendants also alleged that the sales manager was negligent in reentering the building. A jury found the employer and its parent company were each 50 percent liable. It awarded the plaintiff about $11.27 million, and the adjoining business $1.49 million (*Mann v. Rhino Linings USA, Inc.*, 2004).

The third case involves a road construction fatality. Two workers, Mendoza and Childress, were placed at either end of a 40-foot pipe while a front-end loader was to pick up the pipe from the middle and move the pipe back away from the road. These two workers were to steady the pipe as the loader moved backward. On the first attempt, the loader dropped the pipe which rolled toward the roadway. On the second attempt, the loader was curling back allowing the pipe to become properly positioned when the loader stalled; the stalling effect made the ends of the pipe oscillate, throwing Mendoza into the path of a speeding truck. Neither worker was wearing a safety vest and Mendoza was killed by the truck.

The court determined that the employer knew about the peril, but its acts or omissions demonstrated that it did not care. In this instance, the employer had policies and procedures and training programs on safety in general (indicating an awareness of a legal duty or standard of care), including monthly safety meetings and "tailgate" instruction prior to work assignments. Contrary to policy and training, the employee was not issued a safety vest while working on a roadway, and was struck and killed by an automobile. Although training had occurred, the employer was still liable for the gross negligence of lack of supervision at the roadway work site (*Granite Construction Co v. Mendoza,* 1991).

The facts in the Granite Construction case are an example of an employer that has two sets of safety rules. The formal safety rules are supported by policies and training for employees signifying that safety is a priority. However, as Paap (2006) pointed out from her research in the construction industry that construction organizations are likely to ignore their own safety policies and procedures.

THE SPECIAL CASE FOR TRAINING SUPERVISORS AND MANAGERS

Supervisors and first-level managers are the first-line trainers in every organization. These action-oriented personnel have operational authority to direct the work of employees. They are often involved in developing job descriptions and typically conduct performance appraisals. For these reasons, supervisors are in the best position to make effective decisions of entry level employees, provide day-to-day supervision of work processes, and influence employees in positive ways that promote retention and reduce turnover of valuable employees. Most supervisors are expected to provide on-the-job instruction for new employees, coaching of experienced employees, and higher level managers often mentor middle-managers into jobs with advanced levels of responsibility. The systems used to promote these activities vary with structure (informal to formal) and policy guidance from the organization. Herein lays a problem for human resource managers and their employers. Supervisors and managers are susceptible to allegations of negligence for the inadequate performance of these duties. Appendix F provides an organization with a supervisory audit for training related liability. Human resource managers are encouraged to use this supervisory audit form to assess supervisors and managers within different units within the organization.

Four of the most often mentioned liabilities in negligence complaints regarding supervisors and managers are defined and discussed below.

Negligent Selection

Negligent selection is defined as a "situation in which an employer is liable to third persons for injury that the employer knew or should have known of the employee's dangerous characteristics" (Soverign, 1999, p. 202). In this instance, third parties may be customers, clients, or others who are injured by those hired by the employer. An employer is liable to others for injuries committed by an employee where the employer knew or should have known that the employee was dangerous or negligent in the performance of job duties. The employer's negligence must have been the proximate cause of the injury to others whom the employer could reasonably expect to have come into contact with the employee (Bennett-Alexander & Hartman, 2001). Such cases often rest on how diligent the employer was in checking pre-employment references and criminal background of applicants. Previous employment in which the applicant was hired and that the applicants' background indicated foreseeable risk of harm or injury to others (Soverign, 1999).

Human resource managers are presented with a paradox. At one moment, a human resource manager is concerned with releasing information in a reference to an inquiring employer that could lead to allegations of defamation of character on a current or previous employee (Risser, 1993). Moments later this same human resource manager may be soliciting reference information from another employer regarding an applicant for a job. According to Swerdow (1991) half of the employers in the United States will only provide limited employment information (verification and length of employment). This very conservative position by an employer provides some measure of protection in avoiding litigation. Unfortunately, this policy places the hiring employer at risk of selecting not only undesirable employees (poor performers), but also those who may have committed criminal acts (theft, vandalism, etc.), have been violent (assault, rape, murder) in the workplace, or who may have harassed (sexually, racially, etc.) other employees or third parties.

According to Soverign (1999), many courts understand the value of the free exchange of information among employers when hiring. He stated that it "is in the public interest to exchange information about employee to discourage hiring undesirable applicants" (p. 201). Courts will grant immunity and several states provide statutory immunity if certain conditions are met (c.f., Arkansas Code Annotated 11-3-204).

For example, in 1999 the Florida legislature enacted a statute that provides employers faced with claims of negligent hiring with a presumption that they acted properly if they perform a background investigation of prospective employees which complies with the requirements of the statute (Florida Statute 768.096). The background investigation must include

a. criminal background investigation;
b. contacting references;
c. completion of a job application which includes questions about criminal convictions and involvement in civil actions for intentional torts where the prospective employee was a defendant;
d. obtaining written authorization from the prospective employee to check his or her driver's license record if such a check is relevant to the work to be done; or
e. interviewing the prospective employee.

Negligent Retention

Employers who are on notice regarding the behavior of employees who pose threats or who have injured others previously may be liable for negligent retention. Under the theory of *negligent retention*, an employer can be held responsible for keeping an employee on its payroll after it was determined that the employee poses a potential danger to other employees, customers, or other third parties. Examples include making violent threats, physical altercations at work, bringing an unauthorized weapon to work, and driving while intoxicated at work. For example, in *Pittard v. Four Seasons Motor Inn* (1984), there was evidence that an employee had a known drinking problem, and while drinking, had assaulted a guest at the motel. The court had no problem finding against the employer for negligent retention.

Negligent Referral

Employers conducting reference and background checks on applicants are well advised not to knowingly select harassers of any type or anyone who has a history of violence in the workplace. Information of this nature may become evident from criminal background checks, but what of the applicant who has no criminal past, and who may have been disciplined or terminated for such behavior by a previous employer? Does a previous employer have a duty to disclose such information to an employer who is conducting a reference check?

Negligent referral involves an employer providing minimal or positive reference for an employee who has serious performance issues related to violence or harassment. Suppose employer A wants an employee to leave because of low performance or violent tendencies. Suppose employer B calls for a reference on the employee, because he has applied for a job. Assume that employer A provides either minimal information about the employee or gives a positive reference employer B. Further assume that employer B hires the employee who subsequently injures someone in his new position. Not only could employer B end up in court for negligent hiring, employer A could also find itself in court defending a negligent referral claim brought by employer B. According to Swerdow (1991), the Supreme Court of California recognizes that employers have a duty to other employers to not misrepresent the facts when describing the qualifications and character of a former employee, if making the representations would present a substantial, foreseeable risk of harm to innocent third parties. So, saying nothing or providing a good reference for a bad employee could be far riskier than simply telling the truth.

Negligent Supervision

Supervisors who knew or should have known that behaviors of employees could result in harm to others (sexual harassment, violence in the workplace, safety hazards) may give rise to an allegation of negligent supervision (Bennett-Alexander & Hartman, 2001; Sample, 1995). *Negligent supervision* occurs when an employer fails to exercise reasonable care in ensuring that employees can work safely at the employer's place of business. Examples include failure to reasonably supervise employees with known violent tendencies or harassing behaviors. Inadequate monitoring of employee performance and failure to take progressive discipline when appropriate could lead to claims of negligent supervision. Negligent supervision is often alleged in complaints involving police and corrections officers.

The employer who promulgates policies to prevent and correct violent, discriminatory, or harassing behavior, for example, will have an affirmative defense available against an action brought under the theories of vicarious liability or negligent supervision.

Make Training Supervisors and Managers a Priority

The EEO, ADA, and OSHA requirements reviewed in Chapters 2 and 3 are representative of only a small portion of the laws and regulations impacting employers and their management. Depending on job responsibilities, supervisors must also be aware of intellectual property law (copyright and trade secrets), the potential for negligence (accidents on the job and other places, such as the classroom), as well as the federal sentencing guidelines for organizations convicted of a federal crime. In this section of the Chapter 4, a special case is made for training supervisors to comply with these requirements for the following reasons:

- Knowledgeable supervisors are the first line of prevention and defense of a legal problem for any organization.
- They have first hand opportunities to observe workplace performance, are (or should be) familiar with individual job descriptions of their employees and they conduct performance appraisals, recommend personnel actions, interpret broader goals and objectives against the various job descriptions.
- Most jurisdictions will hold employers and their supervisors li-

able for what they know, and sometimes for what they did not know.

Take for example harassment, which comes in many forms: sex, age, race, religion, national origin, handicap, etc. If a supervisor knew of a situation involving sexual harassment that was contrary to law and the employer's policy, and he or she failed to intervene properly, then a court could hold the harasser, supervisor, and the employer liable to some degree (Meritor *Savings Bank v. Vinson*, 1986; Carbonell, Higginbotham & Sample, 1990). But what if the supervisor did not know of the harassment? Many jurisdictions will hold supervisors accountable for what they did not know! If a supervisor "should have known, but did not know" of harassment, (or other areas of liability for that matter) he or she could be held liable in many jurisdictions. The rationale for this tough position is that supervisors will not be allowed to look the other way in the performance of their duties.

Human resource management, training and development units have a responsibility to train supervisors on applicable laws and regulations impacting the scope of work of the company and its managers, supervisors, and employees. In some industries, a general overview of employment law would be sufficient, whereas a different business context might require training in several areas of the law. Since ignorance of the law is no defense for the employer, reasonable training efforts should be incorporated into supervisor and management development curriculum.

The following are examples of legal requirements impacting many jurisdictions for which most supervisors and managers have a "need to know."

- *Negligent hiring, retention, and failure to supervise to standard.* Not only must supervisors be aware of EEO and ADA requirements for selection, they must also know that selecting employees without adequate background checks could result in negligent hiring. Failure to monitor employee behavior and provide progressive discipline for violence and harassing behaviors could result in negligent supervision.
- *Appraising employee performance.* Conducting employee performance appraisals is one of the most important requirements of supervisors and managers. The resulting documentation from employee appraisals is used throughout the human resource management, training and development cycle. According to

Cascio & Aguinis (2005) performance appraisals that do not demonstrate job relatedness may produce adverse impact if such appraisals are used as the basis for personnel decisions (promotions, terminations, layoffs). In *Watson v. Fort Worth Bank and Trust* (1988), the court addressed such issues as the subjective nature of appraisal interviews and concluded that such processes are subject to the same types of applied research analysis as are applied to objective techniques, such as standardized tests. Industrial psychologists who research the legal aspects of performance appraisal advocate the following requirements (Barrett & Kernan, 1987; Cascio & Aguinis, 2005, Malos, 1998):

1. Conduct a job analysis to determine relevant requirements for successful job performance that are incorporated into the performance appraisal.
2. Identify essential functions and task statements that specify job expectations precisely (not broadly) that are under the control of the employee.
3. For each critical job, provide standards of performance that are measurable and observable that distinguishes levels of performance (meets expectations, exceeds expectations, requires improvement).
4. Select a performance appraisal process that is consistent with the nature of the job (management by objectives for higher level managers; behavioral ranking scales for jobs in which behavior is key to performance; graphic rating scales for lower level positions).
5. Provide specific written policies and training on how to conduct accurate performance appraisals.
6. Provide corrective guidance for poor or marginal performers.

- *Overtime Pay for Training.* Employees may be required to attend meetings and events that have training or educational components. The question of paid overtime turns on the status of an employee (Handoo, 2005). The U.S. Department of Labor enforces the Fair Labor Standards Act which requires that nonexempt employees must be compensated for work that exceeds 40 hours per week with overtime pay of 1 1/2 times regular pay (Fair Labor Standards Act, 29 U.S.C. 201). Exempt employees in the private sector (managers, administrators and professionals) are not subject to this requirement. Nonexempt employees required to attend training and/or to complete training assignments that exceed their normal 40-hour work week must be compensated for overtime. According to Freedman (2002)

> "If the employer requires its employees to attend such programs, then clearly the time must be paid. However, if the employer does not specifically require attendance, the time may still be deemed compensable if the employee reasonably believes the employer will take into account, such as in evaluating job performance or during salary reviews, whether the employee has attended such programs. If the employee reasonably believes he or she will benefit or suffer a detriment at the hands of the employer depending on whether he or she attends, the time spent at these programs may be treated as compensable. An employer wishing to minimize the possibility of having to pay an employee for attending programs should make it absolutcly clear that attendance is totally voluntary and that the employee will receive neither a benefit nor a detriment based on attendance at such program" (p. 55).

- *Email and Internet Abuse.* Supervisors and mangers must be aware that inappropriate use of email and Internet usage may violate several state and federal laws (Mills, Srikanth, & Clay, 2001). Emails may be used as evidence in allegations of defamation, invasion of privacy rights (Attran, 2000), harassment (race, sex, religion, age, etc.), violence in the workplace, criminal acts by executives and other employees, and copyright infringement (Eyres, 2005). Additionally, businesses run the risk of security breaches regarding trade secrets, proprietary businesses operations and highly sensitive communications regarding mergers, acquisitions, and layoffs. An extreme example of potential liability for a business involved the systematic displaying on a company intranet of a copyrighted financial newsletter. The plantiff was awarded a judgment of almost $20 million by a federal jury (*Lowry's Reports Inc. v. Legg Mason*, 2003). Businesses should consider the use of monitoring software as a preemptive strike against such abuses. According to Policy (2000), "Employees should be forewarned that their use of the company's computers is not confidential, even though they may be issued a private password to log on" (p. 22). Training for supervisors and managers should include email etiquette and prohibitions regarding Internet usage that is outside the scope of an employee's job and the nature of the business.

- *AIDS in the workplace.* Many states have enacted comprehensive laws encompassing a wide range of AIDS and health-related topics. Florida's AIDS Act includes informed consent for HIV testing, confidentiality of test results and a prohibition of discrimination against those infected with the AIDS virus. An employer may not require an individual to take an HIV-related test as a condition of hiring or continued employment unless the absence of the HIV virus is a bona fide occupational qualification for the job in question. The ADA recognizes AIDS as a qualified disability. OSHA has extensive regulations on the AIDS virus and other bloodborne viruses. The Handicap Rehabilitation Act of 1973 prohibits federal agencies and employers doing business with the federal government from discriminating against the handicapped. AIDS, AIDS-related complex, or HIV positive status are protected as handicapped persons under this Act.

MUNICIPAL LIABILITY FOR NEGLIGENT TRAINING

Governmental agencies may be sued for negligence using two legal theories. The first approach is to seek relief for injuries and damages in a state or federal court having civil jurisdiction to decide a negligence complaint. A second approach is to file a civil rights allegation using the provisions of the Civil Rights Act of 1871, Sec. 1983. This section of Chapter 4 will focus Section 1983 civil rights actions brought against governmental agencies, primarily law enforcement and corrections.

Municipal law enforcement, correctional agencies, and fire departments are often targeted for this type of litigation (Berringer, 1987). Examples of high-liability tasks in the police arena include the use of fire arms, vehicle operation, defensive tactics, first responder, and civil rights (Means, 2005). Analogous high-liability tasks in other governmental sectors include handling and disposal of toxic waste, proper care of children in state foster care, residential treatment for the mentally and emotionally disturbed, emergency room practices in public hospitals, stringing electrical wires by a public utility, and safe operation of machinery, such as fork-lifts in a municipal warehouse (Steinglass, 1988).

According to Ross (2000), over 1500 Title 42 Section 1983 cases have been litigated against law enforcement agencies from 1989 to1999, with the agency prevailing about half the time. Winning such a suit is little comfort to the agency and its personnel. They are irritating, stressful and time-consuming endeavors that threaten careers, personal finances, and health of dedicated officials (Means, 2005).

One would expect with this level of litigation that law enforcement agencies would better prepare through effective risk management programs. Not so, according to Archbold (2005) who determined that only "14 of 354 (0.039 percent) law enforcement agencies identified risk management as one of several tools they use to control police-related liability" (p. 38).

One of the more straightforward strategies for preventing and reducing training liability is recommended by Gallagher (1990a; 1990b). His "six-layered" liability protection system for police is composed of the following components: (1) the development of policies and procedures, (2) adequate training for the task, (3) competent supervision, (4) progressive discipline when necessary, (5) policy and training review and revision on a regular basis, and (6) legal support and services. Gallagher contends that each component must be well developed, and that all six components must be tightly integrated for this approach to work effectively. Organizations other than police agencies are encouraged to adopt a similar approach where appropriate.

Case Example: Reality Training in a County Jail

A corrections officer in a California jail responded to a suspicious person in the facility. The officer was kidnapped at gunpoint by a masked man who terrorized the officer and visitors in the outer lobby of the jail. The intruder then forced the officer into the jail. The officer repeatedly pleaded for his life.

After five or so minutes, the armed intruder revealed himself as a police officer who was participating in a "reality-based" training exercise designed to evaluate the jail officer's compliance with jail procedures related to hostage situations in the jail. The event was staged without advance notification to any jail personnel; visitors were not aware that the masked gunman was part of a training exercise. Jail officers who were observing the incident from behind a gate were not aware that the event was a planned simulation.

The effect of this reality-based simulation was to traumatize the officer who had been taken hostage, the visitors in the waiting area, as well as the police officer who portrayed the masked kidnapper. According to Clardy (2004), the jail officer who was taken hostage was eventually awarded a $580,000 settlement for intentional infliction of emotional distress.

Case Example: Negligent Training in a Police Academy

This case example involves a police department and a police academy in which both were sued for negligent training arising out of the same incident. Officer Parr was employed by the City of Woodland Park in January 1979 and he was trained for police work at the Colorado Springs Training Academy from May 9 through June 29, 1979, at which time he became a certified police officer.

The deposition of the officer in charge of the Colorado Springs Training Academy, Lieutenant Otis Kirkbridge, indicated that the academy showed a film to the police class, entitled "Introduction to Crime Prevention." The film shows a police officer, armed with a shotgun, stop a suspect during an attempted burglary. The officer had the suspect lie spread-eagled on the ground and then, holding the shotgun to the suspect's head with one hand, used his other hand to handcuff the suspect. This was the exact procedure Officer Parr used when he arrested and killed Bryan Scott Sager.

Kirkbridge testified that he purchased the film for the Colorado Springs Police Department in 1976, from the Motorola Corporation and that the film was shown to all police trainees at the Colorado Springs Training Academy, including Officer Parr. The film was shown in a course on crime prevention. Lieutenant Kirkbridge indicated that the procedure shown in the film and subsequently followed by Officer Parr was improper and that a shotgun should never be used in that manner. He further testified that the film was shown for the purpose of pointing out improper technique and generating class discussion, but to his knowledge the class was not informed that such technique was improper. The plaintiffs, from this testimony, allege that Officer Parr saw the film, was never instructed that such technique was improper and unsafe, and used this improper and unsafe technique on the suspect, which resulted in his killing him.

The police academy attempted to argue that it owes no duty to those who are injured by graduates of its academy and that its acts, even if negligent, cannot be deemed the proximate cause of those who are injured. The court disagreed and found that, as a matter of law, the risks created by the police academy alleged failure to properly train its officers on shotgun-arrest technique are unreasonable, that the police academy owes a duty to properly train its officers, and that such duty foreseeably extends to those wrongfully injured as a proximate result of such improper training (*Sager v. Woodland Park*, 1982).

Civil Rights Act 1871, Section 1983

The Civil Rights Act of 1871 section 1983 was passed by Congress to protect citizens from unfair interpretation state of laws (Steinglass, 1988). A state official, "operating under color of state law" cannot deprive someone of his or her constitutional rights, privileges and immunities by applying the law unfairly. "An example would be the police officers who were videotaped beating Rodney King during his arrest in Los Angles in 1991. While performing their duties as government employees, they were alleged to have deprived King of his rights by using excessive force and thus depriving him of his rights as if it were a legitimate part of their duties" (Bennett-Alexander & Hartman, 2001, p. 199). What would otherwise have been a case of negligent supervision and training in the California civil court becomes a civil rights case that is heard in a federal district court.

In 1971, the U.S. Supreme Court extended by case law Section 1983 proceedings to include not only state statutes, but also "policies and governmental customs" enacted or utilized by state and local governing bodies, even though such custom had not received formal approval through the body's decision making channels (*Monell v. Department of Social Services of the City of New York*, 1978). Under this ruling, it must be shown that the department adopted or promulgated (however informal) a "custom" or policy that was the driving force behind the employee's violation of constitutional rights of others. In essence, this is the doctrine of *respondeat superior*, since a policymaker (or "custommaker") has to be found to declare the department liable from the actions of the employee. A "pattern" of constitutional violations and an awareness of them by high-ranking officials must be demonstrated.

This particular decision opened the trap door for a plethora of potential litigation against public agencies. Especially vulnerable would be police, correctional agencies, and fire departments.

Case Example: City of Canton v. Harris

On February 28, 1989, the United States Supreme Court ruled unanimously in *City of Canton v. Harris* that a city may be held liable for failure to train its employees properly (Whitt, 1990). The legal theory for the decision is one of a negligence claim brought as a civil rights action, more specifically Sec. 1983 of the Civil Rights Act of 1871.

Geraldine Harris was arrested in 1978 on a speeding violation which occurred while driving her daughter to school. Upon arriving at the station, she was found sitting on the floor of the patrol wagon, and when asked if she required medical attention, she responded with an incoherent remark. She was brought inside for processing, and during this time, she slumped to the floor on two occasions. Finally, the police officers in charge left her lying on the floor to prevent her from falling again. No medical attention was ever summoned for her. She was released within an hour from custody, and was taken by a family-procured ambulance to a hospital. She was diagnosed as suffering from several emotional ailments, and was hospitalized for one week. She required subsequent outpatient treatment for an additional year.

The legal issue is whether the civil rights of Ms. Harris were violated when she was deprived of necessary medical attention while in police custody. The Due Process Clause of the Fourteenth Amendment provides the constitutional basis for this federal civil rights action.

A municipal regulation in the Canton Police Department required that police officers assigned to act as "jailers" at the police station "shall, when a prisoner is found to be unconscious or semi-unconscious, or when he or she is unable to explain his or her condition, or who complains of being ill, have such person taken to a hospital for medical treatment, with permission of his supervisor before admitting the person to City Jail."

Testimony was given during the lower court jury trial that shift commanders in the Canton Police Department were not provided with any special training (beyond first-aid training) to make a determination as to when to summon medical care for an injured person in custody.

The Supreme Court held that the inadequacy of police training may serve as the basis for Sec. 1983 liability only where the constitutional rights of persons are violated with whom the police come into contact. Such a standard is consistent with failure to train, which amounts to deliberate indifference. In *Monell v. New York Department of Social Services,* the Supreme Court held that a city is not liable under Sec. 1983 unless a municipal "policy" or "custom" is the moving force behind the constitutional violation. Only where a failure to train reflects a "deliberate" or "conscious" choice by the municipality can the failure be properly thought of as an actionable city "policy."

According to the Supreme Court, it is not enough to merely allege that a training program represents a policy for which the city is responsible. Focus must be on whether the training program is adequate to the tasks the particular employees must perform, and if it is not, on whether such inadequate training can justifiably be said to represent "city policy." Furthermore, the identified deficiency in the training program must be closely related to the ultimate injury, which the injured party still must prove, and that the deficiency in training actually caused the indifference, in this case, to the medical needs of Ms. Harris.

Examples of gross negligence or accumulations of mere negligence constitute *deliberate indifference.* This standard is usually satisfied by looking at whether or not the agency administration engaged in supervisory negligence. Virtually every decision a law enforcement agency makes subjects it to possible liability. In addition to the forms of negligence already discussed, the police and correctional institutions are at risk for additional types of negligence:

- Negligent entrustment—inadequately preparing employees prior to entrusting them with responsibilities; a synergistic combination of failure to train and negligent supervision.
- Negligent assignment—assigning known problem employees to critical or inappropriate duties; reckless drivers to patrol; racist officers to ghetto areas; sexist officers with a female partner.
- Failure to direct—not giving officers clear, articulated guidance in how to perform their duties; not having policies and procedures; having officers "sign off" on same without understanding them.
- Failure to discipline—not having an effective discipline process; not following progressive discipline principles.
- Failure to investigate—also a liability of officers; with supervisors; not having an effective Internal Affairs unit, inspections or

integrity checks, a difficult complaint process for citizens, or a difficult grievance process for employees.

- Failure to protect—also a liability of officers and correctional managers; not inspecting safety conditions; allowing victims or witnesses to come in contact with suspects; (protection of public is an individual liability addressed with failure to direct for supervisors or *writ of mandamus*).
- Failure to treat—also a liability of officers and jail manager; not providing first aid, ambulance service, or counseling (given the foreseeability of suicide).
- Negligent classification—liability of correctional managers; mixing adults in with children, or dangerous inmates in with nondangerous ones (Berringer, 1987).

RECOMENDATIONS FOR DESIGNING TRAINING THAT REDUCES THE POTENTIAL FOR NEGLIGENT TRAINING

The recommendations sections for Chapter 3 (OSHA-related compliance issues) and Chapter 4 (negligent training) overlap considerably. The standards used to establish safe work environments by OSHA complement the statutes and case law used to define and litigate negligence in the workplace. The educational principles and practices used to educate a workforce about safe employment worksites are similar for both improving safety and reducing negligence. The difference between these two in terms of legal theory is that OSHA has the regulatory power to investigate, enforce, and sanction employers for unsafe work practices. The law of negligence allows personal legal actions against employers for negligent training and related issues.

The recommendations section for Chapters 3 and 4 will be combined in terms of educational principles and practices. The recommendations section for Chapter 4 will focus on identifying tasks that carry the potential for liability.

The following example from Sample (1995b) describes a method for identifying tasks that have the potential for liability. The context for the example is a mid-sized law enforcement agency. Although the law enforcement context for this example may be foreign to many readers, the process may be easily modified and replicated in large and small businesses and governmental agencies.

Sources for task lists vary and in many instances, do not exist at all.

A well-written job description will typically have three types of information—essential functions, task statements, and KSAs (knowledge, skills, attitudes). The Americans with Disabilities Act requires that essential functions be defined for any job position for which someone with a qualified disability may be recruited, selected, promoted or supervised (Bennett-Alexander & Hartman, 2001). The most logical place for statements of essential function is in the job description and they are typically broad in scope.

Tasks are usually clustered under essential functions and each task defines a discrete unit of work. Minimally each task will be composed of a verb and a behavior. "Make arrest" is a task statement as is "Seize or confiscate illegal apparatus (such as distillery, traps, drugs and drug paraphernalia, or gambling devices)." A well-written task statement is composed of (1) the conditions under which the task is performed, (2) the action to be performed, and (3) a criterion by which performance is assessed (Mager, 1997). KSAs are grouped under the various tasks, and are very useful for instructional designers.

Tasks are descriptions of "what" an employee is expected do on the job. There is nothing inherent in a task that explains "how well" a task is to be performed, and that is the purpose for writing standards of performance for each task. Criteria address level of acceptable performance using some type of measure, such as "below expectations, "meets expectations" and "exceeds expectations." The development of tasks with accompanying performance criteria are useful throughout the human resource cycle—recruitment, selection, placement, performance appraisal, training and development, supervision, and certain personnel actions, such as transfers, promotions, and terminations.

If it is "foreseeable" that a business practice could be or has been harmful in the past, then the employer is expected to take "reasonable" measures to protect employees and the public from harm by doing the following:

1. Identify potentially dangerous business practices and tasks.
2. Develop policies and procedures that guide the training and supervision of employees.
3. Train employees periodically in the correct manner in which tasks are performed.
4. Use progressive discipline if necessary to correct and reinforce performance.

Failure to establish policies to prevent foreseeable harm may be evidence of an arrogant business attitude; furthermore, to establish a policy and then fail to communicate and train to the policy accelerates the arrogance in the eyes of the court.

Identifying High Liability Tasks in Law Enforcement

The conventional wisdom in law enforcement is to group potentially high liability tasks into several general areas: driving, first responder/ first aid, use of force, firearms, and sometimes civil rights issues (Berringer, 1987; Means, 2005). These broad areas serve to put administrators, supervisors, and training personnel on general notice about potential liability. What has been lacking is a specific process for the identification of tasks within those broad areas that carries potentially high liability.

Given the above framework, the first step is to develop an inventory of tasks performed by sworn personnel in the sheriff's department. The second step, the needs assessment, is to analyze routinely kept risk management and personnel records for tasks associated with the following: auto accidents, workers' compensation claims, professional liability, and internal affairs complaints. The third step is to have subject matter experts (SMEs) review the results of the needs assessment to determine which tasks have the most potential for high liability.

Step 1 - Development of a Task Inventory. The task inventory used in this study was generated from the "Job and Task Analysis of Florida Law Enforcement Officers." The original task list of 528 items was updated by 18 representatives of the department. This group identified an additional 22 tasks performed by sworn personnel in the department.

An inventory consisting of 550 tasks and 11 demographic variables (sex, assignment, etc.) was distributed to sworn deputy sheriffs and their sergeants. Each "Law Enforcement Task Inventory" included a mark-sensitive optical scanning scoring form. Instructions for completing the task survey were also included, and the respondents were given two weeks to complete the assignment. Each booklet and scoring form was assigned a number that corresponded to the deputy's identification number.

Every deputy was to determine if he or she had performed each task during the past year, and if so, then to use a 5-point scale to estimate

Table 4.2
Ranking of High-Liability Tasks by Subject Matter Experts.

Rank	NGT Technique Rank	TASK DESCRIPTION
1	4	Pursue vehicles or vessels
2	2	Apprehend suspects
3	3	Control disorderly or irate persons
4	1	Make Arrest
5		Confront or monitor groups
6	6	Conduct felony stop
7	7	Administer first aid
8		Rescue trapped persons
9		Act or respond to extortionist or kidnapper
10		Use animals to control crowds
11		Conduct traffic stop
12		Detain suspect vehicle or vessel
13		Participate in the execution of arrest warrants or make return of to proper authority
14		Protect victim or other threatened person
15		Seize or confiscate illegal apparatus (such as distillery, traps, drug equipment or gambling devices)
16		Guard prisoners outside of jail
17	8	Search for explosives related to bomb threats
18		Use animals to detect or apprehend intruders
19		Transport ill or injured persons from remote area to meet emergency medical team
20		Investigate hazardous materials violations
—	5	Conduct active patrolling of assigned areas
—	9	Set up road blocks

Source: Sample, J. (1995b). Using subject matter experts to identify high liability tasks. Performance & Instruction, 34, 5, 34-37. Reprinted with permission of the International Society for Performance Improvement. Copyright© 1995. Reprinted with permission of John Wiley & Sons, Inc.

"relative time spent" on the task (1 = very much below average; 5 = very much above average). One-hundred fifty-four (92 percent) task surveys were returned to the personnel unit for processing. The optical scanning forms were scored and analyzed by the testing and evaluation center at a major state university.

Step 2 - Needs Assessment and Data Analysis. A representative of the staff services unit of the sheriff's department and I (Sample, 1995b) reviewed incident reports to determine what specific tasks were being performed at the time the incident occurred. In this context, incident means any single occurrence of an automobile accident, professional liability claim, internal affairs/citizen complaint, or workers' compensation claim. A summary report was written for each of these areas. In many instances, multiple tasks were performed during each incident. Both analysts had to agree that one or more tasks were performed before a task(s) was assigned to a specific incident. Incidents were determined for an 18-month period.

Step 3 - Use of Subject Matter Experts (SMEs). Subject matter experts (SMEs) are those individuals who have specialized expertise and whose judgment and professional opinion will withstand rigorous scrutiny. In a law enforcement context, SMEs must have the experience and ability to provide credible testimony and to withstand cross-examination if they ever had to testify in their area of expertise. SMEs must be chosen carefully for a department's future liability may turn on their expertise. It was recommended that the sheriff's department use external and internal SMEs for a specific type of expertise. In this regard, the use of SMEs is similar to using external observers for assessment center activities.

In this instance, the sheriff requested the assistance of seven internal and external subject matter experts. The SMEs for this project represented driving, firearms, first responder/first aid, defensive tactics, and general law enforcement administration. Included as SMEs was a representative of the state sheriff's association and an attorney from the insurance company that represented the department. They did not receive any compensation for their assistance.

The SMEs met for a half-day to assist the department in identifying tasks with high liability potential. As a group, the SMEs reviewed the summaries of the automobile accidents, internal affairs complaints, professional liability, and workers' compensation claims. The next objective for the SMEs was to determine a practical definition of high liability tasks.

After lengthy discussion, the SMEs agreed upon the following working definition. A high-risk for liability task

- results in claims involving death or significant injury to members of the public or deputies; or

- results in a loss (settlement or judgment) of $50,000 or more; or
- results in multiple incidents of the same task or deputy, each incident $5,000 or more loss; or
- a combination of the above.

Having reviewed the report summaries and given the above definition, the seven SMEs were instructed to examine the task inventory to determine potentially high-liability tasks for the department. Working independently, each SME used his or her experienced judgment to determine tasks with potentially high liability. For tasks of their choice, the SMEs assigned an "H" (for High), an "M" (for moderate), or an "L" (for low) potential liability.

The SMEs were also instructed to determine potentially high liability tasks using an alternative method, nominal group technique (Delbecq, Gustafson, Van de Ven, 1986). This approach to group decision making requires that subject matter experts identify high liability tasks and silently vote to determine a priority ranking. In this instance, each of the seven SMEs were instructed to assign 10 votes to the 10 tasks having the potential for the highest liability. The task with the highest liability received 10 votes, the next highest liability task received 9 votes, and so on.

Triangulation: Task List, Needs Analysis, Subject Matter Experts. The following list of tasks is the consensus of subject matter experts from the above-described procedures for determining high liability tasks for the sheriff's department.

(1) The rank order in the left-hand margin is the result of the SMEs assessing each task in terms of high liability potential.
(2) The second list of rankings represents the rank order from the nominal group technique (NGT).

Note that the NGT method resulted in two additional tasks that were not identified by the first method: (1) Conduct active patrolling of assigned areas, and (2) Set up roadblocks, ranked 5th and 9th respectively.

It is of some significance that the two methods resulted in essentially similar rankings. Multiple methodologies are always preferable in applied research of this nature, and in this instance, confidence is increased in the validity of the final task list since both methods yielded very similar results (Cascio & Aguinis, 2005). There is no particular magic to be attributed to the final consensus list of potentially high liability tasks reported in this article. A different group of equally competent subject matter experts could have identified a different ranking of tasks. What is defensible is the process by which the tasks were systematically and rigorously identified. In this instance, the sheriff's department has confidence that a grand jury or civil trial jury would conclude that reasonable steps were taken to identify high-risk tasks.

The results of this applied research project cast the identified high liability tasks into what the courts refer to as foreseeable field incidents that officers could be reasonably expected to experience (*Canton v. Harris*, 1989). Having identified high liability tasks, the sheriff's department is now on notice to adequately prepare sworn deputy sheriffs and their supervisors to respond competently to situations in which these tasks are required. Failure to do so could result in civil liability against the department's insurer and the county for failing to train to standard.

CONCLUSION

Litigation arising from negligence is a private civil action brought against those who have breached a legal duty or standard of care that has been established by common law or statute. Negligence may be intentional or unintentional by definition. Those who may be sued for negligence include individuals, businesses, corporations, and governmental agencies. The workers' compensation system is a no-fault legal remedy for employees who suffer job related-injuries. Given the existence of the workers' compensation system, employees may not sue their employer for negligence unless the incident causing the injury was due to gross, reckless or intentional negligence.

Negligent training is a recent legal cause of action having evolved during the 1980s. Injuries and damages sustained during training in classrooms, laboratory simulations, and work sites, and include the proper use of dangerous equipment, working with noxious chemicals, and in unsafe work environments. Employers may be held criminally responsible for the reckless indifference to the safety of employees and third parties.

A special case is made for training supervisors and managers in practices that prevent or reduce the potential for job-related negligence. Adequate instruction on the following topics is recommended: how to avoid allegations of negligent hiring, supervision, training, retention, and referral; accurate ratings of employee performance, overtime pay for training based on the Fair Labor Standards Act, email and Internet abuse, AIDS and related health matters. Documentation of training for supervisors and managers strengthens the employer's argument for an affirmative defense if negligence is alleged.

State, local and municipal governments are not immune from civil rights violations that would otherwise be considered an instance of negligence in a state court. The Civil Rights Act of 1871, Section 1983, has been interpreted through a series of appellate court cases to allow citizens to sue police departments and correctional institutions. The plaintiff must prove that a public official was *deliberately indifferent* to an otherwise lawful "policy" or "operational custom" that resulted in serious injury or death to someone.

Chapter 4 concludes with an explanation of a process for using subject matter experts to identify job tasks that have the potential for liability if not performed correctly. The example is from a law enforcement agency, and the process has applicability to employers in both the private and public sectors.

Chapter 5
Adventure Training and New Age Experiential Learning

Chapter Objectives

Having reviewed the information in this chapter, the reader will have

1. a practical understanding of the purposes and principles underlying adventure training and experiential learning,
2. analyzed legal issues and case examples associated with adventure training and new age experiential learning, and
3. reviewed recommendations for preventing and reducing the potential for legal challenges and litigation.

INTRODUCTION

A very popular approach to employee and management development programs utilizes experiential learning methods. These programs focus on developing personal self-confidence and collaborative teamwork, typically with supervisors and managers. One such experiential approach used by organizations is adventure training. Colleges and universities also use adventure-based curriculum for students in undergraduate programs and often market these programs to the public. A second approach to experiential learning involves "new age" experiential learning. These programs employ a variety of techniques, such as encounter and confrontation, transcendental meditation, hypnosis, and other approaches designed to change individual belief systems. Both of these approaches are susceptible to various forms of litigation (Eyres, 1990; Kezman & Connors, 1993).

Both adventure training and new age learning approaches have advocates and critics. Advocates include businesses, consulting firms, and outdoor outfitters that market a variety of related programs to public and private sector organizations. Critics cite two general issues: (1) a lack of evidence that these programs add value for the employer or employee, and (2) the potential for litigation based on several legal theories.

EXPERIENTIAL LEARNING

Experiential learning in the United States has deeply embedded roots in the seminal writings of John Dewey. Dewey (1938) voiced the belief that "all genuine education comes through experience" (p. 25). David Kolb's (1984) "experiential learning cycle" has been an influential model used by adult educators and human resource development professionals since its inception. Furthermore, for adult educators, experience is one of the key facets for Knowles's (2005) treatment of "andragogy," the art and science of facilitating adult learning experiences.

Typical classroom methods for experiential learning are role playing, guided discussions with reflection, and various forms of group-based learning, such as Tavistock groups (Sims, 1990; Gould, Stapley, & Stein, 2004). These mainstream methods continue to be part of the accepted theory and practice of adult education and human resource development. Two methods not considered mainstream are corporate adventure training programs and new age experiential learning approaches.

New age experiential learning may take several forms. Meditation, guided visualization, self-hypnosis, out-of-body experiences, and biofeedback are examples cited by Sample (1997). Mitchell (1990) included the teachings of mystics and faith healers who read "auras" of employees to improve personal vitality. Eyres (1998) also listed therapeutic touch and induced altered states of consciousness. This form of personal development training typically occurs in a workshop or classroom setting.

Legal issues include the potential for discrimination based on religious beliefs, intentional infliction of emotional distress, and invasion of privacy. Mainstream experiential learning methods are recognized and widely accepted by adult educators, although use of new age and adventure-based training remains controversial. Advocates cite a litany of contexts where adventure programming has been used in schooling (K-12 and higher education), including teaching inclusivity and cross-cultural tolerance, working with at-risk youth, older adults and women's outdoor programs, and challenge courses for persons with disabilities. Other contexts include adventure-based therapeutic environments (Davis-

Berman & Berman, 2002), integrating ecotourism with travel, and leadership development and team building for organizations (Miles & Priest, 1999).

ADVENTURE TRAINING PROGRAMS

Adventure training in the broadest sense is also known as "experienced-based training and development," "outdoor training and development," "outdoor leadership training," or "outdoor management development." Participants run the gamut from school age children and adolescents to adults, including special populations such as delinquent youth and the physically disabled. Miner defines these forms of experiential learning as a "process which uses challenges, adventure or risk (perceived or actual, physical or psychological) combined with participant processing, usually in an outdoor or wilderness setting, to improve employees' workplace performance" (T. Miner, 1999, p. 396).

Adventure training had its origins in World War II seamanship and survival training for British sailors, and Kurt Hahn is generally regarded as the progenitor of the movement. Weigand (1995) noted that sailors referred to these experiences as being "outward bound." The model was introduced to the United States as part of Franklin D. Roosevelt's New Deal and became part of the Civilian Conservation Corps in the 1930s. The Colorado Outward Bound School was formed in the 1960s and used wilderness experiences for the personal development of adolescents. The outward bound model for personal and professional development has flourished for more than 40 years (J. Miner, 1999).

The fundamental purpose of adventure training is to increase the likelihood that personal growth, successful leadership, and effective team skills will become embedded in the behavior of participants. "The basic proposition underpinning this type of activity is that learning and growth occur as a result of having to deal with real situations which are shared by group members, with consequences which are important to everyone" (Burnett & James, 1994, p. 16). McKenzie (2000) stated that adventure training creates a state of dissonance or anxiety in which mastery of physical challenges leads to growth. Hattie, Marsh, Neill, & Richards (1997) as part of a meta-analysis of outcomes associated with adventure training identified six domains (academic, leadership, self-concept, personality, interpersonal, and adventuresome).

Adventure programs take many forms and may involve wilderness excursions and extended hikes, canoeing trips, white water rafting, and offshore jaunts on large sailing craft in which participants are placed in charge of sailing the vessel. Most wilderness programs are short term,(three to five days), and often are repeated by those drawn to such adventure for a variety of reasons. Residential wilderness programs are designed to physically and emotionally remove participants from the stresses of everyday life. Some programs are quite lengthy, extending 20 or more days in the wilderness. Day (2006) described how to develop residential programs for adults in which participants are encouraged to reevaluate their lives, values, beliefs, and relationships.

Adventure training typically involves a series of physically and emotionally taxing experiences. Adaptations include "high" and "low ropes" or challenge courses (most challenges today use cables, not ropes). High challenge courses are more physically taxing and emotionally stressful for the participant. In this category are rock climbing (in either natural settings or using fabricated walls with hand and toe holds), rappelling down cliffs, walking rope or cable bridges or traversing a narrow horizontal beam situated at various heights above ground.

Examples of "high challenge" exercises include the following:

- The "pamper pole" challenge consists of "climbing to the top pf a 30- to 70-foot vertical pole or log, standing on top of the pole unsupported (but on belay), and diving for a suspended trapeze that hangs a tempting six to eight feet from the precariously balanced climber" (Rohnke, 1999, p. 349).
- Participants walk a single cable that is 30 or more feet above ground. Two parallel cables about chest or shoulder high are held as the participant walks the cable. All three cables are connected by vertical support cables that add stability to the exercise (Miles & Priest, 1999).
- The "trust fall" requires that a participant use a ladder to access a platform at the top of a 10-foot pole. The participant then jumps a short distance to the next platform which is situated atop an 8-foot pole, and then jumps to the next platform which sits on top of a 6-foot pole. At this point, the participant stands at the edge of the platform, and with eyes closed, falls backward onto the outstretched arms of other participants. During the complete exercise, participants are stationed in a safety ring around the poles (Vogel, 1991).

A "low challenge" course is less physically demanding and emotionally stressful. Examples of low "challenge" exercises are as follows:

- Two participants at opposite ends of a cable attempt to cross a 30-foot expanse. The cable may be attached to two trees (or pole supports if indoors). Participants walk on a single cable while holding on to two parallel cables. The foot cable is about two feet off the ground and team members act as spotters. Variations on this theme include having the option of wearing a blindfold while completing this exercise.
- Participants in the "spider web" exercise are expected to negotiate a series of ropes or cables tied between two trees that resemble a spider's web. The lower level of the web is shoulder high. Teams are instructed to lift and pass participants through certain holes in the web and to pass through each hole only once. To add to the drama, participants pretend that certain ropes are electrified (Vogel, 1991).
- A team is provided with several planks of varying measured lengths. A team of 7 to 10 participants begins the challenge standing on a plank that is anchored on each end to provide stable support. The plank is about 1-foot off the ground, is only 6 inches wide and approximately 10-feet long. There are several 1-foot-high stanchions arranged in a straight line extending from the plank that holds the team. The distance between each stanchion is measured to fit only one of the several planks provided each team, and each plank varies by only inches. Each team must build a bridge using only the planks provided to them. The boards must not touch the ground, and no team member should touch the ground, otherwise the exercise must begin anew. The team that finishes first with the fewest mishaps wins the competition (Miles & Priest, 1999).
- The "swinging log" challenge requires that a team stand on a large log that is suspended about 18 inches above the ground. The log is designed to sway back and forth on suspended cables. Physical movement by the team working in unison will make the log sway (Sample & Hylton, 1996).

The Allure and Assumption of Risk

Adventure training is unique in that risk is integral to the process and represents a two-edged sword. It is the allure of risk that motivates individuals to accept challenge in their quest for growth and development (Davis-Berman & Berman, 2002). Overcoming the challenges of life requires risk-taking behaviors, the outcomes of which are increased confidence and robustness for life. Elation and thrill are often associated with successful risk taking, as is evidenced with the recent spate of the extreme sporting events. Crafting experiences for adults that emulate opportunities for controlled risk-taking is the dilemma for program development in adventure education. The other side of the sword is that adventure training carries the risk of injury, or even death and the resultant public outrage. Risk management is central to a viable adventure education program.

Participants in adventure training programs are presumed to have given legal consent to risk if certain requirements are met. Primary assumption of risk applies to participants who consent to risk and who if injured may be barred from any recovery of damages. According to Barton (2003), 44 states have statutory provisions that protect operators of recreational programs if a "well-written waiver, voluntarily signed by an adult" (p. 22) is executed prior to the event. Such consent must be "free and voluntary" for those risks inherent in the challenge exercise, and is based on "knowledge of the activity, understanding in terms of one's own condition and skill, and appreciation for potential injuries" (van der Smissen & Gregg, 1999, p. 288). Secondary assumption of risk or contributory negligence does not extend to the challenge exercise, but does extend to the conduct and behavior of the participant that contributes to the injury. Examples include not heeding warning of event instructors, failure to follow rules and use safety equipment. Waivers of liability may protect the operator of the recreational activity, even if the operator is negligent (Barton, 2003; Vogel, 1991). "The prime objective of adventure risk management is to minimize the potential for physical, social, emotional, or financial loss arising from participation in an unusual activity in an unfamiliar environment with unknown outcomes" (Brown, 1999, 273).

Adventure education is supported by certification guidelines for those who facilitate adventure programming and by an accreditation process sponsored by the Association for Experiential Education (www.aee.org). Both of these initiatives were a direct result of issues relating to professionalism, litigation, and the need for insurance coverage (Gass, 1999). Finally, the field of practice is informed by several scholarly journals, as well as colleges and universities that offer undergraduate and graduate degrees in experiential and adventure education.

Corporate Adventure Training Programs

Corporate adventure training programs differ in several respects from other forms of adventure programming for adults. Individuals may volunteer to participate in white water rafting, rock climbing, or other forms adventure education. Their voluntary assumption of risk is offset by signed waivers that provide outfitters and vendors with an important form of protection in the event of an accident or fatality. Individuals get to select the adventure programs of their choice, for reasons that they choose, and at self-determined levels of comfort for their physical and emotional abilities. Reasons for the selection of such programs range from recreational to spiritual enhancement, and include creative forms of exercise, the thrill of risk and danger, and the opportunity to interact in the natural world. The operative concept is individual voluntary choice in the type of program and level of intensity.

Corporate adventure training programs are paid for by the employer who selects the type of adventure training program, the level of intensity, as well as who will attend. The employer makes all the choices, with or without expert guidance, as to the risks and perceived benefits of such programming.

Vogel (1991) argued that this form of leadership and management development manufactures types and levels of stress that are not related to most corporate environments. This lack of fidelity between the reality of the world of work and adventure training programs makes transfer of learning unlikely, if not impossible. Voluntariness on the part of participants and the availability of alternative modes of development present additional problems, many of which have implications for litigation.

LEGAL ISSUES WITH EXPERIENTIAL LEARNING PROGRAMS.

Adventure training programs and new age experiential learning run the risk of liability under a number of legal theories: injury or death due negligent design and supervision, intentional infliction of emotional distress, invasion of privacy, wrongful discharge, false imprisonment (Eyres, 1998, Kezman & Connors, 1993, Mitchell, 1990, Vogel, 1991). Designers of adventure-based education should be aware of several legal concepts that are basic to understanding risk in the context of litigation.

Foreseeablility, Reasonableness, and Standard of Care

The civil justice system expects employers and providers to foresee the risk involved in potentially dangerous activities, both as part of the routine nature of work, as well as inherent in adventure-based education programs. It is foreseeable that certain activities carry a higher risk of serious injury or death than do others. White water rafting carries higher risk than a hike in the woods on a well defined trail. The judicial system expects reasonable—not perfect—behavior from individuals and their organizations. People make mistakes and accidents happen. Reasonableness enters the picture when the courts attempt to assess the extent of culpability and damage to an injured complainant. Given the nature of the adventure-based challenge exercise and an injury, could a "reasonable and prudent professional" conclude that the accident causing the injury in this situation was foreseeable? (van der Smissen & Gregg (1999, p. 287). The more foreseeable and severe the risk, the more the sponsoring organization and provider will be held to a higher standard of care.

As discussed in Chapter 4, proof of a standard of care is required in order for an injured party to prevail under a legal theory of negligence. In the context of adventure training, the injured party must establish that the sponsoring organization and/or provider breached the duty, and that the breach was the proximate cause of the injury. These types of negligence cases are typically heard in state courts using established common law or statutory tort law and previous case law. The courts may draw upon expert witnesses (*Langston v. Kidder*, 1995) as well as industry standards to establish an applicable standard of care. An example of industry standards for adventure based education is the Manual of Accreditation Standards for Adventure Programs (Williamson & Gass, 1993).

Negligent Design and Supervision

Failure to properly design, maintain, and supervise challenge activities may result in incidents for which a claimant may sue. Such incidents are actionable under negligence theories (see Chapter 4 for a more information about negligence). Vogel (1991) stated that "if an employer sponsors the program and expects employees to participate and if the employee is physically injured, the employer will be liable under the workers' compensation system" (p. 658).

In addition to workers' compensation, most state statutes allow injured employees or their survivors to bring a cause of action against the employer in certain circumstances. These situations include grossly negligent conduct by the employer, a serious violation of safety statutes, or exposing employees to excessive hazards that jeopardize their safety and health (Soverign, 1999).

It is common knowledge that older employees may not be physically fit and many have serious health problems. To require employees in these conditions to embark on strenuous and risky programs requiring fitness and agility could result in grossly negligent conduct by the employer if an employee is seriously injured or dies (Gahin & Chesteen, 1988). The case study from Chapter 1 involving Mr. Smith, a contract trainer with a telecommunications employer, exemplifies how injuries may be litigated in a state court. Recall that an older female employee was seriously injured while participating in "the swinging log" team building challenge. She collected both workers' compensation and damages for negligence!

In a more recent example, a Florida state agency used challenge courses at a military training camp for leadership development and team building. Cotterell (1999) recounted the consequences of poor managerial decision making that resulted in injuries to three state employees, ages 63, 48 and 47. The agency had successfully implemented several of these "team-building" programs at the states National Guard training facility. More than 1200 employees from several state agencies had successfully completed the program in past years. The National Guard facility had both a "leadership reaction" course and a "confidence" obstacle course. The leadership course utilizes logistical and operational challenges, and the confidence course uses standard issue military obstacles. The state sponsored "team building" consisted of both classroom discussions on team building and the leadership reaction course.

The participants in the program consisted of employees from a computer and technical services unit of the state agency. A miscommunication in the planning phase failed to notice that the "leadership reaction" (low challenge) course would not be available for this program. The training manager from the state agency decided to have these employees use the high challenge "confidence" obstacle course as an alternative. The confidence course is typically used by military personnel as part of their physical and agility training. According to Cotterell (1999), one of the employees said later that "Let me be clear about one thing: The decision to go out on that obstacle course was, at best, a dumb one" (p. A1).

This employee recounted that the course facilitator walked the participants through each obstacle, stating further that some of the obstacles were too dangerous. It was understood that each obstacle could be skipped or attempted.

One employee suffered a compression fracture of two vertebrae and had to wear a waist-to-shoulder back brace for over two months. He dropped nine feet landing in a sitting position. A second employee broke his collarbone while swinging on a rope when attempting to reach a cross bar. A third employee had to have surgery to repair a shattered lower leg bone. Cotterrell (1999) estimated that thousands of dollars in medical bills were absorbed by the state, along with workers' compensation costs.

In addition to serious injury, there are instances in which fatalities associated with corporate adventure programs have been litigated. One tragic instance in 1987 involved a white water rafting trip organized by DDB Needham, a world wide advertising agency. This excursion was designed to lure clients to the agency; the underlying logic was that the adventure-based experience would result in strong business relationships between potential new clients and Needham account executives. The "bonding" experience turned horribly tragic (Hume & Teinowitz, 1990).

During a particularly treacherous stretch of the Chilko River in British Columbia, the raft hit a rock, overturned and threw 11 of the 12 participants into the river. Five high-level executives who were guests of DDB Needham were drowned, along with a retired Needham employee. Two of the surviving widows sued in a U.S. district court asserting wrongful death claims. They alleged that Needham failed to provide adequate safety devices, had overcrowded the raft, and failed to hire a licensed river guide or outfitter (*Fasules v. DDB Needham Worldwide*, 1989; *Goldstein, et al. v. DDB Needham Worldwide*, 1990).

Attorneys for DDB Needham argued that signed waivers by the deceased should result in dismissal of the widow's claims. Both district court judges disagreed, concluding that the "decedents did not fully understand and comprehend the risks involved in their whitewater rafting expedition. The waivers were supposed to have been mailed and signed prior to leaving on the trip. However, they were not given to them until they were at the airport in Vancouver, British Columbia. The language of the release included a clause that the participants should obtain insurance to cover injury or illness. The actual release form was general in nature and nowhere in the agreement was there mention of white water rafting, the risks of white water rafting, negligence in general, or the negligence of DDB Needham Worldwide, Inc. The document contained serious ambiguities and therefore could not be the basis for dismissing the widow's claims" (Barton, 2003, p. 25).

Intentional Infliction of Emotional Distress

Stress-related illness may result in claims involving workers' compensation or civil suits for "emotional distress" or "intentional infliction of distress." According to the Second Restatement of Torts, intentional infliction of emotional distress requires extreme and outrageous conduct on the part of the employer that intentionally or recklessly caused severe emotional distress to an employee.

The world of work is stressful and incidental to job performance. Employers are given leeway by the courts to "inflict distress [including] a degree of brusqueness or even insensitivity . . . when necessary to assure performance of essential tasks" (Vogel, 1991, p. 674). The level of stress induced by participation in a required adventure based education program may significantly eclipse the stress from that of normal day-to-day work. Under certain circumstances this could be considered outrageous conduct. Risk taking and stress levels are designed into such programs, and for some participants, the anxiety and fear they experience may border on intentional infliction of emotional distress. "When an adventure program forces employees to expose and confront their fear of falling or drowning or suffer public humiliation, the stress produced seems no less outrageous than that suffered by an employee forced to confess to a crime" (Vogel, 1991, p. 677). Kezman & Connors (1993) conclude that "The more 'outrageous' (out of line with actual job duties) the activity the employee is asked to perform, the better the chance of a successful claim for damages for such an employee" (p. 71).

False Imprisonment

Liability for false imprisonment or detention of a participant could lead to criminal charges as well as a civil complaint (Kezman & Connors, 1993). If a participant decides during the course of a program, that he or she wishes to leave the premises or property, then no physical force should be used to detain the participant. This presents a very complex problem for the program facilitator who is in the middle of a white water rafting trip. Failure to accommodate a request to be put ashore could result in claims against the employer and outfitter.

Invasion of Privacy and Religious Discrimination

Constitutional issues of right to privacy and religious freedom may be infringed upon when participants are forced to discuss personal values and religious convictions or participate in activities that offend their religious beliefs. Both adventure training and new age experiential learning methods are at risk for this for of kind of litigation. Pressure to adopt values inconsistent with personal values and religious convictions may place an organization legally at risk based on state and federal civil rights laws. As Vogel points out, "Employees have a reasonable expectation of privacy regarding their persons, beliefs, property, personal relationships and other off-work activities" (p. 686).

In *Kim v. The Dekalb Farmer's Market, Inc.* (1988) Kim and seven other employees filed Title VII complaints alleging that the management training required by DeKalb was a "religious cult" that was contrary to the religious beliefs of the plaintiffs. The plaintiffs were members of the Roman Catholic, Baptist, Hindu, Jehovah's Witness, Jewish, Muslim and Presbyterian faiths (Mitchell, 1990). The complaint filed a U.S. district court alleged that plaintiffs were forced to attend the "Forum" program, and were expected to adopt the values and beliefs of the cult, including the recruitment of new converts (employees and their family members) into the Forum.

In this instance, the cult was a self-development program popularized in the 1970s by Werner Erhard. The program was part of the "est" (i.e., Erhard Seminar Training) which put forth a belief in the "the supremacy of man, a belief which by its very existence denies the centrality of God and historical concepts at the heart of so many established religions . . . This concept rejects the possibility of a deity higher than self" (Mitchell, 1990, p. 414).

The $525 cost of the program was charged to each employee through payroll deduction, and each employee attended 50 hours of instruction that included two weekends. Not to attend the program resulted in intimidation, as well as direct and indirect threats of loss of job. According to Mitchell (1990), a "committed listener" was assigned to each Forum member; "This listener pries into every aspect of an individual's life, including their sex lives" (p. 414). This case was settled without benefit of a trial that would have litigated the issues, thus providing future guidance to employees and their organizations.

Mandatory new age training programs, designed to improve employee motivation, cooperation or productivity through meditation, yoga, biofeedback or other practices, may conflict with the nondiscriminatory provisions of Title VII. Employers must accommodate any employee who gives notice that these programs are inconsistent with the employee's religious beliefs, whether or not the employer believes there is a religious basis for the employee's objection (EEOC, 1998).

Another example of an extreme approach to experiential learning concerned the Federal Aviation Administration's use of new age training in its management development program (Sample, 1995a). A federal agency used extreme confrontation and principles of radical psychology as part of a management development program. Participants were exhorted to break down traditional barriers to communication with expectations of sleeping together and taking showers together. The CNN Moneyline television program obtained a copy of a secretly videotaped class session with a psychologist who advocated tying people together for long periods of time and having them take showers tied together. In one excerpt of the video, the psychologist was observed to say, "I want it to get so uncomfortable for all of you that when you hear one of your people in this room speaking like a snake, speaking indirectly, speaking like a victim, accusing, miscommunicating their personal truth or universal truth, I want it to grate like fingernails on a chalkboard. I want 23 voices in unison to go, 'Aaah, don't do that'" (Anonymous, 1994, p. 5).

Accommodating Disabled Participants

Including the disabled employee in adventure-based training may result in several positive outcomes. McAvoy and Lais (1999) cite research concluding that participation by the disabled results in enhanced self-concept and increased social adjustment and cooperation, enhanced body image and positive behavior change. Integrating the non-disabled with disabled participants resulted in "increased understanding of the capabilities of persons with disabilities, more positive attitudes about persons with disabilities, and increased tolerance of differences among people" (p. 404).

Recall the discussion in Chapter 2 regarding the Americans with Disabilities Act (ADA) and training. "Just as a disabled employee who cannot overcome inherent barriers in the test [selection] is entitled to a reasonable accommodation, so too is the disabled team member who cannot fully participate" in adventure training programs (Eyres, 1998, p. 193). An example of a reasonable accommodation might be to provide alternative challenges to those that present physical or emotional threats. Any policy that makes adventure-based and new age training mandatory should be examined for alternative programs that would result in similar outcomes. Issues such as accessibility to sleeping quarters, eating and bathroom facilities, as well as program sites must be investigated in advance with outfitters and vendors (Sample, 1995a).

Wrongful Termination

Termination of employment for failure to participate in organization-mandated programs could result in wrongful termination suits. The employment-at-will doctrine continues as a well-established employment law policy. Unless there is an agreement to the contrary, such as a personnel policy or employment contract, the employee and the employer may terminate the employment relationship at any time "for good cause, for no cause, or for cause morally wrong, without being guilty of legal wrong" (Hartman, Homer, & Reff, 1998, p. 246). Statutory restrictions have evolved over time tending to reduce the harshness of this doctrine. Employees who are fired for whistleblower activity or who are fired for failure to perform an illegal act are protected from wrongful termination in most states. Terminations based on exercising statutory rights or for membership in federally protected groups (race, sex, disabled) may allege wrongful termination. Finally, defamation, fraud and intentional infliction of emotional distress may be litigated as a wrongful termination (Soverign, 1999).

In *Hiatt v. Walker Chevrolet Company* (1987), the plaintiff alleged wrongful discharge for refusing to participate in a new age training program. Hiatt attended a new age training course in February 1984. At first, Hiatt had a very positive attitude towards the new age motivational program. By the fourth day, however, his view had changed. At that point, Hiatt became convinced that the program was anti-Christian, and conflicted with his Christian beliefs, and he left the program.

He was scheduled to attend a business meeting in California following the new age training course. He continued on to that meeting without notifying his employer that he had left the training session on the fourth day of a five-day program. When he arrived in California, he called his employer and explained that he had terminated his participation in the course because the program was anti-Christian, and he could not participate in it.

Shortly after Hiatt returned from California, he was fired by his employer, Walker Chevrolet. Hiatt in turn filed suit against his former employer, alleging discrimination in violation of both state law and the Federal Civil Rights Act The employer denied the allegation, and countered by saying that Hiatt's attitude, inability to communicate with management and his peers, his failure to implement his sales plan, and excessive absenteeism were the basis for his dismissal.

The federal law applicable in this case is Title VIII of the Civil Rights Act of 1964. This Act makes it an unfair practice for an employer to discharge, refuse to hire, or otherwise discriminate against an individual with respect to compensation, terms, conditions, or privileges of employment because of the individual's race, color, religion, sex, or national origin. An employer may demonstrate that it is unable to accommodate an employee's religious observance without undue hardship on the conduct of the employer's business. In this case, Hiatt had to prove that

1. he had a bona fide religious belief that conflicted with an employment practice;
2. he had informed the employer of that conflict; and
3. he was fired because he refused to comply with the employment requirement.

Hiatt was not able to meet all of the court's requirements, and was not able to meet the burden of proof. In fact, the court found that Hiatt had volunteered to attend the training course, and that his request to terminate the program was immediately granted by Walker Chevrolet. The court summarily dismissed his Title VII argument in favor of Walker Chevrolet.

In the next case, a public policy argument was used in an Arizona wrongful termination case to negate the firing of a nurse. The nurse, along with mostly other hospital employees and her supervisor, embarked on an eight-day camping and rafting trip. During the trip, group pressure mounted to have her and others participate in public urination and bathing, heavy drinking, and related activities. One of the activities involved a skit in which participants "mooned" each other while singing "Moon River." The nurse who refused to participate in these activities was harassed by her supervisor and was fired for refusing to resign. There were no previous performance issues with the nurse. The Arizona Supreme Court found the firing against public policy in that the pressures to behave badly contravened Arizona's prohibition against indecent exposure (*Wagenseller v. Scottsdale Memorial Hospital*, 1985).

HOW EFFECTIVE IS EXPERIENTIAL LEARNING

Empirical research reviewed by Gosen and Washburn (2004) concluded that mainstream experiential learning appears effective, but noted that "results reflect a long-standing trend of not meeting the highest of research design and measurement standards" (p. 270). A search for credible research on the "new age" experiential approaches failed to produce any relevant research.

A meta-analysis by Hattie, Marsh, Neill, and Richards (1997) of adventure education programs using the outward bound model concluded that the average *effect size* at the end of such programs was .34 and an *effect size* of .17 in follow-up assessments. This study was based 1,728 effect sizes drawn from 151 samples across 96 studies. Multiple research outcomes were assessed, including self-concept, locus of control, and leadership. The study population consisted of primary school and adolescent students, as well as adults on two continents. According to the researchers the "most effective programs were for adults in the Australian Outward Bound longer (20+) day courses (.51) . . . For all programs with school-aged students and for all shorter programs, the mean effect was .26" (Hattie, et al., 1997, p. 70). The study concludes that given the moderately impressive effect sizes, much is to be determined about why such programs are effective. McKenzie (2000) concluded from her extensive review of the literature that outcomes and benefits of adventure-oriented programs are based more on theoretical expectations rather than on findings from empirical research.

Efforts to research and evaluate the effectiveness of corporate training programs are mixed at best. Jones and Oswick (1993) reviewed 45 studies purporting to assess outcomes and determined that 53 percent of the studies had been conducted by those who provided the program. These researchers concluded that these studies are contaminated by systematic bias on the part of the researchers. Any claims of positive outcomes are suspect because of such bias.

Burnet and James (1994) used both quantitative and qualitative methods to test the extent to which outdoor programs facilitate personal change in managers. Using the outdoor development outcome matrix proposed by Dainty and Lucas (1992), Burnett and James hypothesized that outdoor management programs would result in increased levels of "openness" behaviors, self-awareness, and learning how to learn, as well as positive changes in self-concept. The study included three groups of MBA students from the UK, as well as members of their "role sets." The experimental group of students participated in a three-day outdoor development project. The second group participated in a one-day version of the outdoor program and the third group was a control group. Participants and members of their role set completed questionnaires prior to their participation, as well as immediately following the program and six months after the program.

Findings from the Burnett and James study were mixed. Three of the four tested hypotheses are not supported by the study. The results of the qualitative portion of the research were much more positive. Participants (and their role set) believed "that change has occurred in the behaviors of those who undertook the [three-day] outdoor development activity" (Burnett & James, 1994, p. 22). The researchers concluded that a number of factors explain their mixed results. Mazany, Francis, and Sumich (1995), Ibbetson and Newell (1999), and Keller and Olson (2000) conducted similar research in corporate settings and reported similar mixed results.

RECOMMENDATIONS FOR PREVENTIING LITIGATION

The following four recommendations for preventing litigation associated with experiential learning are consistent with Eyres (1992), Kezman and Connors (1993) Tarullo (1992), van der Smissen and Gregg (1999), and Vogel (1991).

1. Link management development to the strategic needs of the employer. There is a tendency in contemporary organizations to establish a "false dichotomy between developing individuals and conducting business. Development is seen as HRD's domain while conducting business is seen as the responsibility of line management" (Seibert, Hall, & Kram, 1995, p. 551). The management development activities often promoted by the HRD community, including experiential learning, are often solutions in search of a legitimate business need. The direct link is often unclear and is therefore a hard sell to senior management, and when implemented, the outcomes seldom meet expectations.

If a particular form of management development is the solution, then what is the strategic imperative that informs the business of this solution? This form of the question presumes a solution to a strategic business need. Robinson and Robinson (2004) advocate postponing the identification of favorite solutions, (i.e., remaining solution neutral) until a strategic business need has been determined.

HRD professionals are advised to "Begin by moving out and up to business strategy" (Seibert, et al., 1995). Human resource development managers are encouraged to think strategically first, followed by program development as a secondary activity! This will be a difficult learning curve for many HRD professionals who may be tied to the classroom. As a practical matter, managers of the HRD unit should become intimately familiar with the employer's strategic business objectives, initiatives, and issues. Use this information to distill competencies and behaviors necessary to accomplish strategic objectives.

Seibert et al. (1995) also advised that management development initiatives should place job experience before classroom activities (not vice versa), keep program development flexible and responsive to changes in strategy, and provide support for experience-based learning. The last statement focuses on the development of a culture that expects, supports, and rewards learning as part of day-to-day challenges of work.

2. Program design should systematically consider scope of learning, potential for risk of injury, and litigation. Adventure-based education programs have been criticized in the past for using a generalized framework as a "one size fits all" approach to management and leadership development. This assumes that outcomes will be effective without regard to context, learning objectives, and links to business strategy.

Gahin and Chesteen (1988) recommend the identification of business related goals or benefits that can be evaluated against the potential for risk. Their classification compares the following benefits against risk: (1) essential job requirement, (2) productivity, (3) stress management, (4) self-concept, (5) physical fitness, (6) recreational. All six benefits can be evaluated using a scale that ranges from "catastrophic" to "negligible" in terms of risk. Gahin and Chesteen (1988) remark that a "firm

Table 5. 1
Outdoor Development Matrix for Adventure Based Training

TASK / PROCESS	Low Intensity	High Intensity
Tight	Quadrant 2 Narrow skills	Quadrant 3 Broad skills
Loose	Quadrant 1 Fun/ enjoyment	Quadrant 4 Self and other evaluation

Source: Dainty & Lucas (1992) *Management Education and Development* 23,2, 106-122.
Reprinted with permission from Paul Dainty.

might easily decide to participate in outdoor executive training, for example if the perceived benefits were considered 'essential job requirements' whereas the risk level was perceived as 'negligible' or 'moderate'" (p. 50).

A useful tool for program developers would be a schema that delineates tasks and processes useful for designing adventure-based education. Dainty and Lucas (1992) suggest that tasks are classified along a continuum ranging from "tightly defined" to "loosely defined." Tightly defined tasks include rock climbing and rappelling challenges which require expert input and monitoring to ensure safety. These tasks have limited range of execution, otherwise success is compromised. Loosely defined tasks require less expert input and have multiple ways to execute for the desired solution. Mountain-rescue challenge operations are an example and rely on managerial skills (requiring delegation, communication, and interpersonal skills).

Process is classified on a continuum using intensity. "High intensity" process focuses on extensive individual feedback, an elaboration of feelings, and the impact that participants have on one another. Feedback is likely to be confrontational with a high intensity process. A low intensity process explores tasks more generally and might focus on broad areas of leadership. This type of feedback is more informational than confrontational.

Dainty and Lucas conclude that personal change is more likely to occur with loosely defined tasks coupled with high intensity process (Quadrant 4). They recommend open-ended activities that allow participants the opportunity to determine what is most important to learn, and to practice the skills most relevant to their development. In this manner, participants will learn to deal with ambiguity, extend their range of behaviors, and develop attitudes appropriate for changing business environments.

According to Brown (1999), given adequate safety requirements, training and equipment, participants in many adventure based education programs are subjected to lower levels of risk than they would be with every-day living. For example, many organized sports report higher levels of injury than found in adventure based programming. Drowning is highest with outward bound programs, and injury rates are the highest for white water paddling, caving and Nordic skiing. Injuries to instructors (rather than participants) are more common with rock climbing and caving.

Sources of risk can be grouped according to the Adventure Risk Exposure Model (Brown, 1999). Table 5.2 describes risk factors and responses associated with (1) the environment in which the challenge occurs, (2) characteristics of the participants, and (3) preparation for the challenge (Brown & Wood, 1997). According to Curtis (1995), the number of risk factors at any one time has a multiplicative (not additive) effect on the potential for injury. For example, two environmental hazards, two human factor hazards and two preparation hazards will combine as a multiplier for a risk factor of eight (2 X 2 X 2 = 8) rather than six (2 + 2 + 2 = 6).

The risk management process includes the following components (Brown, 1999):

- risk identification – an assessment of hazards based on the environment, participant preparation, and the challenge of the environment;
- risk evaluation – an assessment of frequency of occurrence and severity of the risk;
- risk adjustment or control – decisions to retain, reduce, avoid, or transfer risk;
- risk management plan – specific choices made that negate risk; and
- evaluation plan and update (including monitoring).

Table 5.2
Adventure Education Risk Exposure Model

RISK FACTORS	For example • Gender • Age • Nationality • Health • Fitness • Attitude • Experience	For example • Risk awareness • Fitness Training • Equipment • Footwear • Clothing • Water	For example • Terrain • Infrastructure • Accessability • Heat • Cold • Solar rediation	For example • Extreme • High • Moderate • Low
	▼	▼	▼	▼
	Participant Characteristics	**Participant Preparedness**	**Adventure Environment**	**Participant Risk Exposure**
	▲	▲	▲	▲
RISK RESPONSES	For example • Preactivity advice • Set age limits • Medical screening	For example • Preactivity advice • Risk information • Sequence experiences • Certification • Guided	For example • Preactivity advice • On-site briefing • On-site management - barriers - belay system - signs - walkways - emergiency alarms	Emergency Response Readiness ▲ Emergency Response Action

Source: Brown, T. J., 1999. Adventure Risk Management in J. C. Miles and S. Priest (Eds.) *Adventure Programming.* State College, PA: Venture Publishing, 273-284. Reprinted with permission of Venture Publishing, Inc. 1999 Cato Avenue, State College, PA 16801 (www. Venutrepublish.com)

Adventure-based education is subject to litigation when participants or instructors are psychologically traumatized or severely injured or die as a result of negligence on the part of the provider. Program designers of adventure based education programs are advised to seek the advice of competent legal counsel for ways to avoid or reduce the potential for litigation. Van der Smissen and Gregg (1999) provided the following guidelines worth considering.

- Require an Agreement to Participate form that explains "the nature of the activity and appreciation for possible injury, which provides a base for assumption of risk defense, and sets forth expectations for the participant, an element in secondary assumption of risk" (p. 290).
- Other tactics to be considered are (1) covenants not to sue, (2) express assumption of risk by the participant, (3) waivers or release not to sue by adult participants, (4) indemnification agreements that distribute risk and potential damages among multiple parties (sponsoring organization, vendor/provider).

3. Consider the needs of program participants. Given job requirements, choices of adventure education programming, and the age and health conditions of participants, require a medical examination to determine levels of fitness as a condition of participation (Gahin & Chesteen, 1988). Employees with disabilities consistent with the Americans with Disabilities Act who request the opportunity to participate in adventure programming should have a medical examination prior to the event. Such a diagnosis is necessary to determine if a "reasonable accommodation" is required. See McAvoy and Lais (1999) for an extended discussion regarding the programmatic aspects necessary for meeting the needs of the disabled while complying with ADA.

Make participation in adventure-based and intense experiential training programs truly voluntary. Require a written consent after fully disclosing the contents of the program. Any other type of consent may not be interpreted as "informed" and is therefore unenforceable. Provide nonpunishing alternatives for employees who do not wish to participate in experiential activities that may intrude on constitutionally guaranteed rights, such as privacy, religion or disability. Design alternative developmental approaches that result in the same learning and performance outcomes (Eyres, 1990; Tarullo, 1992).

Never force an unwilling employee to continue an experiential activity or exercise, and make every effort to avoid embarrassing an employee, both during training and back on the job. This includes general classroom facilitation as well as extended residential or other forms of intensive experiential training.

4. Select instructors and vendors carefully. Employers who use adventure-based programming should carefully screen and select instructors and vendors. Two methods are important to consider in this regard: certification and accreditation. Certification is designed to guarantee that a specified level of competency has been met or exceeded by an individual instructor based on an evaluation by the certifying authority (Senosk, 1997).

Certification of individuals is problematic. According to Gass (1999), poor program design and inadequate or faulty equipment will likely undermine the most competent instructor. The alternative to individual certification is program accreditation which:

1. provides adventure programs with the ability to achieve standards without losing the flexibility to decide and design how these standards are met;
2. takes a "systematic" view of adventure programming rather than dividing it into individualized categories;
3. encourages improvement through internal and external review;
4. assures clients, agencies, and the custodians of the lands that a program has clearly defined and appropriate objectives, and
5. maintains conditions under which their achievement can reasonably be met (Gass, 1999, p. 248).

The Association for Experiential Education (AEE) provides a four-phase, 17-step accreditation process that normally takes 12 to 18 months. Qualifying programs are eligible for a variety of benefits including increased recognition, liability insurance premium discounts, access to certain public lands, and the use of the AEE Accredited Seal (van der Smissen & Liddle, 1997).

Check provider references, program content, and if possible, observe a program in progress for safety and emergency precautions. Determine if a vendor has a history of litigation or OSHA safety citations. Reduce to writing how you expect the vendor to handle instructional content and conflict, and the availability of evacuation strategies for emergencies. Based upon job-related data, require vendors to modify the design and development of media and content of their curriculum to meet the work-related requirements of the sponsoring employer (Gahin & Chesteen, 1988).

Expect the provider or contract instructor to follow supervisory "best practices" when conducting adventure based education. Sources for best practices will be found in the AEE Manual of Accreditation Standards for Adventure Programs (van der Smissen & Liddle, 1997). Consider requiring insurance and performance bonds for vendors and private contractors. Read the fine print on vendor contracts to make sure that liability does not automatically transfer to the sponsor in the event of an accident or litigation. Include indemnification clauses that distribute causes of action across several parties (employer, vendor). "Address every aspect of the program, from when to excuse participation by a trainee who falls ill, to providing emergency services, to accommodating special needs of disabled participants" (Eyre, 1997, p.198).

Document the steps in the planning process used to select an adventure training program. If necessary, have the employer's safety officer, risk manager, and/or training manager be responsible for planning and documenting the complete experience, from beginning to end. Appoint a middle-manager to the role of liaison with the vendor during the event. Document any instances of safety violations during the event, and especially patterns of lapses in judgment and expertise by instructors and vendor personnel.

Hold the vendor accountable for a complete array of emergency equipment and alternative ways to access emergency services. It is foreseeable that more than first-aid will be necessary to stabilize a participant who falls during a rock climbing exercise and breaks a leg. Relying on just one source for communicating with emergency services could be a problem; batteries must be recharged for cell phones, hand-held two-way radios are limited to line of sight transmission, and are therefore limited in range. The vendor must have emergency telephone numbers, radio frequencies, and alternative communication sources in working order at the start of the event.

In the event of an accident, move the other participants away from the injured party and make the individual as comfortable as possible. Summon emergency assistance immediately and make arrangements for transfer to a medical facility if necessary. If cameras or cell phones with video capability are available, take pictures of the area where the accident occurred. If there are no cameras, then draw a representation of the accident scene and be sure to include the month, day and year on any drawings or notes. Indicate the names of any witnesses (participants and vendor staff); however, do not offer any explanations regarding the cause of the accident to anyone. As Eyers realistically points out, "It is an unfortunate aspect of litigation that your friends, business partners, and colleagues may later be called upon to testify truthfully and in good faith about communications surrounding an incident, and your genuine post accident concern may be mischaracterized as an admission of liability" (p. 203).

CONCLUSION

Experiential learning methods continue to be practiced in adult education and human resource development settings. Mainstream techniques such as role playing, group discussions and self-reflective activities carry a low risk for personal injury and potential for litigation. Radical new age experiential learning techniques resulting in intentional infliction of emotional distress and invasion of religious and personal privacy carry a higher risk of potential litigation.

Adventure training is not considered a mainstream approach to experiential learning. The risk of litigation is heightened if such programs are designed, supervised, or facilitated without regard for safety of participants or their legal rights. Organizations that sponsor these types of programs should also be aware that credible research generally fails to support the promised benefits of either corporate adventure training or new age experimental learning methods.

Employers that consider adventure programming as a development option are advised to provide nonpunishing alternatives for employees, supervisors, and managers. The more outrageous and extreme from the reality of the world of work, the more likely the potential for litigation for the employer. The failure to make the "job-relatedness" connection between adventure training and the realities of the job puts the employer at risk.

The chapter concludes with recommendations for preventing or reducing the legal risk associated with both of these methods of experiential learning. Planning and documentation of such events are necessary for ensuring the safety of participants, as well as for providing an affirmative defense if an accident occurs or if there is complaint alleging transgression on an individual legal right.

Chapter 6
Intellectual Property: Copyright and Trade Secrets

Chapter Objectives

Having reviewed the information in this chapter, the reader will be able to

1. identify and explain the laws that govern the use of copyrighted material and trade secrets in the United States;
2. define the rights of employers and the responsibilities of employees in the use of copyrighted material and trade secrets;
3. explain the purpose for the "work for hire" provision in the copyright act;
4. explain the doctrine of "fair use" and how to secure the right to use copyrighted material;
5. identify options for how an employer may protect business secrets;
6. identify issues associated with the inappropriate use of emails, Internet usage, and software piracy by employees; and
7. summarize the essential elements of a business strategy to reduce infringement, protect trade secrets, and other related issues.

The following additional materials are located in Appendix G. Checklist for Compliance with the TEACH Act, Appendix H. Checklist for Compliance with the Fair Use Privilege for Educators, Appendix I. Examples of a Copyright Permission Request Letter, Appendix J. Guidelines for Registering a Copyright, Appendix K. Example of a Non-Disclosure Agreement for Training Materials, Appendix L. Example of a Nondisclosure of Trade Secrets Agreement, and Appendix M. Example of a Noncompete Agreement.

INTRODUCTION

Intellectual property is any tangible outcome of someone's intellect that has commercial value, and includes copyright, patents, trademarks, and trade secrets. It is the right of the originator to control the use of his or her intellectual creations for commercial purposes. Copyrights—like patents and trademarks—protect ownership by public pronouncement as a warning not to infringe (Fishman, 2004). Trade secrets are an attempt by an employer to keep competitive advantages confidential. Chapter 6 will focus only on copyrights and trade secrets as these two sets of legal principles have the most impact on the training and development function in an organization.

Instructional designers and training and development professionals will have occasion to develop training that is protected by copyright and trade secret laws. Programs developed by an employer for employees, suppliers, vendors, and subcontractors may have implications for both of these laws. For example,

- original and creative training and development programs created by employers should be considered for full copyright registration,
- external consultants and internal trainers may have access to proprietary information of a competitive nature that must be kept secret,
- external consultants who author their own training and development programs should consider protecting their original works with copyright, and
- external consultants and internal trainers should understand and conform to the "work for hire" provision of the copyright act.

Adult educators who work for not-for-profit accredited educational institutions and governmental agencies that design and conduct training using digital technologies for distance learners, should be aware of their responsibilities under the TEACH Act. This complex law both extends and limits the use of copyrighted material in the digital transmission of learning applications by instructors in the public sector.

SUMMARY OF THE LAWS GOVERNING COPYRIGHT AND TRADE SECRETS

The primary law governing copyrights in the United States is the Copyright Act of 1976. The rapid development of computer technologies during the 1980s and the explosive growth and global use of the Internet beginning with the 1990s spawned two additional pieces of legislation — the Digital Millennium Copyright Act (DMCA) and the TEACH Act. Trade secrets are covered by the Uniform Trade Secrets Act (USTA).

The U.S. Copyright Act of 1976

The fundamental public policy underlying copyright laws is that products of intellectual creativity by individuals have commercial value. The federal law governing copyright is located in Title 17 of the United States Code. A copyright provides the originator of a creative work the exclusive rights to perform or display the work as well as control over use and distribution of the work. It is important to note at the outset that only tangible original or creative expressions of the producer's work are subject to copyright. Ideas, facts, and concepts are not subject to copyright. Names and addresses in a telephone book are facts; however, the "display" of all the names and numbers from a page in a telephone book is a "tangible expression" that would be subject to copyright protection. Use of copyrighted material requires consent from the the copyright holder and may involve payment of a fee and notice of use.

Works that are copyrighted enjoy a relatively long life; 70 years beyond the life of the creator. Works made for hire last for 95 years from the first year of publication or 120 years after the year of creation (17 U.S.C. §302). After the specified duration of time, the works belong in the *public domain* and may be used freely by anyone. There is a "fair use" provision in the copyright law that enables the public to use—within strict limitations—of copyrighted material.

Adult educators and training and development professionals are more likely to work with copyrighted material than anyone else in their organization. They are very much at risk for committing an infringement if not careful, thus putting themselves and their employer in harms way for potential litigation.

Digital Millennium Copyright Act of 1998

Siskind (2003) stated that "Perhaps the hottest issue in copyright law is the scope of liability for high-tech infringement" (p. 25). High-stakes court cases involving file sharing and search engine infringement led to passage of the Digital Millennium Copyright Act in 1998. This law implements two 1996 World Intellectual Property Organization (WIPO) treaties. The DMCA also criminalizes the development, production, and dissemination of technologies that circumvent measures to protect the copyright holder in web-based online environments. The act increases criminal penalties for infringement occurring under these circumstances on the Internet (Strickland, 2003).

Federal causes of action may be brought against those who

- circumvent computer programming technologies designed to control access to a copyrighted work;
- create any technology for offer to the public that is intended to circumvent technology designed to control access to a copyrighted work; and
- create any technology offered to the public designed to counter act technological measures that protect the rights of a holder of a copyright (Siskind, 2005).

It is unlikely that adult educators and training and development professionals will need to know in depth the provisions of the DMCA. Since the DMCA carries criminal penalties, any questions regarding the potential infringement by an employer or contract employee should be discussed with an attorney.

The TEACH Act of 2002

TEACH is an acronym for The Technology, Education, and Copyright Harmonization Act. This law attempts to mediate legitimate concerns of owners of copyrights (primarily publishers) and the needs of educational institutions and governmental agencies to make information available to students who learn via the various digital modes of transmission. Adult educators, their agency managers, information technologists, and employees, who receive instruction by digital transmission over the Internet must be conversant with the TEACH Act. This complex act requires significant planning and control over technology used to transmit instruction. Not-for-profit colleges and universities are allowed to transmit performances and displays of copyrighted works as part of a course using an online medium if certain conditions are met. If these conditions cannot be met, the materials will have to qualify as fair use under the original Copyright Act of 1976, or permission from the copyright holder must be obtained.

Uniform Trade Secrets Act (UTSA)

Trade secrets are part of a competitive business environment. Employees, including instructional designers and training and development professionals, owe a legal duty to their employers not to disclose proprietary or competitive business information. A trade secret is defined by the Uniform Trade Secrets Act (1985) as any "information, including a formula, pattern, compilation, program device, method, technique, or process, that: (i) derives independent economic value, actual or potential, from not being generally known to, and not being readily ascertainable by proper means by, other persons who can obtain economic value from its disclosure or use, and (ii) is the subject of efforts that are reasonable under the circumstances to maintain its secrecy." This definition includes information held in databases, marketing plans and strategies, names of vendors and suppliers, and methods and processes for conducting business, all of which may be defined by an employer as confidential or secret.

The Uniform Trade Secrets Act is a model act that has been adopted by more than 40 states, and the remaining states have adopted portions of the UTSA or continue to follow common law (Restatement of Torts, Sec. 757). The theft of trade secrets is also a federal crime (Economic Espionage Act of 1996). These laws prohibit employees (current and former) or others from obtaining trade secrets through misappropriation.

Training and development professionals are in a position to have knowledge of their employers' business secrets. They may be directed to design, develop, implement, and evaluate training that is based on proprietary and highly competitive information that must be treated as secret. Examples include sales and marketing training, new product orientation, business processes, and technical training for new products.

COPYRIGHT

The most well-known intellectual property protection is by far the copyright. The holder of a copyright has the legal right to keep others from using the original and creative works unless permission is granted. Copyright automatically attaches to all types of original works, such as diagrams and flowcharts, software, CD ROMs, graphic designs, and text. It is not necessary for the creative or original work to be registered in order to enjoy the protection of the copyright law. If a tangible description, explanation, or illustration exists, then a copyright is secured immediately and automatically when the work is "displayed" in some tangible form, such as a printed copy or a picture. The exact words (such as sentences or paragraphs) or diagrams as displayed in a book may be copyrighted; ideas, processes, procedures, methods of operation, concepts, and principles cannot be copyrighted (Fishman, 2004).

The holder of a copyright has five exclusive rights (17 U.S.C., §106):

- to reproduce the copyrighted work;
- to prepare derivative works (adaptation) based upon the copyrighted work;
- to distribute copies of the copyrighted work to the public by sale or other transfer of ownership, or by rental, lease, or lending;
- to perform the copyrighted work publicly, in the case of motion pictures and other audiovisual works; and
- to display the copyrighted work publicly, in the case of audiovisual work.

Works in the "public domain" are not protected by the copyright laws, which mean that anyone can use the work without obtaining permission from the author or the author's heirs. Work is considered in the public domain when (Fishman, 2005)

- the duration of the copyright has expired;
- the work is based on facts and ideas;
- the work was published prior to 1978 and lacked proper copyright notice, or between 1978 and 1989 and a defective notice went uncorrected;
- the copyright owner intentionally placed the work in the public domain with a notice such as "I (author) grant this work to the public domain"; or

- the work was created by the federal government.

Of the above-mentioned exclusive rights, the ones most sensitive to the owner of the copyright is the extent to which the commercial market will be impacted by unauthorized use, such as copying. Making just one copy of an article from a magazine or periodical for which you have a paid subscription is a technical violation of the copyright law, and would typically be deemed fair use. The author of a manuscript accepted for publication in which he or she grants the copyright to the publisher no longer can claim the copyright, unless there is an agreement to the contrary. This means for the most part that any claimed fair use is really an affirmative defense to the act of violating the copyright law!

Employees may copyright their original creations as long as the work occurred outside the scope of work expected by the employer. For example, a trainer may have occasion to develop material that he or she uses to teach a continuing education program, or an instructional designer may submit an article for publication. In the first example, the trainer will own the copyright; in the second example, the instructional designer will be asked to assign rights to the article to the publisher (or they may jointly own the copyright).

The Fair Use Privilege

The exclusive rights of the copyright owner are qualified by the privilege known as "fair use." The fair use exception allows others—within strict guidelines—to use works otherwise covered by a copyright. The following exceptions to the federal copyright statute spell out fair use. Unauthorized copies may be made under the following conditions (17 U.S.C. §107):

- in connection with the review and criticism of the work (as in a book review in a scholarly journal or trade publication);
- in the course of reporting the news;
- as part of scholarship or research activity; and
- for teaching purposes in educational institutions that are non-profit.

Adult educators in not-for-profit educational institutions (public colleges and universities) enjoy an expanded fair use privilege that is explained in Appendix G. This provision applies to the use of copyrighted material in traditional class room instruction. The TEACH Act (explained later in this chapter) further extends and limits the fair use privilege for adult educators in educational institutions and governmental agencies who design and offer instruction for digital transmission over the Internet.

If one of the above fair use exceptions is not available, then permission from the owner of the copyright must be obtained. The copyright holder may be the originator (author) or the publisher. The extent to which the fair use exception can be asserted depends on the following four factors (17 U.S.C. 107):

1. the purpose and character of the use, inlcuding whether such use is of a commercial nature or is for nonprofit educational purposes;
2. the nature of the copyrighted work;
3. the amount and substantiality of the portion used in relation the copyrighted work as a whole; and
4. the effect of the use upon the potential market for or value of the copyrighted work.

Let's consider several examples of fair use:

- Angela, the trainer in a vocational trades program at a local not-for profit community college, copies and distributes several pages from a copyrighted periodical. She provides a credit line and the price. In the second example, Sam the trainer, working for a for-profit utility, copies and distributes the same pages, including the credit line, as part of his vocational skills training program at the utility. For Angela, her actions would very likely be within the scope of fair use. Appendix H provides additional explanation and a checklist for educators such as Angela.
- Not so for Sam! He would have likely infringed on the copyright of the publisher of the periodical. The significant difference between the two examples is that Angela is employed by a not-for-profit educational institution, and teachers (adult educators) have an expanded fair use privilege. Sam will not be able to claim fair use since he is employed by a for-profit business. Sam is obligated to seek permission from the owner of the copyright.
- Monica, a private consultant, submits a contract proposal for a team-building session to a potential client. In her proposal, she indicates that handouts will be provided free of charge and that she will only charge for her group facilitation. She knows that

one of her handouts is covered by copyright, but erroneously believes that it is fair use if she does not charge for it. Not charging the client will not absolve Monica as she cannot give away something that is not hers.

- Jorge is directed by his training manager to develop a manual that will be used in a future training program. He is coming up on a deadline and is rushing to complete his assignment. Much of the content is based on principles found in industrial technology texts and journals. He decides to use "quotation marks" for several long passages because he does not have time to accurately paraphrase the technology principles. Jorge provides a correct citation for the quotes; however, his manager is concerned that the quoted passages may not fall within the guidelines for fair use—and she is correct. Quotation marks should be used for brief statements properly attributed to the author, not whole passages, such as several paragraphs quoted verbatim. Longer passages may require permission from the holder of the copyright.
- Alexis is a computer programmer who has been temporarily assigned to the training unit as a technical writer. Her business sells several lines of advanced high-end telephone systems, and each system comes with technical specification information necessary for installation, as well as manuals for how to operate the equipment. She has been assigned the responsibility to write a series of "job aids" for each of the systems. These guides will be used to market the equipment and to provide simple operational guidelines for customers. Alexis notes in her close reading of the vendor's operational information that a copyright notice has been prominently placed on all of the documents. She believes that her business has a fair use privilege since they are marketing and selling the vendor's telephone systems. Nothing could be further from the truth; equipment specifications and underlying technology and operational guidelines are proprietary and usually copyrighted. Her employer should seek permission to restate the vendor's documents into "job aids."

The "Work Made for Hire" Doctrine

Employers have the right make use of the work completed by their employees, whether it is the fruits of manual labor, the written code for a computer program, or a training manual for how to select employees. Work completed in a tangible form or expression belongs to the employer. For purposes of the Copyright Act of 1976, "In the case of a work made for hire, the employer or other person for whom the work was prepared is considered the author for [purposes of Title 17, sec. 201] unless the parties have agreed expressly otherwise in a written instrument signed by them, owns all of the rights comprised in the copyright." In this context, work created within the scope of employment belongs to the entity that commissioned the work (the employer), not the person (the employee) who created the work (Fishman, 2005).

Many training and development personnel spend significant amounts of time and energy writing and editing instructional materials and modules, handbooks, orientation manuals, tests and answers for the tests. If completed at the direction of the employer during work hours defined by the employer and absent an agreement to the contrary, then such works belong to the employer. In this context, employment is considered full or part-time employment or as an independent contractor, such as a consultant.

A few publishers will allow the public to freely use their copyrighted works in limited quantities. An excellent resource for instructional designers and trainers is the *Pfeiffer Annual Training* and *Pfeiffer Annual Consulting* (published by Pfeiffer/Wiley). This two-volume set expressly allows consultants and trainers to select experiential exercises, inventories, questionnaires, and surveys, as well as theory-to-practice articles to be copied and distributed for educational and training events in limited quantities. In order to qualify for fair use, Pfeiffer/Wiley requires that a credit line be stated on the copied materials. Large-scale copying and distribution of *Pfeiffer Annual* materials is prohibited unless permission is granted by the publisher.

Training and development professionals are encouraged to share their knowledge and expertise by publishing in a variety of sources, such as *T & D* (American Society for Training and Development), *Training* (Lakewood Publications), *Performance Improvement* (International Society for Performance Improvement), and *Adult Learning* (American Association of Adult and Continuing Education). Not only will your articles share your knowledge, you will also be marketing your talents, and you might be paid for your submission! Each of these publications will require that the author agree to assign the copyright to the publisher.

Copyright Infringement and Penalties

Remember that a copyright attaches the moment the originator makes a tangible expression of an idea, process, or concept. Accidental infringement is likely since many authors do not immediately affix a copyright notice to their works, and sometimes never do. In the case of the *innocent infringer*, it is more likely that no civil or criminal penalties will accrue to the infringer; however, the infringement must cease immediately (Fishman, 2004).

Examples of serious copyright infringement include

- making unauthorized copies of an original work for commercial purposes;
- using someone else's copyrighted computer code in another computer program;
- adapting someone else's copyrighted work from one source (such as an article or book) for use in another medium (such as a CD-ROM or video); and
- outright and deliberate plagiarism of another's previously copy righted work.

Federal courts may issue restraining orders or injunctions to cease the infringement as well as assess civil penalties which may include actual damages or damages set by federal statute. Under certain circumstances the plaintiff may be awarded attorney fees. Criminal penalties exist for those who deliberately infringe on the copyright of others and may result in prison sentences between 1 and 10 years upon conviction (Copyright Act, 1976, Title 17 Sec. 501 & 506 and Title 18 U.S.C. Sec. 2319).

There are several defenses to an allegation of copyright infringement. If the use of the work was a critical commentary (as in a book review), or was used in a nonprofit organization, then the fair use exemption probably applies. The alleged copyright infringer could argue that his or her work was original or creative in nature and scope, or the owner of the copyright failed to bring action before the statute of limitations had run (three years). Works that are in the *public domain* are no longer copyrighted.

Case Examples: Making Unauthorized Copies

In this first case, consider the human resource management and development department of a major manufacturing company. The internal consultants, instructional designers, and training personnel regularly photocopied articles from technical, trade, academic, and professional publications. Sometimes, the copies were sent to regional offices of the corporation, or were used as handouts in corporate training programs. The corporation was designing and developing a comprehensive training program for its technical and support personnel. The project required the extensive use of subject matter (SMEs), internal and external consultants, and computer-based instructional designers. The corporation had only one subscription per journal.

The rationale for making copies from journals was simple—the original journals got lost in the shuffle of circulation among those on the various teams of the project. Personnel also stated that they preferred copies so they could make notes in the margins of articles or highlight sentences or paragraphs from the journals. One of the quarterly journals was quite bulky—usually more than 150 pages per issue. It was argued that copying a 10-page article was easier for personnel to carry and store for future use.

The argument for using the articles in training was that corporate personnel were the authors of the articles. The corporation's orientation program used the articles for indoctrinating new employees and impressing suppliers. Other articles about technical innovations were regularly copied and circulated in training programs for technical personnel.

Is there a violation of the federal copyright law? Does any provision of the fair use exception apply to this case? A federal court would likely conclude the following (*American Geophysical Union v. Texaco Inc.*, 1992):

- The corporation systematically made and distributed multiple copies of articles from journals and magazines. Nothing new or different was created from the original copyrighted work.
- The corporation as a sole subscriber might argue that making one copy for taking notes in the margin was not a violation of the copyright law. In this instance, many people were using copies from a single journal, trade publication, or magazine.
- In this case, the reason for transforming the copyrighted infor-

mation into a more useable form is overshadowed by the primary aspect of making multiple copies.
- The copying was done for commercial gain. Entire articles had been copied for a variety of uses, all of which were designed to increase the competitive edge of the corporation. Internal marketing (employee orientation) and external marketing (suppliers), instructional designers—all were recipients of copyrighted articles.

This is a clear case of copyright infringement. The corporation intentionally thwarted the federal copyright laws.

In the second example, Legg Mason, a global asset management firm illegally made copies of a financial market services newsletter produced by *Lowry's Reports*. Legg Mason had purchased three $70-subscriptions and by license agreement was prohibited from copying and distributing. Legg Mason not only made multiple copies, but had them distributed by email to over a thousand co-workers—on multiple occasions. Even after receiving a cease-and-desist letter from Lowry's Reports Inc. to immediately stop the unauthorized copying, Legg Mason continued the practice of distributing unauthorized copies until sued by the publisher (*Lowry's Reports v. Legg Mason,* 2003).

During the trial, the publisher of *Lowry's Reports* requested a special copyright remedy known as special damages. The jury concluded that Legg Mason had knowingly and recklessly disregarded legal responsibilities not to infringe on the Lowry newsletter. The much larger global business believed that it could disregard the copyrights of the six-person Lowry's publishing business. Statutory damages in the amount of $50,000 were assessed for each infringement that occurred prior to the publisher's cease and desist letter, and $100,000 for each infringement after the notice was given. The total judgment against Legg Mason was just under $20 million, and the appeal by Legg Mason to reduce the amount of the judgment was unsuccessful.

FAIR USE AND THE TEACH ACT

Adult educators who are employed in the public sector and who offer online instructional programs are a special group for purposes of copyright and fair use. They enjoy particular copyright privileges specified under the fair use provisions of the Copyright Act of 1976 and the TEACH Act of 2002. These acts assume that educators are employed by a not-for profit accredited educational institution or governmental agency. Included in this category are public schools, vocational technical and community schools, community, four-year colleges and universities, and all governmental agencies. Instructional designers and training and development specialists (both in terms of traditional classroom and digitally based online instruction) who work for for-profit business will not come under the purview of the TEACH Act. Nonaccredited and for-profit educational institutions are exempt from the TEACH Act, and therefore must seek lawful use through the original fair use provisions of the Copyright Act of 1976.

Educational institutions that meet the requirements for the TEACH Act offer credit and noncredit continuing and professional education programs. These institutions and governmental agencies currently use—or plan to use in the near future—digital technologies to transmit instruction and information over the Internet. Instead of offering courses for academic credit, these educational providers market noncredit programs to business and governmental agencies. Examples include frontline supervision, communication skills and sales training, and basic and advanced computer and software applications.

Most of the professions (medicine, law, accounting, etc) call for mandatory continuing education (MCE) and participants must report their continuing education units (CEUs) for evaluation on a timely basis. For example, Florida State University offers two online programs for the professions—The Certified Financial Planner (CFP) certificate and Continuing Legal Education (CLE) for attorneys.

Governmental agencies at all levels are using and developing online instruction. The federal government leads the way with the Office of Personnel Management and the Defense Acquisition University. Additionally, the U.S. Departments of Energy, Agriculture, Interior, Defense, and the IRS offer a variety online instructional program (Gallaway, 2006; Gold, 2003). The Colorado Division of Housing replaced a thick training manual for housing and community staff with an online inspection training programs; Barron, 2006 and Isaacs, (2003) provided examples from county and municipal governments.

The TEACH Act both extends and limits the fair use provisions of the Copyright Act of 1976, and it applies specifically to "mediated instructional activities" that use online and distance learning technologies. "The statutory language itself is often convoluted and doesn't necessarily flow gracefully" (ALA, no date, p.3). This very complicated legislation requires extensive policy development and planning at the institutional level. Each sector of the institution including the highest level policy-making administrators, management system information managers, and related technology specialists, librarians and information managers, faculty, and students are expected to comply with the provisions of this legislation. See Appendix H for a compliance checklist for the TEACH Act as it applies to governmental agencies.

The TEACH Act applies to adult educators in the public sector who are developing and delivering instruction using digital technologies for noncredit continuing education programming. Examples include the following:

- Local vocational and technical schools and community colleges that receive the majority of workforce development funding. These programs provide entry-level and intermediate skill building in high demand jobs necessary to support the developing economics in a community or region. Given that more and more students exiting high schools are computer literate, it makes sense for adult educators to capitalize on online instruction.
- Community colleges are very involved in supporting the training and professional development of employees and supervisors for small and medium-sized businesses as well as governmental agencies. Employees in both sectors require entry-level computer and software application training, as well as programs in supervision, human resource management, sales training, and so on. Public safety training programs are typically housed in two-year colleges. Utilizing online programs for these clients is a natural extension given the digital revolution taking place in both sectors.
- Universities and four-year colleges also offer noncredit continuing professional education programs for a variety of professions—attorneys, accountants, engineers, doctors, and financial planners, to name only a few. Advanced certification in high-end computer applications and technology platforms are also available from these institutions in online formats.
- The TEACH Act specifically identifies "governmental bodies" in the same language that it identifies not-for profit accredited educational institutions. This language supposes that governmental bodies other than educational institutions are to comply with this Act. Governmental bodies include state and federal agencies, municipalities, townships and parishes, county govern-

ments, and a myriad of other agencies (district water boards, public hospitals, and government health care facilities, correctional and community control agencies). Adult educators and training and development professionals working with these "governmental bodies" and who use digital transmissions for educational purposes are subject to the TEACH Act.

The following qualifications and limitations define the scope of the TEACH Act for adult educators and related instructors (§110(2). Previous laws limited the use and transmission of copyrighted works to classrooms. Such works may now be digitally transmitted to any location using online and distance learning applications.

Under the Copyright Act of 1976, any type of work could be "displayed" under fair use, but only "performances" of nondramatic literary works and nondramatic music could be digitally transmitted to students at a distance. Excluded were many dramatic works, including performances of audiovisual materials and sound recordings.

The TEACH Act allows an expanded range of allowed works:

- performances of nondramatic literary works;
- performances of nondramatic musical works; and
- performances of another work, including dramatic works and audiovisual works, but only "in an amount comparable to that which is typically displayed in the course of a live classroom session.

Some works are still excluded. Works that are marketed "primarily for performance or display as part of mediated instructional activities transmitted via digital networks" are excluded. This exclusion is meant to protect the commercial market for educational materials designed specifically for online instruction for students at a distance or that are already available through an online database. Also excluded are performances or displays unlawfully made ("pirated") if the instructor or institution "knew or had reason to believe" that they were not lawfully made and acquired (§110(2).

Instructors are required to participate directly in supervision of students, meaning that

- the performance or display "is made by, at the direction of, or under the actual supervision of an instructor";

- the materials are transmitted "as an integral part of a class session offered as a regular part of the systematic, mediated instructional activities of the institution"; and
- the copyrighted materials are "directly related and of material assistance to the teaching content of the transmission." (§110(2)

Mediated Instructional Activities

The TEACH Act makes no distinction between traditional classroom instruction and digital transmission in the use of media and instructional materials. Both modes utilize instructors who meet over a period of time for the purpose of delivering a "course of instruction" for educational purposes. Any "mediated instructional activity" must be "an integral part of the class experience, controlled by or under the actual supervision of the instructor and analogous to the type of performance or display that would take place in a live classroom setting" (§110(2). The TEACH Act makes illegal the unauthorized digital transmission of commercially developed instructional materials that are created expressly for a distance-learning market. (§110(2).

The digital conversion from an analog to a digital format is predicated upon three provisions in the TEACH Act (§110(2):

1. an institution or governmental body may digitize only "portions" in amounts consistent with the revisions stated in section 110(2);
2. only if there is no digital version of the work already available; and
3. if a digital version is already available, the material is subject to security measures that keep it from being inappropriately used.

Educational institutions and governmental bodies are prohibited "from keeping copyrighted materials on any network [or server] that is open to students beyond those who are in class for which the material is being used" (Dames, 2005, p. 28). Reasonable steps must be taken to assure that students use the mediated instructional materials for educational purposes and that they not appropriate the materials for uses other than educational purposes.

Institutional Security Measures

Educational institutions and governmental agencies must be aware of the requirements for establishing institutional use policies. Failure to communicate fair use policies to faculty and students (adult learners in the case of governmental agencies) and to establish practical controls puts the institution or agency at risk. Appropriate technologies, instructional and governance policies must be in place and enforced to prevent students from retaining the copyrighted works beyond lawful instructional use and from any further distribution outside the instructional domain. Finally, those institutions governed by the TEACH Act must not interfere with technological measures required to prevent retention and distribution of copyrighted works.

The institutional policy requirement for implementing a legal fair use application that conforms to the TEACH Act and the Copyright Act of 1976 is one more obstacle for educational institutions and governmental agencies to overcome, and it is a potentially costly one at that. Failure to provide security measures will invite infringement litigation. Given the prescriptive requirements of this law, expect that the "oops, I didn't know . . ." defense will only serve to anger plaintiffs and their attorneys.

SOFTWARE AND INTERNET PIRACY

Training and development professionals continually rely on computers and software in the design, development, implementation, and evaluation of instructional programs for customers, suppliers, employees, and managers. Print-based instructional materials are being developed that use sophisticated word processors, authoring software, and specialized graphics programs. The advent of training and development for the learner at a distance means that computers and learning management systems (LMS) are the future of learning. Training and development professionals and their employers are well advised to consider the serious nature of software and internet piracy.

Software piracy is a serious form of copyright infringement. According to the Business Software Alliance (BSA, 2005), the global piracy rate in 2002 was 39 percent compared to 23 percent in the United States. The Alliance reports that worldwide losses due to piracy were estimated at $13 billion dollars in 2002, and in the United States, the industry lost nearly $2 billion, more than 105,000 jobs and $5.3 billion in lost wages. Software companies such as Microsoft, Macromedia, SAP, Network Associates, and Autodesk have established elaborate processes and educational promotions to fight piracy of their products. Several of these businesses have their own compliance personnel who audit and enforce licensing agreements and pursue software pirates. These companies encourage anonymous reporting of infringement; BSA offers up to $200,000 for leads from confidential sources that report software piracy.

Illegal software usage is controlled primarily by two mechanisms: software license agreements and copyright laws. Software piracy in the United States may result in stiff civil penalties up to $150,000 for each software program copied and criminal penalties up to $250,000 along with possible imprisonment of up to five years.

Software vendors are stepping up enforcement of licensing agreements that allow the vendor to audit businesses that purchase their products. A typical audit clause allows the vendor, or someone hired by the vendor, to conduct one software audit year. According to Bigler (2002), such clauses may give the vendor "the right to charge audit fees, penalties, and full retail prices for licenses deemed required if the company is found not to be in compliance. Depending on the type of software audit, audit fees can range from a few thousand to several hundred thousand dollars" (p. 64).

It is a myth to believe that material found on the Internet is exempt from the copyright laws. Copying screens, graphics and content from Internet websites is a clear violation of the copyright laws. Once something is in cyberspace, it available to millions of people who may make unlimited copies! This problem has grown to such epidemic proportions that the Federal Bureau of Investigation in cooperation with several other federal and local agencies has specialized teams investigating everything from terrorist communications, intellectual property crimes and identity theft, hackers who produce and distribute viruses, child pornography, Internet scams, and other white collar crimes.

Instructional designers who conduct desktop publishing as part of their job should be aware of software license agreements limiting the manipulation of copyrighted clip art. Some software companies license the owner to use its clip art for most purposes—except resale or wide scale distribution. In these instances, printed material or products may require permission from some software companies for the use of clip art. Other software companies freely allow unlimited reproduction and distribution of their clip art.

Digital manipulation of clip art or scanned photographs does not remove the possibility of infringement, as some training and development specialists may believe. The original copyright holder has the right to make derivations of the original work. Slightly modifying a piece of clip art does not make the artwork original and creative.

TRADE SECRETS

Employees as agents of their employer have a duty to maintain confidentiality regarding business methods, practices, and dealings with customers, vendors, and suppliers. The duty is predicated upon the importance of free communication between principals (owners/employer) and agents (employees) in a business. Loyalty of employees to their employer is the bedrock of commerce; loose lips by employees to parties outside the business may threaten the financial survivability of the enterprise. According to Reisser (1993) an employee has a duty not only to protect "information labeled confidential but also to any information which the employee should know is confidential" (p. 268). This duty arises out of the law of *agency* and is independent of laws requiring confidentiality of *trade secrets.*

Employers typically maintain competitive advantages by not allowing others access to certain types of information (Halan, 2004). One way to protect such an advantage is to veil the information in secrecy by requiring all employees never to release such information to competitors. To this end, the Uniform Trade Secrets Act (UTSA) has been adopted by more than half the states, with the remaining states still following common law principles. These laws prohibit employees from disclosing competitive business information, such as "a formula, a pattern, a compilation, program device, method device, or process" that accomplishes the following: (1) provides the owner or employer with a realistic competitive economic advantage, that (2) is kept secret in ways that do not allow the public or competitors access to the information (Restatement of Torts, § 757).

Examples of items commonly treated as secrets include (Risser, 1993)

- salary information,
- sales, marketing, and pricing information,
- manufacturing processes and project designs,
- customer and vendor lists,
- chemical and biological inventions not covered by a patent,
- computer hardware and software,
- mechanical medical devices,
- formulas—food, cosmetic, chemical, and

- procedures, methods, and expertise.

Training and development professionals will become privy to information deemed secret. Instructional designers, classroom and distance learning instructors, and program evaluators will also have access to this information. Examples include certification programs and sales training programs, harassment prevention and diversity programs, instruction of a technical nature, including maintenance for the repair of specialized equipment, and process control center operations. Job aids simplify complex machine and process operations and to monitor and interpret dials, meters, gauges, and screens on computer monitors should also be considered proprietary information.

Case Analysis: *ISC-Bunker Ramo Corporation v. Altech, Inc.* (1990). This case is a good example of how a hardware and software development business protected its business and trade secret assets through

- effective confidentiality agreements signed by previous ISC employees,
- timely nondisclosure notices and, and
- copyrights of its training and support materials.

In addition to software, the ISC product support group developed service manuals and technical bulletins, as well as formal training programs designed to facilitate service and use of ISC products by its field service engineers.

Altech, the defendant, was found to have misappropriated trade secrets and interfered with several confidential agreements held by ISC. Altech purported to service banks and financial institutions using hardware and software designed by ICS. Altech had no training programs or services manuals other than those developed by ICS. Altech obtained ("found") one copy of the software guide and service manual and made additional copies for its field service engineers, and also made unauthorized copies ISC software disks.

In anticipation of illegal business practices by third parties, ISC copyrighted all of its service and instructional materials. Additionally, ISC protected the hardware and software guide, service manuals, and technical bulletins with confidential information notices. Reasonable steps were taken to ensure continuing secrecy of the design and logic of its computer programs and only licensed its software products to customers. Former ISC employees were under no obligation "not to compete," but all were bound by ISC confidentiality agreements.

Several factors are used to determine the extent to which a business practice is a secret:

- Is the secret information generally known outside the confines of the business?
- Is the secret available to employees and others in the business?
- What measures have been taken by the business to ensure the secret is kept secret?
- How valuable is the secret to the competitive success of the of the business?
- How easily could the secret be replicated or acquired by others outside the business?

A potentially serious problem arises when the HRD professional accepts an employment offer from a competitor of his or her employer. During the course of employment, an instructional designer or trainer may learn of proprietary information that is considered "secret" by the employer. What rights does the employee have regarding the acquisition his or her skills and abilities necessary for higher level responsibilities leading to new opportunities and jobs? How can the employer provide protection against disclosure of proprietary information held to be secret?

Employers must remember that every employee has a right to earn a living. A cornerstone of adult education philosophy is that of training and development of employees for the current job requirements which may also be useful to other employers. General knowledge and skills are not subject to trade secret legislation. Employees are not prohibited from using their skills and abilities with a new employer. Trade secret laws only protect secrets!

So how might the employer protect legitimate business secrets?

- One option is to require employees to sign confidentiality or nondisclosure agreements. Vendors, independent contractors, and consultants could also be included in these types of agreements. Such agreements require employees who are privy to trade secrets not to disclose them. If the nondisclosure contract is violated, the employer can file an infringement action, obtain an injunction to stop further use of the secret, and recover monetary damages, which may include punitive and treble damages (Barnes, et al., 2003). Under some circumstances, such agreements may be implied, such as in research and development operations or the acquisition of patents. An example of a nondisclosure is provided in Appendix L.

- A second option is to enforce the law of *principal* and *agent.* In the context of a business, HRD specialists are agents of their employer, the principal. Relationships between principal and agent are defined by the law of agency which states that disclosure of confidential inormation to others not associated with the business is actionable under the law of *agency* (Barnes, et al., 2003).
- A third option is to require the employee at the time of hire to sign a noncompete agreement. A typical noncompete agreement provides that for a stated period of time, (i.e., one to three years) the employee will not engage in any competitive business or accept employment with any competitor of the employer. Such agreements will generally be upheld by courts if the geographic restrictions and duration are limited. An example of a noncompete agreement is provided in Appendix M.

The owner of a trade secret may choose to notify a former employee's new employer advising that the former employee is legally bound by nondisclosure agreement not to disclose trade secrets. If such secrets are disclosed, the new employer would be directed not to use them (Reisser, 1993).

RECCOMENDATIONS FOR REDUCING LIABILITY ASSOCIATED WITH INTELLECTUAL PROPERTY

The following recommendations are designed to assist managers of human resource development programs with the sometimes confusing legal requirements associated with copyright and trade secret infringement.

Copyright

1. Obtaining permission. Gaining permission to reproduce materials covered by a copyright is not as difficult as one might imagine. Individuals or their employers may directly contact the owner of a copyright for permission to reproduce the work. Oftentimes the author or publisher will grant permission to reproduce at no cost, or there will be a demand for a royalty payment. The following guidelines will assist and document the permissions request:

a. Make the request in writing. Many permissions editors will accept an email request, while others will expect a written request. See Appendix I for an example of a permission request letter.
b. Specify what the content is covered by the request. Send either a copy of the document or passage to be reproduced, or indicate specifically the passage to be reproduced in the request. Is the request for a book or article, a manual for a training program, handouts for a training program? The owner of the copyright, especially publishers, will want to have some idea of the scope of intended use.
c. Keep a copy of all correspondence, faxes, emails and notes of telephone conversations with the owner of the copyright. If a royalty payment is required, make copies of payments for your records.
d. Consider keeping a usage log if material is used for consulting or for multiple workshops. Be sure to abide by any agreements as to how many copies can be made or for how long the work may be reproduced.
e. It is not enough to gain permission to use copyrighted works; the holder of the copyright will require a citation (credit line), usually with specified wording, on at least one page, of the reproduced work. Different publishers may require different wording in the citation. Note two examples:

    - Used with permission from J. Sample, *INFO-LINE Legal Liability and HRD: Implications for Trainers*, American Society for Training and Development, Washington, D.C., 1993.
    - SOURCE: From "Transfer of training: A review and directions for further research" by T. T. Baldwin & J. K. Ford, 1998, Personnel Psychology, 41, p. 65. Reprinted by permission

The Copyright Clearance Center provides a service for those who need permission quickly. For an annual fee, service from the Center allows your organization to make immediate authorized copies without having to obtain permission directly from the holder of the copyright. Contact the Copyright Clearance Center by mail (222 Rosewood Drive, Danvers, MA 01923), or telephone (978-750-8400), or the Internet at http://www.copyright.com/.

2. Establishing a copyright. In the case of works that are creative, innovative and original, a copyright attaches immediately upon development, and there is an extra measure of protection afforded the copyright holder when the copyright is registered. For additional information, Contact the Library of Congress Copyright Office, 101 Independence Ave., S.E., Washington, DC. 20559-6000 (or access at http://www.copyright.gov/). The Public Information Office telephone number is (202) 707-3000 and the Forms Hotline telephone number is (202) 707-9100 (or access forms at http://www.copyright.gov/forms/). See Appendix I for guidelines on how to write a permission request letter. See Appendix J for guidelines for registering a copyright.

3. Managerial oversight. A system of managerial oversight of issues related to intellectual property should be developed. This function may be delegated to support personnel, but there must be constant monitoring by the training manager. Managers who did not know, but should have known, or knew of actual infringement violations and who looked the other way, may be subject to an allegation of "negligent supervision." Instructional designers and technical writers will have cause to use specialized software in the development of instruction. Establish internal compliance policies similar to those recommended for harassment prevention training (see Chapter 2). This requires the (1) development of a compliance policy regarding intellectual property issues that apply to the training and development function, (2) communicating the policy to all instructional designers, trainers, technical writers, program evaluators, and support staff, (3) training to the policy including signing for a copy of the policy, and (4) provide progressive discipline as appropriate. Ensure transfer of learning by reinforcing the policy during regularly scheduled meetings, on-the-job training, coaching, and yearly performance appraisals.

Although it is likely that the employer's IT specialists will organize and manage the purchase and monitoring of computer systems, peripherals, and software, it is still a good idea to maintain copies of the following documentation by the training and development unit:

- software licensing agreements used in the development of instruction (Bigler, 2003),

- hardware and software technical manuals particular to the context of the business for which instruction will be developed,
- original permissions for use of copyrighted material, along with copies of correspondence, faxes and emails detailing negotiations for royalty payments and compliance, and
- original signed copies of confidential trade secret agreements and noncompete agreements required of professional and support personnel.

The training and development unit should produce a standard policy and procedures for documenting sources as well as a standard citation procedure. Several systems are available from the American Psychological Association (APA), the Modern Language Association (MLA), and the Council of Biology Editors (CBE) for scientific citations. Select one that meets the needs of your business. Require anyone who develops instruction to document primary and secondary sources, and this individual must make them available upon request for review.

Designing and requiring the use of a standard copyright permissions form is essential. Each publisher (books and periodicals) will usually have a designated permissions coordinator, and many will accept a permissions request by email. Use the Internet to locate websites of publishers.

4. Legal obligations to previous employers. Instructional designers and training and development employees have been known to quit their jobs with the intent of conducting training and consulting services for other companies. If this should occur, the individual should not use material that was developed for his or her previous employer, though this may be tempting. Since the employer owns the right to material developed by its employees, those wishing use materials must secure an agreement from their current or former employer. Remember that the new hire may have signed a noncompete agreement or a confidential trade secrets agreement that can be enforced as contractual.

Trade Secrets

1. Keep trade secrets secret—really secret—really! Establish policies and procedures that identify and document business secrets. Identify and document proprietary instructional designs, materials and media, employee performance support systems (EPSS), and results of program evaluations and return on investment studies (ROI). Use new employee orientation programs and exit interviews to reinforce legal duties to maintain secrecy. Distribution of instructional materials must be tightly controlled. Once a trade secret becomes public knowledge, and therefore no longer a secret, then the protections afforded it no longer apply.

2. Mark required information as "confidential" or "secret" on training materials. Adopt a written statement that appears on all instructional documents of a confidential nature. The notice should cover both copyrighted material and trade secrets. An example of a nondisclosure agreement for training materials will be found in Appendix K. Each participant in the instructional program signs the document which is later safely stored. During the training program, the instructor provides reminders to reinforce the notice and the importance of compliance.

3. Maintain control of instructional materials deemed secret or confidential. Training and development personnel should be required to check materials in and out on an as needed basis. Maintain a log of who has access to confidential documents, making sure that those who have access have a "need to know." Control access to copy machines, optical scanning devices, and shredding machines. Require the encryption of confidential information on employee computers and reinforce the importance of preventable and nonpreventable breaches; apply progressive discipline if necessary to reinforce.

4. Protect trades secrets with nondisclosure and noncompete agreements. Employers are encouraged to have instructional designers, training and instructional personnel, and program evaluators sign nondisclosure (confidentiality) agreements to protect the employer from the disclosure of training and development-related business secrets. A signed agreement by an employee focuses attention on the seriousness of trade secrets and spells out employee responsibilities. Such an agreement also protects the employer if the employee later claims ownership of a trade secret that is enumerated in the nondisclosure agreement.

Examples of a nondisclosure of trade secrets agreement and a noncompete agreement are provided in Appendix L and Appendix M. Consult an attorney for specific language that is consistent with the laws of your particular state.

5. Reduce the potential for software piracy. The Software Publishers Association suggests the following eight strategies for reducing software piracy (cited in Sample, 1995, p 197):

a. Appoint a software manager to implement all aspects of company software policy.

b. Implement a software code of ethics.
c. Establish a procedure for acquiring and registering software.
d. Establish and maintain a software log.
e. Conduct periodic audits.
f. Establish a program to educate employees.
g. Maintain a library of software licenses.
h Enjoy the benefits of complying with software agreements.

10. Reduce employee motivation to breach trade secret and copyright laws. Take seriously the philosophy and practice underpinning human resource development. Treat employees with dignity and respect, rewarding them for their creativity and innovation. Reduce opportunities for employees to feel disrespected, discounted, and unfairly treated. Be reminded that disgruntled employees who leave the service of an employer angry are more likely to (1) steal without guilt and (2) to file employment related litigation.

CONCLUSION

Managers of instructional design and training and development units are expected to comply with U.S. and international copyright, patent, trademark, and trade secret laws. This chapter has focused on applicable sections of copyright and trade secret laws most likely to impact the training and development function in an organization.

Infringement of a copyright is a serious violation of federal and international law. The fact that the various laws are complicated does not relieve a training manager from monitoring the development and delivery of instruction. Many businesses have taken opportunities to copyright and export their training programs.

Recent federal legislation has addressed issues associated with illegal file sharing (DMCA of 1998) and the use of digital transmission technologies typically associated with online and distance learning (TEACH Act of 2002). Training managers in the government sector are encouraged to become familiar with the provisions of the TEACH Act that control the use of copyrighted material when used with digital technologies (online instruction by governmental agencies).

Training managers in the private sector must also be aware of the implications for inadvertently sharing business trades secrets. Employers may require that training and development personnel sign nondisclosure and noncompete agreements.

Chapter 7
Corporate Ethics and the Federal Sentencing Guidelines

Chapter Objectives

Having reviewed the information in this chapter, the reader will have

1. summarized issues associated with ethical conduct and illegal business practices;
2. identified the key requirements from the Sarbanes-Oxley Act of 2002 that call for the existence of codes of ethics for public accounting firms and other types of businesses;
3. explained the purpose for the Federal Sentencing Guidelines, including types of crimes and organizations covered;
4. identified the seven components for an effective compliance and ethics program as defined by the Federal Sentencing Guidelines;
5. explained the incentives and disincentives organizations have when designing and implementing a compliance and ethics program; and
6. analyzed recommendations for designing, implementing and evaluating the effectiveness of a compliance and ethics program.

INTRODUCTION

The most recent round of financial scandals in the United States to plague the corporate landscape had their beginnings in the late 1990s. Examples include Enron, Adelphia, WorldCom, HealthPlan Southeast, Tyco International, and several others. These scandals, and especially the Enron debacle, caused panic in the stock markets, eroded investor confidence, and left thousands without pensions (Petrick & Scherer, 2003). Several high level corporate officials were prosecuted and found guilty of a myriad of federal crimes. One of the largest and most trusted accounting firms, Arthur Anderson, was indicted by federal prosecutors and convicted for obstruction of justice for its part in the Enron fiasco.

Although the conviction was later overturned by the U.S. Supreme Court, this former accounting giant finds itself with few employees and virtually no clients as it moves slowly into dissolution (*Arthur Anderson LLP v. U.S.*, 2005).

Chapter 7 explores issues related to ethics, criminal activity by organizations, and the programs designed to address those issues. Federal legislation, such as the Sarbanes-Oxley Act and administrative rules promulgated by the United States Sentencing Commission, require the development of compliance and ethics programs designed to increase ethical conduct and reduce criminal activity.

CORPORATE ETHICS—A SURVEY OF THE LANDSCAPE

The often stated slogan, "If it's legal, it's ethical" may lead to embarrassing revelations of unethical business practices. In 1991, executives for Solomon Brothers, one of Wall Street's largest securities firms, believed that it had no legal or ethical mandate to report unlawful activities within the government bonds trading section of the business. Failure to disclose and report in a timely manner by the executives "prompted a serious crisis of confidence among employees, creditors, shareholders, and customers" in the government bond market (Paine, 1994, p. 110). Five highly placed officers left Solomon Brothers. Warren Buffet, a significant investor in Solomon Brothers, temporarily filled the vacuum of moral leadership by becoming the interim chairman until successors could be selected (Malkin, 1991). The lapse of ethical oversight eventually cost Solomon Brothers an estimated $1 billion in legal costs, increased funding costs, and lost business.

Multinational businesses are not exempt from unethical conduct and criminal activities. Rampant copyright, trademark, and patent infringements internationally have significantly impacted legitimate businesses in the United States. According to the 2005 Price Waterhouse Global Economic Crime Survey, "45% of companies worldwide have fallen victim to economic crime in the past two years" (Skalak & Nestler, 2005, p. 2). Critics of globalization are demanding integrity standards that make foreign investments more transparent to the international business community (Kennedy-Glans, 2005). Logsdon and Wood (2005) called for a value-driven approach to global business citizenship that includes the voluntary development of codes of conduct applicable to multinational businesses.

The U.S. business sector continues to be besieged with serious business-related criminal conduct. The *New York Times* reported in 2004 that Citigroup had been removed from private banking business in Japan following allegations of money laundering and other irregularities (Kubal, Baker, & Coleman, 2006). A study of business news reports between January 1, 2000 and June 30, 2005 concluded that 40 of the *Fortune* 100 companies had committed acts considered unethical (Clement, 2006). The acts reported by Clement included three types of fraud (accounting, securities, and consumer), discriminatory practices, undisclosed executive pay, antitrust activities, patent infringements, and other violations of law.

To understand these breaches of integrity, we must also explore what causes people to allow or engage in unethical activity. Recent surveys of the ethics landscape in business will help build a framework for understanding this important issue. The Society for Human Resource Management (SHRM) reported a study by Spherion Workplace (www.spherion) that explored whistle blowing and ethics. "Although 34% of the respondents said they had seen unethical activities at the workplace, only 47% said they are likely to blow the whistle for such activities" (*HR Focus*, 2006 p. 9). The Ethics Resource Center compared survey data from 1994 through 2005. The study concluded that in 2005, 52 percent of employees observed at least one type of ethical misconduct and 36 percent observed two more instances of ethical violations. "Of the employees who observed misconduct at work in 2005, just over half (55 %) reported it to management, a ten percentage point decrease since 2003 and a backsliding to levels similar to those in 2000" (ERC, 2005, p. 1).

The term "business ethics" connotes an active tension between the words themselves. The competing goals that pit free-market enterprise and short-term financial gain against ethical business conduct are not likely to be resolved any time soon. Recent legislation mandates the development of codes of ethics that inform and shape financial accountability at the highest levels of corporate America. Yet compliance for the sake of satisfying a legal requirement is not the only reason for behaving ethically and legally. Certainly some ethical behavior stems from a personal sense of doing what is "right," but choosing to act ethically can also be the result of weighing the advantages and disadvantages of not doing so. The following examples show that ethical behavior can be good for business.

- The fallout from negative publicity and the accompanying media frenzy may be as costly as damages awarded for illegal corporate conduct. National and local news media will sometimes conduct "sting" operations in which unethical business practices are caught with hidden cameras and microphones. A typical example is charging for auto parts not installed during routine auto maintenance. A later visit by a news journalist catches hapless employees stammering for an explanation while they are being videotaped for all to see.

- Businesses that enjoy continuing positive reputations for ethical business have an advantage when it comes to attracting and retaining talented employees. For example, a study of 800 MBA students concluded that intellectual challenge, financial package, and reputation for ethics and caring (in that order) were priorities for selecting a job. The study also indicated that 94 percent of these students would take 14 percent in reduced pay to work for such a business (*HR Focus*, 2006).
- One of the ways to increase customer loyalty is to have a focus on priorities other than profits. According to Hatcher (2002), "almost 100 percent of the population [from a national survey] wants companies to focus on more than profits and over 50 percent of the respondents said they form an impression of a company based on its social responsiveness, or lack thereof" (p. 4).
- Employees who have a personal code of conduct and values consistent with his or her employer are less likely to flaunt personnel rules. Examples include taking unauthorized sick leave and absenteeism, theft of time and business assets, harassment and other counterproductive behavior (Spector, 2006). A strong ethics brand for a business will signal to applicants the importance of value-based employee performance.

SARBANES-OXLEY ACT AND RELATED REQUIREMENTS

The Sarbanes-Oxley Act of 2002 is designed to increase the culpability of corporate officials, especially chief financial officers and any other executives who make misstatements about the financial matters of public companies. Strict guidelines are in place to insure that accounting firms conduct honest audits and report irregularities (Pohlman & Mujtaba, 2007). Section 301 of Sarbanes-Oxley Act requires audit committees to establish procedures for confidential and anonymous reporting of complaints about audit and financial issues. Section 406 of the Sarbanes-Oxley Act requires public accounting firms to establish and report the existence of an adopted code of ethics for "senior financial officers, applicable to its principal financial officers and comptroller or principal accounting officer, or persons performing such similar function" (Sarbanes-Oxley § 406). This section also directs the Securities and Exchange Commission (SEC) to establish rules that guide the development of standards, which were issued in 2003. For these purposes, the term "Code of Ethics" is a set of written standards reasonably designed to promote the following (Sarbanes-Oxley Act, 2002, § 406):

- honest and ethical conduct, including the ethical handling of actual and apparent conflicts of interest between personal and professional relationships;
- full, fair, accurate, timely and understandable disclosure in reports and documents that a company files with or submits to the SEC and in other public communications made by the company;
- compliance with applicable governmental laws, rules, and regulations; and
- the prompt internal reporting of any violation of the Code of Ethics.

A close reading of the Sarbanes-Oxley Act reveals that public accounting firms are not required to adopt a Code of Ethics; however a firm must disclose whether it has adopted a Code, or explain why it has not done so.

The New York Stock Exchange (NYSE) and Nasdaq Stock Exchange (NASDAQ) have been approved by the SEC for new governance requirements, including the establishment of codes of conduct. Section 303A (10) of the NYSE Manual calls for the adoption and disclosure of a code of conduct and ethics for directors, officers, and employees. NASDAQ Rule 4350(n) has similar requirements.

Several laws impact international commerce. The Foreign Corrupt Practices Act of 1977 prohibits payments by U.S. businesses to foreign officials to obtain or keep business. Other laws include embargos that prohibit trade or limit commerce with specified countries and export control laws that prohibit the sale of certain goods, technologies and equipment to specified countries (Kriesberg, 2006).

FEDERAL SENTENCING GUIDELINES

The sentencing pattern of convicted federal criminals in the United States has varied widely from jurisdiction to jurisdiction in the past. Leniency might be granted to one person or a very long prison term might be imposed another, and they could have been convicted of similar crimes. This disparity in sentencing practices by federal judges led to the Sentencing Reform Act of 1984. The United States Sentencing Commission was established to develop guidelines for the federal courts to follow in sentencing of all felons convicted in the federal courts.

In 1987 the Commission mandated that federal judges begin using the Federal Sentencing Guidelines (hereafter referred to as Guidelines) on persons convicted of violating federal statutes. Judges were expected to use a "sentencing table" consisting of a vertical axis (offense level) and horizontal axis (prior criminal history) to determine the number of months for a prison sentence, up to and including life in prison. Other possible sentences include probation, supervised release, restitutions, fines, and forfeitures. The Guidelines were amended in 1991 to include the sentencing of organizations convicted of a federal crime.

The Guidelines were declared unconstitutional by the U.S. Supreme Court in *U.S. v. Booker* in 2004. The Booker decision turned on the issue that federal judges use information for sentencing based on facts that a jury would not have had an opportunity to hear and consider for concluding reasonable doubt. The impact of *Booker* was that federal judges were no longer bound by the sentencing guidelines. Shortly after the *Booker* decision, the Supreme Court concluded in *U.S. v. Fanfan* that although problematic, the Guidelines should continue to shape sentencing decisions. The use of the Guidelines would become voluntary. Federal judges are free to decide longer or shorter sentences for those individuals and organizations convicted of federal crimes. Federal judges appear not to have exercised their new found freedom to ignore the Guidelines. Fewer than one in ten sentences by judges were outside the Guidelines as of 2005 (Fields & Cohen, 2005).

Organizational Sentencing Guidelines

Effective November 1, 2004, the Guidelines specify that organizations must develop "effective compliance and ethics" programs along with other requirements. Chapter 8 in the Federal Sentencing Guidelines is designed to modify the conduct of organizations by seriously increasing the negative cost of unethical behavior and criminal activities (U.S.S.G. 2005, § 8A1.1). According to Biegelman and Bartow (2006):

> The guidelines were an attempt to lessen the harshest aspects of federal sentencing for crimes if an organization could demonstrate that it instituted an appropriate compliance program prior to being charged. There was a substantial reduction in fines for corporations that have vigorous fraud prevention and detection programs in place prior to the offense and that self-report the crimes. (pp. 55-56)

The Guidelines define "organizations" as corporations, partnerships, associations, joint-stock companies, governmental entities, as well as unincorporated and nonprofit organizations. All organizations, regardless of size, convicted of a federal felony or a Class A misdemeanor are subject to sentencing under the Guidelines (USSG, 2005, §8A1.1). Although organizations cannot be sent to prison, they can be fined, placed on probation, required to complete community service, and ordered to pay restitution (U.S.S.G., 2005, § 8C1). Typical offenses include fraud, environmental pollution (e.g., water, air, toxic pollutants), money laundering, antitrust violations, and food and drug violations (Desio, 2004).

Organizations sentenced under the Guidelines are expected to conform to the following four principles (U.S.S.G., 2005, introductory comments to § 8A1):

1. the organization must remedy any harm caused, not as punishment, but as a "means for making the victim whole for the harm caused";
2. an organization operated primarily for criminal purposes shall be fined "high enough to divest the organization of all its assets";
3. probation will be used to ensure compliance with sanctions or when the likelihood of future criminal activity is diminished; and
4. culpability of the noncriminal organization and the seriousness of the offense are used to determine sentencing.

Culpability and seriousness are determined by "*pecuniary gain*, the *pecuniary loss*" or the level proscribed by the table of fines, the extent to which the organization was tolerant or intolerant of criminal activity and its prior criminal history, the violation of any related court orders, or obstruction of justice. The ultimate severity of the sentence may be mitigated by (1) the existence of an effective compliance and ethics program, and (2) self-reporting of criminal activity, cooperation with investigating authorities, and/or (3) acceptance of responsibility for criminal activities (USSG, 2005, § 8B2.1).

The sentencing of organizations convicted of criminal activity begins with a base level fine that ranges from $5,000 to $72,500,000 (U.S.S.G., 2005, § 8C2.4). A series of worksheets are used to increase or decrease fines based on culpability scores and minimum and maximum multipliers.

Federal judges sentenced 72,408 persons for conviction of a federal crime in 2005 compared to 38,377 in 1995. One hundred forty-two organizations were sentenced in 2005, compared to 108 in 1995. The lowest number of organizations sentenced under the Guidelines was 86 in 2004, compared to a high of 255 in 1999. The 10-year average for 1995-2005 for organizations sentenced under the Guidelines is 217. Given the larger scope of federal law enforcement activities, the investigation and prosecution of organizations pales in comparison to holding persons responsible for criminal conduct.

According to the U.S. Sentencing Commission Annual Reports for 2005 (www.ussc.gov/annrpts.htm):

- Fines were ordered in 112 of the 142 organizations for an average of $3,870,330.
- The highest fine imposed was $32,890,455 million for an antitrust violation, followed by substantial fines for fraud and environmental water pollution.
- Forty-five organizations were ordered to pay an average restitution of $569,042.
- One-hundred thirty organizations were ordered to pay an average fine and restitution of $3,531,414.

The following two cases exemplify the power of the Department of Justice and the federal courts to hold organizations accountable for criminal acts. Daiwa Bank was fined $340 million in 1996 for banking irregularities. Diawa discovered that a trader had lost over $1.1 billion in unauthorized sale of securities over an 11-year period. The trader secretly sold government bonds held in custody by the bank to cover pension fund accounts. Daiwa investigated and upon confirming the losses, replaced the funds using its own financial resources. The bank failed to make a public disclosure or notify the federal regulators in a timely manner, resulting in criminal charges. Further disclosures to federal investigators determined that executives in the bank falsified records, failed to disclose a similar incident from the early 1980s, and had made other misrepresentations into the 1990s (Copeland, 2000).

The highest criminal fine imposed thus far under the Guidelines was against the Hospital Corporation of America (HCA), the nation's largest for-profit hospital chain for a reported $880 million. The settlement with the Department of Justice capped a nine year investigation into allegations of Medicare and Medicaid fraud involving false claims and payoffs to doctors for patient referrals. The total amount of fines and criminal penalties over the nine years came to $1.7 billion (Hospital Chain, 2002).

According to the Association of Corporate Counsel (ACCA, 2005), organizations most likely to be sentenced under the Guidelines are smaller companies. These companies are less likely to have expert compliance counsel, are less likely to have a compliance and ethics program, and instead of plea bargaining, are more likely to do battle with federal prosecutors.

Having an effective compliance program may reduce an organization's culpability score by three points at the time of sentencing and may increase the likelihood of probation (U.S.S.G., 2005, § 8C2.5). According to Hasnas (2006), the importance of the culpability score cannot be emphasized enough. An organization's culpability score "can reduce the organization's fine 95 percent or increase it by 400 percent" (p. 46). Given a hypothetical conviction and assuming that the business self-reported the criminal activity and had a compliance program in place, Bowman (2004) concluded that a potential fine of $20 million to $40 million would be reduced to $4 to 8 million. This estimate is based on a 5,000-employee business involving sales managers and the loss of $10 million.

Case Study – Sentencing of Organizations Under Varying Conditions.

The following case explains the structure of fines used by federal judges prior to and after the implementation of the revised sentencing guidelines for organizations.

The defendant auto rental company systematically charged customers, who damaged rental vehicles, more than the actual cost of repairs.

The company was convicted of mail fraud. The defendant also billed some customers for the cost of repairs to vehicles for which they were not responsible. Prior to adjudication, the defendant auto rental car company paid restitution in the amount of $13.7 million.

If this case had been prosecuted to conviction prior to the Guidelines, a federal judge would have imposed a fine of $6.85 million (about half of the pecuniary loss suffered by the bilked customers). The current Guidelines would have allowed a judge to fine the defendant company from 5 to 200 percent of the loss suffered by the bilked customers, depending on the extent to which (1) the company had an effective ethics and compliance program to detect criminal activity, (2) whether or not it reported the crime, (3) the extent to which it cooperated with investigators and federal prosecutors, and finally (4) the extent to which the defendant company accepted responsibility for the unlawful conduct.

If a high ranking official at the defendant business was found to have been criminally involved, the maximum fine could have been as large as $54,800,000 or four times the loss to customers of the defendant rental car company (U.S.S.G, 1991). Table 7.1 describes the range of fines for each of four circumstances.

What Constitutes an Effective Compliance Program?

The language in the Federal Sentencing Guidelines provides an extremely general framework for the design, implementation, and enforcement of an organization's compliance program. Such programs are complex and will vary by industry and laws that regulate them. Wellner (2005) contends that the complexity of the differing types of organizations populating the corporate, nonprofit, and public sector landscape of this country requires that each entity design a compliance program that meets its specific needs. The courts and the United States Sentencing Commission cannot be expected to— nor should they be have to—fill in all the blanks in the design and development of a compliance program.

The seven necessary elements for an effective compliance and ethics program designed to prevent and detect criminal conduct are summarized below. *Due diligence* requires that the following be addressed (USSG, 2005, 8B2.1, pp. 478-483):

1. Standards and Procedures to Reduce Criminal Conduct. Organizations must establish a rigorous code of ethical conduct that is supported by unequivocal standards, procedures, and internal controls de-

Table 7.1
Fine Structure for Defendant Organization Under Varying Conditions.

	Minimum fine	Maximum fine
Existence of compliance, self-reporting, cooperation with investigators, responsibility for criminal acts	$685,000	$2,740,000
Existence of a compliance program only	$5,480,000	$10,960,000
No compliance program, no reporting, no cooperation, no acceptance of responsibility	$13,700,00	$27,400,000
No compliance program, no reporting, no cooperation, no acceptance of responsibility, and criminal involvement of high level official	$27,400,000	$54,800,000

Source: Based on Case No. 88-266, United States Sentencing Commission Supplementary Report on Sentencing Guidelines for Organizations (1991), p. C-81.

signed to detect criminal behavior and to reduce the likelihood of such behavior. Standards and procedures must take into consideration the uniqueness of the organization, the industry in which it does business, and any related compliance requirements. Codes of conduct should be written for understanding, not couched in legal jargon, and include an identification of possible conflicts of interest and the identification of any other applicable laws (such as payments to foreign governments) (Pell, 1996). Organizations that conduct business internationally should be prepared to revise important documents into foreign languages.

2. Establishing a Culture of Compliance by Senior Leadership. The "governing authority" of an organization includes the board of directors and the highest level governing authority knowledgeable about the content and operation of the compliance and ethics program. Specific executives will be assigned the responsibility for monitoring the ethics compliance program. Day to day operational responsibility will be assigned to specific individuals who must report periodically to higher level managers as necessary to ensure compliance. Individuals assigned these responsibilities will be provided adequate resources, the necessary authority, and direct access to senior managers.

3. Reasonable Efforts to Prohibit Illegal and Unethical Activities by Employees. An organization must take *due diligence* to exclude from the compliance planning and operational structure anyone that the organization knew or should have known to have engaged in unethical conduct or criminal activities.

4. Training and Communication. An organization is expected periodically to communicate and train personnel in the standards and procedures that constitute the ethics and compliance program. "It is thus no longer enough to have a lawyer pack some judicial opinions into a briefcase and give a few lectures about the law" (Murphy, 1997, p. 361). Training that meets the seven criteria discussed in this section must be provided to "high-level personnel of the organization," designated employees, and agents of the business (USSG, 2005, § 8A1.2).

5. Monitoring, Auditing, and Evaluating Program Effectiveness. An organization is expected to take reasonable precautions to ensure that the compliance and ethics program is followed and that the training is effective. Employee monitoring to detect criminal conduct is part of the evaluation process. Program evaluation also includes a process that allows employees and agents of the organization to seek advice or report criminal and unethical conduct without fear of retribution.

6. Provide Incentives to Comply and Progressive Discipline. Compliance and ethics programs are to be positively promoted and consistently enforced throughout the organization. Progressive levels of appropriate discipline should be used for anyone engaging in illegal activities. Reasonable measures must be taken to prevent and detect criminal activity.

7. Taking Remedial Measures. If unethical behavior or criminal activity is detected, the organization must take reasonable steps to stop such actions and take measures that prevent similar conduct. The organization will periodically determine the risk of criminal conduct, and as necessary, revise the compliance and ethics program where appropriate. Any ethics compliance program that significantly diverges from the seven criteria provided by the Guidelines will suffer a higher culpability score (Wellner, 2005).

There are several provisos in the language of the Guidelines that further define the scope of what constitutes an effective compliance program. "The failure to prevent or detect the instant offense does not necessarily mean that the program is not generally effective in preventing and detecting criminal conduct" (U.S.S.G. 8B2.1, p. 478). The emphasis is on prevention and detection of unethical and criminal conduct, the self-reporting of criminal activity by an organization, and cooperation with investigative authorities, including attorneys for the U.S. Department of Justice. The compliance program must have been in place prior to any charge alleging unethical or illegal activities before a judge will consider the adequacy of a compliance program as a mitigating factor in sentencing.

Effective compliance programs are expected to incorporate applicable governmental regulations and industry practices and to consider the size of the organization (USSG, 2005, § 8B2.1). Larger organizations are expected to have a formal compliance program structure and to allocate more resources than would a smaller organization.

Although smaller organizations are expected to meet the same degree of ethical conduct and compliance as are larger ones, these organizations may rely on more informal and "existing resources and simple systems" to demonstrate compliance. Smaller organizations may use senior managers to directly manage the compliance program, instead of delegating responsibility to lower level personnel. Informal staff meetings, monitoring by regular "walk-arounds or continuous observation while managing the organization," using available personnel instead of hiring additional staff, and modeling the organization's own compliance and ethics program and "best practices" of similarly situated organizations are additional options (U.S.S.G. 2005. § 8B2.1). The costs for establishing and maintaining a compliance program may be greater for smaller organizations than for larger ones (Bowman, 2004).

There are very few reported examples of compliance training programs designed to meet criteria established by the Federal Sentencing Guidelines. Murphy (1997) provides a cogent review of methods and techniques useful for communicating and training "in a practical manner." Jordan and Murphy (2004) reviewed 36 cases that were settled without a trial to better understand what the government expects from compliance and ethics programs. Their conclusions were highly generalized and varied by type of offense and organization, although they did conclude that judges did rely heavily on the Guidelines.

Copeland (2000) states that the first compliance program at Tyson Foods focused on the fiduciary responsibilities owed by directors, officers, senior managers, consultants, and lobbyists. Training in specialized topics is provided throughout Tyson, including the Foreign Corrupt Practices Act, and for food quality assurance and environmental compliance. As the director of ethics, Copeland monitored continuous training of all "team members" on a yearly basis at Tyson's world headquarters and all other facilities. A 25-minute video was developed and distributed to all locations in order to ensure uniformity. Copeland also notes that The Tyson Management Development Center was inaugurated in 1999 as a way to integrate leadership development, strategic goal setting, and ethics and compliance training.

Incentives and Disincentives for Developing a Compliance Program

The incentives for adopting a compliance program at first view would appear significant. Adoption of such a program reduces the potential for vicarious liability for corporations for the criminal acts of their employees and fines that might be imposed. The revised fine structure and calculation schema are designed to reinforce and reward organizations that self-report, cooperate with investigators, and who have an "effective compliance and ethics" program in place prior to any criminal activity. Corporations may be less likely to be indicted if an effective compliance program is in place prior to criminal acts by employees (Hasnas, 2006; Wellner, 2005).

Are there disincentives for establishing compliance programs? One might speculate that given the incentives to organizations to comply with the Guidelines that most organizations would opt for the development of compliance programs. However, this is not the case, as not one of the 167 organizations sentenced in 2002 was on record for having any type of compliance programs. Two of the 92 organizations sentenced in 2001 were deemed to have inadequate compliance programs; the remaining 90 organizations had no compliance programs whatsoever (Wellner, 2005). Bowman (2004) reviewed the United States Sentencing Commission Annual Reports for the years 1992 through 2002. He determined that out of 1,880 organizations sentenced under the guidelines, only a "grand total of three organizations have ever received a sentence reduction for an effective compliance program" (p. 684). The sentencing guidelines provide a downgrade penalty for corporations that developed a shadow of a compliance program, one that lacks substance and commitment by senior level employees (U.S.S.G., 2005, 8C2.5; Wellner, 2005).

Research on the effects of compliance programs is at best mixed. Parker and Atkins (1999) "failed to find evidence of a statistically significant change in either the levels or the structure of monetary corporate penalties . . . when comparing the 1991 Guidelines with baseline data from 1988" (p. 448). Alexander, Arlen, and Cohen (1999) concluded that corporations sentenced under the Guidelines received fines 470 percent higher than for pre-Guidelines cases.

By agreeing to the sentencing Guidelines, organizations essentially hand over the keys to investigators and Department of Justice attorneys. There is no place to hide; the organization becomes an open book. Complying with the Guidelines means that the organization cooperates fully from the onset of the investigation, including full disclosure of "all pertinent information known by the organization in sufficient quantities that investigative personnel may identify the nature and extent of the offense, including those responsible for criminal misconduct" (U.S.S.G. § 8C2.5). Under certain circumstances, an organization may have to forfeit the attorney-client privilege. In this context, "Acceptance of responsibility essentially requires an organization to plead guilty to an offense charged without putting on a defense" (Hasnas, 2006, p. 48).

Are Compliance Programs Fair or Effective?

What constitutes a test for evaluating compliance program effectiveness in the eyes of the legal community is described by Urofsky (cited in Wellner, 2005) who advises the following standards:

1. the program is an off-the-shelf program or is specifically tailored to detect and deter criminal conduct within an organization;
2. the organization has devoted sufficient resources, including audit and investigative staff; and
3. the program provides for reporting to the highest levels of management; the organization has imposed discipline upon officers, employees, and agents found to have violated its compliance policies.

These criteria are very subjective and will likely promulgate the kind of disparate conclusions that the Federal Sentencing Guidelines are designed to discourage. Take for example two assistant United States attorneys who both have access to the same information regarding a convicted organization that is about to be sentenced under the Guidelines. Assume further that neither attorney was actively involved in the prosecution of the defendant organizations. Given the subjectivity of the Urofsky standards, each attorney could come to different conclusions regarding the effectiveness of the defendant organization's compliance program. The potential for such disparity among federal prosecutors is very important considering that they must provide recommendations to the federal judge prior to sentencing an organization (USSG, 2005, § 8C2.5). Part of the recommendation will address rating the "effectiveness" of the organization's compliance and ethics program. Federal Sentencing Guidelines were designed to assist judges in sentencing; however, what guidelines are available to federal prosecutors to assist them in evaluating compliance programs when making sentencing recommendations?

This form of "interrelator unreliability" is not an unusual phenomenon specific to judges and prosecutors. Industrial psychologists have wrestled with the "rating problem" by supervisors of employees since the 1940s. Inaccurate ratings by supervisors lead to a number of undesirable "effects," including halo, strictness, leniency, and contrast effects (Cascio & Aguinis, 2005). Unless there is a specific frame of reference to guide the rating of employees, it is highly probable that two supervisors observing the same employee could commit one or more of the effect errors mentioned above (Sample, 2006). Given the wide latitude allowed federal prosecutors under the Guidelines, shouldn't they be required to form "ratings" of compliance programs as "effect" free as possible? Are there professionally developed guidelines for evaluating programs that could guide assessment of the effectiveness of an ethics compliance program?

We might be reminded at this juncture that the Equal Employment Opportunity Commission mandates the use of the following external sources in validating selection decisions: the *Principles for the Validation and use of Personnel Selection Procedure* (SIOP, 2003) and *Standards for Educational and Psychological Testing* (American Educational Research Association, 1999). Would it not be in the best interests of all involved in the sentencing of organizations if an external authoritative frame of reference was in place for determining the effectiveness of a compliance and ethics program? One such resource is *The Program Evaluation Standards* (Sanders, 1994) which is also approved by ANSI—The American National Standards Institute (http://www.ansi.org/).

A legitimate use of qualified expert witnesses would be to assist the federal courts in determining the effectiveness of compliance and ethics programs. Expert witnesses are used in several states in OSHA claims, either to defend a personal injury claim or to appeal an OSHA citation. In those instances, expert witnesses are used to prove that safety programs are "effective in practice" (Clarke, 2006). The Federal Sentencing Commission could adopt a similar process in which qualified expert witnesses are engaged by the federal courts to opine the effectiveness of a compliance and ethics program.

Kraweic (2003) asserted that there is little evidence that those internal compliance programs, such as those required by the Guidelines, are effective. This is disturbing given that ethical conduct and the establishment of an ethics based compliance program is the Rosetta stone of Chapter 8 of the Federal Sentencing Guidelines. Other studies support problems with the effectiveness of compliance and ethics programs (Matthews, 1987; McKendall, DeMarr, & Jones-Rikkers, 2002; Schwartz, 2001; Trevino et al., 1999).

Even the United States Sentencing Commission has conceded that

> Any discussion assessing the degree of success in attaining the ambitious Commission goals for its organizational sentencing guidelines must begin with a significant concession. With regard to the hoped for goal of deterrence/crime control, there apparently is no empirical data that comprehensively charts changes in organizational crime rates over time. (Steer, 2001, p. 9)

Moving From Compliance to Integrity Based Programs

The failure of compliance programs to alter and sustain behaviors and attitudes may lie within the strategy itself. Programs that are based on a "compliance" strategy rely on mandated conformity to externally imposed standards with the goal of preventing unethical and criminal activities. According to Paine (1994), such programs rely on lawyer-like leadership that assumes employees are independent actors guided by material self-interest which requires internal policing up and down the ranks. Program development using a compliance strategy focuses on regulatory and criminal law as the foundation for educating the workforce to conform the externally mandated standards. Such programs typically reduce individual discretion, increase auditing controls, and penalize unethical and illegal activity. A typical formula is to write and communicate organizational policies, train to policy, monitor performance, and provide progressive discipline when necessary (Paine, 1994).

Given the evidence cited above that compliance strategies are ineffective, what alternatives are available to training and development personnel and their managers for designing and implementing an effective compliance program?

To answer this question Trevino and her associates (1999) administered a survey to more than 10,000 randomly selected employees at various levels within six large U.S. corporations. The purpose of the survey was to determine what ethics and compliance programs actually accomplish. Variables for the study included four types of strategies: integrity/values focus, compliance focus, external stakeholder focus, and a focus on protection of top management.

Although all four strategies were determined to influence the outcomes of interest to the researchers (Trevino et al., 1999, p. 138), it is clearly most important to have a "program that employees perceive to be values-based . . . Unethical behavior was lower, awareness of ethical issues was higher, and employees were more likely to look for advice within the firm, to be willing to deliver bad news to management, and to report ethical violations. They were more committed to the organization and more likely to believe that decision making was better because of the ethics/compliance program."

Three of the four research variables in the study were highly correlated—values, compliance and stakeholder—suggesting that a combination of the three approaches may be effective. Clearly not supported by the findings was protecting top management (Trevino et al., 1999).

The alternative to a compliance strategy is one that is "integrity and values-based." This strategy promotes self-governance to organizationally selected standards and is management—not lawyer—driven. According to Paine (1994) the assumptions that underlie this strategy are that employees at all levels are social beings, and although guided by material self-interest, they are also motivated by values and ideals, and may be influenced by their peers and leaders. Program development methods emphasize leadership, accountability, a systems approach of understanding organizations, and decision making. Auditing and control processes are driven by internally derived values, not externally mandated standards.

A similar conclusion was reached by Pell (1996) in his review of "leading edge practices" by *Fortune* 250 companies. Compliance-based programs fail to address "root causes of misconduct . . .Integrity-based programs, whereby management's commitment to ethical values and promotion of ethical behavior creates an organization in which exemplary conduct is encouraged . . . Companies in our survey with leading edge practices all employed integrity-based programs" (Pell, 1996, p. 2)

RECCOMENDATIONS FOR DEVELOPING AN EFFECTIVE COMPLIANCE AND ETHICS PROGRAM

The following recommendations are derived from a variety of sources, including Murphy (1997), Paine (1994), Pell (1996), Trevino et al., (1999), and Wick et al., (2006).

1. Conduct a comprehensive ethics audit and risk assessment. Conduct surveys and focus groups with employees, vendors, suppliers, and other agents of the organization to find out what is happening at lower levels. Honesty from the trenches will depend on perceived ethical leadership of those asking the questions and nonpunishing opportunities to speak up about issues involving ethical violations and criminal activity (Paine, 1994; Badaracco & Webb, 1995). Risk assessment includes an estimate of the significance of risk, predicting the likelihood or occurrence of risk, and determining how to manage the risk (Pell, 1996). Risk assessment must take into consideration the industry in which the organization operates and all other regulatory and compliance requirements.

2. Avoid fast-fixes; focus on values and organizational culture. Avoid the "duct-tape" model of quick fixes. Consider carefully the consequences of using overly broad or narrowly conceived "off-the-shelf" programs that are often recommended and used by external consultants or purchased by naive internal trainers. Focus first on growing a culture of ethics followed by policies, standards, and programs. Use a value-based strategy in concert with compliance and concern for stakeholder strategies when designing an effective ethics compliance program. The emphasis should be on strengthening shared values that drive organizational behaviors.

Emphasize follow-through on ethical codes, policies, and reporting procedures. Executives and senior managers are expected to "model the way" and to "challenge the process" (Kouzes & Posner, 2002) by demonstrating shared norms that support an ethical culture through words and actions. Many organizations will develop the hardware first without concern for issues related to culture and follow-through. Failure by management to follow up on reported ethical violations and criminal activity will only result in disdain for the process and the organization (Paine, 1994; Trevino et al., 1999).

3. Select employees, senior managers, contracted professional personnel, and vendors, who are ethical and have no criminal history re-

garding fiduciary duties or criminal behavior. The focus of the federal sentencing guidelines is to prevent criminal activity, and if such activity occurs, to aggressively resolve the illegal conduct by appropriate means. Selecting personnel for high-level governance responsibilities who have no criminal history or predilection to act with unethical or criminal intent is a giant step in the right direction. Those in charge of selecting employees must "develop guidelines for evaluating the values and character of potential hires, as well as their experience in demonstrating ethical behaviors" (Loescher, 2006, p 95). This includes not only background checks, reference checks, and criminal history assessment, but also investigation into serious professional missteps (i.e., federal and state bar associations for attorneys). Applicants who have had fiduciary responsibilities subject to federal or state regulation may have been investigated and disciplined (i.e., Securities and Exchange Commission). Finally, accounting and auditing firms must be selected using best business practices in accordance with the Sarbanes-Oxley Act.

4. Keep the compliance and ethics program in the organization. Consider carefully who develops and manages an ethics compliance program. Some human resource management functions can be outsourced with little impact on an organization's performance. The management of an ethics compliance reporting and investigation process should remain an internal function of the organization. An outsourced compliance reporting system may send the wrong message. Strict compliance models are typically developed and managed by attorneys who are trained to reactively defend the assets of an organization. The development of a cultural/values-based approach requires a broader view of an organization as a social system that relies on shared norms to guide employee behavior. A highly-placed and credible senior manager with line management experience is more likely to engender the social support required for a values-based compliance program (Trevino, 1999).

5. Make the business case for developing a compliance and ethics program. Avoid the inclination to quickly dispose of a "legal compliance" requirement by meeting minimal standards. Hiring an "ethics officer," providing an anonymous tip-line, and using "off-the-shelf" training materials may be viewed as "window dressing," thus increasing—rather than decreasing—the organization's culpability score (Hanas, 2006; Wellner, 2005). Any "program" whether it be compliance training, capital expansion, market penetration, new product development, or any other effort designed to propel the business forward, must be directly linked to organizational profitability and growth. Thinking in terms of "what business needs will be met" (Wick et al. 2006, p. 32) broadens the scope of the effort from merely designing a compliance program to addressing legitimate business needs. A business must consider a myriad of factors other than just those related to compliance.

It is not too early in the planning to begin thinking about how to monitor, audit, and evaluate program effectiveness, as required by the Federal Sentencing Guidelines. Balanced scorecards (Kaplan & Norton, 1996) and dashboards (Prevatte, 2006) are very useful for managing information compliance (Kahn, 2004).

6. Design an effective compliance and ethics program that is systemic and complete. The design of a program within the meaning of the Federal Sentencing Guidelines means to systematically include all seven factors into a comprehensive framework that addresses and documents the detection, reporting, and disciplining of unethical and criminal activity, as well as cooperating with investigative and judicial authorities. Training and communications (number four of the seven factors) do not constitute "the program," but are a critical part of it. This distinction is important because many factors other than training influence performance outcomes (Brinkerhoff, 2004).

The terms "systemic and complete" mean that a "cross-functional" design team must oversee the development of the organizations compliance and ethics program. Larger organizations should consider some combination of the following:

- A senior level VP or manager who has extensive experience as a line operations manager, sterling credibility for ethical practices, and visibility within the organization.
- A representative of the organization's legal staff, presumably an attorney with regulatory and compliance experience.
- A representative from corporate communications (or equivalent position).
- A representative from the human resources management, training, and development unit that has program design and evaluation expertise.
- An experienced fraud and audit professional (may be internal or external).
- A representative of the union if there is a current contract to manage.
- Representatives from key suppliers or vendors with whom the

organization has an agency relationship.
- A documents and data management specialist to address how to automate the monitoring and auditing requirements.

Large and multifaceted organizations may need multiple teams, with each team managing the design and development of a compliance and ethics program that meets the unique requirements of a division or function within the organization. This will certainly be true for organizations that conduct business internationally. Smaller organizations are typically constrained by resources and will have fewer employees and managers responsible for various components of the design.

The design team is charged with establishing a framework that addresses the following minimal requirements within the context of identified business objectives:

a. Develop of a code of ethics and a mechanism for encouraging the reporting of unethical behavior and criminal activity.
b. Develop standards and procedures for detecting and reporting criminal activity of all employees, including high level employees.
c. Development of positive incentives to comply with regulatory and legal requirements.
d. Develop a monitoring system that captures efforts to prohibit illegal and unethical activities.
e. Develop procedures for applying progressive discipline and taking remedial measures, including reporting illegal criminal activity and cooperating with investigative authorities.

The development of a framework that meets the needs of a specific organization calls for patience, continuous dialogue, and above all—*due diligence*! It is during this stage of the design process that senior managers are expected to state clear and unequivocal expectations for the integrity of the compliance and ethics program, including the imperative to "follow through." Each of the five components of the framework when "worked over time" by the design team will become integrated into a system of complementary parts. The design team must resist the temptation to develop the training and communication component until the framework has been completed. To do otherwise may result in false starts that will necessitate significant redesign and deployment of resources.

A transfer-of-learning matrix proposed by Broad and Newstrom (1992) exemplifies the level of planning necessary to move a compliance and ethics "framework" from "words on a page" to a systemic, complete and documented compliance and ethics program. Note the relative importance to managerial involvement compared to others in the matrix.

The completeness and systemic integrity of the framework for a compliance and ethics program can be tested by "stapling yourself [as the program designer] to the learner [employee]" (Wick et al. 2006, p. 68). Imagine the journey of the participant from the beginning of the compliance and ethics program into the future by six months or a year. Consider the following questions that employees might ponder:

a. Am I clear about my responsibilities to the organization regarding ethical behavior and criminal activities?
b. Will I be punished or ostracized for reporting unethical or criminal activities of others?
c. What is my support system for clarifying possible unethical behavior by others or myself? Who do I contact and can I trust the system to maintain confidentiality?
d. Where does my manager stand on the importance of the compliance and ethics program?
e. Is this stuff really important to higher-ups in the organization? How will I know that my ethical behavior is valued?

Finally, consider the remote possibility that these same questions, and many others, will be asked by investigators from multiple agencies if allegations of criminal activities are reported by the organization or are uncovered by some external source. Under those circumstances, investigators and Department of Justice attorneys will become "stapled" to employees! Given these circumstances, how would your employees respond to questions regarding the "effectiveness of the compliance and ethics" program?

7. Deliver the compliance and ethics program for on-the-job application. In order to assure application from a compliance and ethics program, it is absolutely essential that employees view effort to learn and perform ethically and legally on the job as instrumental for receiving a valued outcome (Vroom, 1964). Simply stated, effort, performance and valued outcomes are interrelated.

It is the WIIFM ("what's in it for me") factor that most managers

Table 7.2
Transfer of Learning Matrix for an Effective Compliance and Ethics Program

Design Teams	Before	During	After
Executive level, senior and mid-managers, with assistance from legal staff, corporate communications, fraud, and adult personnel.	Designs the framework, writes code of ethics, and communicates expectations to organization, including the detection and reporting of unethical and criminal activity.	Senior leadership models ethical leadership behaviors. Reinforces the importance of ethical job performance at various points during training and through continuing corporate communications.	Senior leadership models ethical leadership behavors. Addresses unethical and criminal activity in a timely manner, including self-reporting of the organization for detected criminal activity, cooperation with investigating authorities, and accepting responsibility for criminal activity Periodically deternines the effectiveness of the compliance and ethics program and revises as necessary.
Human Resource management, training, evaluation. and documents/data mangement pesonnel; union representatives.	Designs means, methods, documentation and evaluation strategies for compliance program, including training participants. Program designers must "get the right people into the room" and "onto the same page" (Wick, et al. 2006, pp 58-59) with planned ongoing support after the training. Consider a variety of delivery methods (classroom instruction, eLearning and electronic performance support systems and coaching).	Implements coodinated program, including attracting and retaining ethical talent, training (new employee orientation, training of targeted groups, such as corporate board members, senior managers, and employees).	Tracks effectiveness as part of a balanced scorecard or similar HR management information system. Provides continuing reinforcement through periodic briefings at "town hall" meetings, eLearning training sessions, and as part of the annual performance appeaisal. Manages and documents the progressive discipline of employees.

Vendor, suppliers, and business that has an agency relationship with the organization	Adopts business policy agreeing to comply with and support the organization's code of ethics. Agrees to conform to ethical business practices, including reporting unethical and criminal activity.	Voluntarily attends briefings and training programs designed to assist vendors and suppliers with compliance.	Vendors and suppliers are reinforced for voluntarily reporting unethical or criminal activities while conducting business with the organization.
Prarticipants of the compliance and ethics program.	Adopts high expectations based on corporate communications. Reviews ethics and criminal activities' policy, and signs agreement of voluntary compliance.	Attends training programs, participates by asking questions, and contributes to exercises designed to inform employees regarding their responsibility for ethical and non-criminal behavior.	Conforms to culture of ethical and non-criminal behavior. Uses the anonymous tip line to seek clarification regarding potential unethical and criminal activity; reports unethical and criminal activity of others.

and human resource development professionals recognize as a universal question to be addressed when designing any training program or change effort (Wick et al., 2006). Failure to identify valued personal outcomes for the recipients of training allows excellent training and development programs to wither from eventual nonattendance and predictable lack of line manager support (Robinson & Robinson, 2004). In this context, a valued coutcome is a tangible reward that comes as a result of effort and performance on the job.

Listed below are several valued outcomes related to a compliance and ethics program for an organization. Which one—from the employee's perspective—might be the valued outcome that most clearly captures the employee's attention in such a way that he or she would be motivated to exert effort to perform well? This question applies equally to members of the board of directors, senior and mid-level managers, key professional staff, internal and external auditors, vendors and suppliers, or other identified employees.

Examples of Valued Personal Outcomes:

a. Increases profits, sustainable growth, customer satisfaction and brand loyalty based on the reputation that the organization has as a corporate good citizen.

b. Protects shareholder investments and loyalty based on a reputation for socially responsible and ethical business practices.
c. Reduces costs associated with regulatory oversight, fines, legal settlements and judgments associated with unethical and criminal conduct.
d. Protects and strengthens essential "business to business" vendor and supplier relationships that are critical to the success of the organization.
e. Increases employee opportunity for recognition for sustained ethical conduct that is instrumental for higher visibility, positive performance appraisals, performance bonuses, and opportunities for advancement.
f. Reduces the potential for personal and/or organizational civil and criminal liability (fines, prison sentence, restitution and probation) as well as a ruined career and reputation.

The valued outcomes stated above run the gamut from protecting the commercial interests of the organization to protecting individual self-interest. Any one employee may be attracted to more than one outcome, and not all valued outcomes have been identified. Selecting a valued outcome also establishes relevance for the employee as a learner. It is central to this particular discussion that one or more outcomes become a motivating factor for increasing effort to perform ethically and legally.

8. Ensure Follow-Through with Goal Setting. Establishing expectations is paramount for gaining control over follow-through for a compliance and ethics program. Program designers should not be shy about building an instructional system that focuses on job performance. Here is an example of an exercise that links effort and performance to a valued outcome:

Transfer of learning requires that participants do the following: (1) select of a valued outcome (see examples listed above), (2) write a performance goal that requires effort to achieve, and (3) elicit the support of the participant's manager to make performance instrumental for achieving the valued outcome. Wick (2006) and his associates advocated allowing enough time in the training portion of the compliance and ethics program for each participant to write a performance goal that will be delivered to his or her manager for review and follow-up. The design of the program should allow sufficient time for participants to recover from the surprise of such a task, and for instruction and support in writing meaningful performance goals. Program designers may want to develop templates that facilitate completion of the goal-setting process. See Wick et al., (2006, pp. 84-93) for assistance in how to develop and manage the setting of performance goals.

Transfer of learning is not ensured by setting performance goals in a vacuum or simply as an exercise in a training session. Delivering the participant's performance goal to his or her manager for review and feedback will begin a continuing dialogue, refinement, and progress checks. Scheduled meetings once or twice a year to discuss progress and ask for advice or clarification will provide opportunities for coaching by managers. The process of clarification and coaching should not be taken for granted.

9. Ensure Active Support of Managers. The active support of managers for integrating ethics into the culture and fabric of the organization is critical for sustained follow-through. A review of Table 7.2 reveals that managers have the most responsibility before, during, and after the development and implementation of a compliance and ethics program. This approach is counter to the research on managerial involvement and its role in supporting change initiatives and training.

Broad and Newstrom (1992) researched the importance of three roles (managers, trainers, and trainees) over three time periods (before, during, and after training) to determine the most effective role/time configuration for ensuring transfer of learning. The researchers concluded that managers ranked one (before training) and three (after training) out of possible nine role/time combinations in importance for influencing transfer of learning. The researchers were disappointed to learn that managers, in actuality, were the least used of the three roles after the training was completed (ranked ninth out of nine possible role/time combinations).

Engaging managers in the early design of the compliance and ethics program (the "before" time period) will create ownership and commitment. Expecting participants (managers as well as employees) to write performance goals "during" training that are sent to their immediate supervisor "after" training will result in dialogue and coaching opportunities.

Managers have other ways to contribute to the continuing success of the compliance and ethics program.

- In their capacity to recruit talented employees, managers can emphasize the importance of corporate citizenship, socially responsible, and ethical business practices.

- Managers can attend new employee orientation sessions to reinforce the expectation of ethical and legal behavior.
- Managers can incorporate a discussion of ethics into the formal appraisal process by recognizing efforts to support a culture of ethical business practices.
- Managers can remind vendors and suppliers of their ethical obligations to the organization, including reporting unethical or criminal activity by the organizations sales and procurement personnel.
- Managers, especially executives and senior managers, can develop a "stump speech" on the importance of ethical and crime-free business practices that can be used within the organization and externally in the community (service and business clubs, regional and national association meetings, community events).

Others important to transfer and follow-through include the organization's human resource management, training, and development personnel. Human resource managers and their personnel have daily opportunities to monitor the organization's landscape for examples of ethical and unethical conduct. Instructional designers, training, and development personnel have continuing opportunities to weave concepts and practices of ethical conduct into the design and facilitation of a variety of instruction. Wick et al. (2006) cited the potential for online blended coaching, peer learning communities, and the necessity for programming prompts and reminders into the organization's communication system.

10. Monitor, audit, and evaluate effectiveness of the compliance and ethics program. Designing an evaluation process that monitors and audits efforts to comply with the seven elements of an "effective compliance and ethics" program will be a necessary, yet insufficient strategy to prove *due diligence.* An evaluation must also directly address the effect of the organization's standards and procedures for preventing, detecting, and reporting unethical and criminal activity at all levels of the organization.

Traditional evaluation approaches rely on measurement and evaluation tools that are viewed by many as overly complex, labor intensive, and requiring advanced skills in statistics and evaluation methods (Swanson, 2005). Consumers of evaluation reports are typically not predisposed to believe numbers and statistics as evidence of program adequacy (Brinkerhoff, 2006).

Evidence that the organization's compliance and ethics program detects and accurately reports unethical and criminal activity should be the primary focus of the evaluation. The fact that an organization has monitoring and auditing procedures in place is less persuasive than reporting the effects of such procedures. For example, maintaining an accurate process that documents unethical conduct and criminal activities by employees, vendors, suppliers, and other agents of the organization, including investigations, progressive discipline, and remedial activities will be persuasive evidence of compliance with the Federal Sentencing Guidelines. Setting goals, explained earlier in this section, can be used to assess the extent to which employees and managers are changing behaviors. Critical incidents of observed behaviors are also useful for documenting behaviors or employees, managers, and executives (Wick et al., 2006).

It is important to learn as quickly as possible if the organization's compliance and ethics program is effective. Traditional evaluation models lack flexibility in this regard. The Success Case Method advocated by Brinkerhoff (2006) enables program developers to quickly and with credibility build a persuasive argument that a program is effective (or not, as the case may be). This qualitative approach begins with the development of a short survey that can be delivered by fax, email, or accessed using an organization's Intranet to complete an online survey. This first step is intended to identify successful and unsuccessful instances of program effectiveness. Follow-up interviews (by telephone or face-to-face) ascertain aspects of the program that are effective, should be modified, or eliminated.

Results in economic terms can be calculated by using a "return-on-investment" (ROI) approach. An ROI study enables an organization to determine the extent to which a compliance program contributes directly to business objectives, as well as measuring the effect of a compliance and ethics program. In an ROI case study published by Hill and Phillips (1997), the client healthcare company found that sexual harassment prevention training resulted in a reduction of internal complaints by 36 percent and the number of claims litigated dropped by 41 percent. Expenses attributed to legal fees and settlement costs fell by 49 percent, saving the company over $800,000 in one year. Additional benefits included a reduction in turnovers caused by harassment from 11 percent to 3 percent in the year of implementing the prevention training.

The development of an "information management compliance system" that tracks the requirements of the Federal Sentencing Guidelines is described by Kahn (2004). The essential elements for such a system are as follows:

a. Good policies and procedures.
b. Executive-level program responsibility.
c. Proper delegation of program roles and components.
d. Program dissemination, communication, and training.
e. Auditing and monitoring to measure program compliance.
f. Effective and consistent program enforcement.
g. Continuous program improvement (Kahn, 2004, p. 32).

The information management compliance system recommended by Kahn may be incorporated into a "balanced scorecard" business strategy (Kaplan & Norton, 1996). This approach measures such key organizational factors as learning and development, customer and shareholder satisfaction, internal business processes, and financial indicators. Each of the four factors is defined in terms of goals, key performance indicators, and measures.

The purpose of a balanced scorecard is to align an organization's business vision and planning with operational goals that are linked to performance indicators. Feedback loops provide information necessary to adjust and realign strategies. Table 7.3 describes a balanced scorecard framework for assessing the effectiveness of a compliance and ethics program.

Using a balanced scorecard that integrates the factors in Table 7.3 within the organization's overall scorecard, enables the compliance and ethics program to be viewed as a "partner in strategy." Information from a balanced scorecard that reports the effectiveness of the compliance and ethics program will enable boards of directors and senior managers to view compliance as part of the organization's commitment to ethical performance (Busco, Firgo, Giovannoni, Riccaboni, & Scapens, 2005; Souissi, 2006).

An innovation that can be utilized in concert with a balanced scorecard system is the digital dashboard (Prevette, 2006). A dashboard enables executives, managers, and compliance officers to access current information regarding key performance indicators. The dashboard can be designed using various business intelligence technologies that are available from a number of software vendors. A well-

Table 7.3
Framework for a Balanced Scorecard for Documenting and Measuring the Effectiveness of an Effective Compliance and Ethics Program.

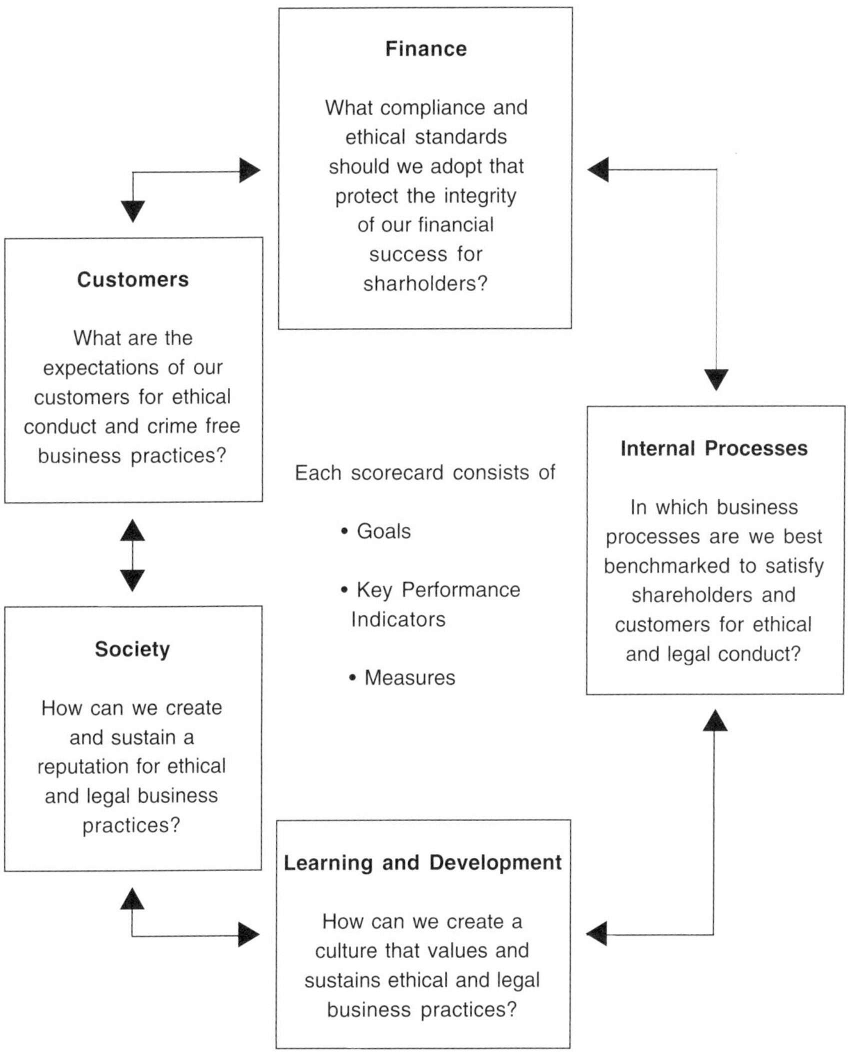

designed dashboard will include the following features (Petrich & Moon, 2005, p. 3):

- The ability to access quickly investigation to relevant reports, documents, information data bases, and scorecards.
- Real-time reporting on key performance indicators that are defined within the compliance program and rooted in operational data.
- Integration capability that supports the delivery of real-time analytic and operational measures from a multitude of business systems.

A digital dashboard can be designed and programmed with color graphics and other attention-getting signals. For example, instead of requiring the compliance officer to send a reminder email to an employee who has not attended compliance training, the digital dashboard could automatically send the email and track attendance of all employees (Bhalala, 2006; Cutright, 2005).

11. Evaluating classroom instruction. Compliance and ethics classroom instruction are unique in that the trainer (corporate counsel, human resource managers, ethics or compliance officer, etc.) must consider the ramifications for evaluating such programs and their instructors. Recall from the *Stender v. Lucky Stores* case (see Chapter 2) that participant notes and used flip charts were subject to pretrial discovery and used as evidence against the defendant. Instructors are advised by Murphy (1997) to "inform classes not to take notes, or at least to take them with keen awareness of their riskiness" (p. 382).

CONCLUSION

The establishment of the Sarbanes-Oxley Act and the revised 2004 Federal Sentencing Guidelines ushered in a new era of accountability for ethics and corporate governance. The requirement for an "effective compliance and ethics program" to detect and report criminal activity will be a challenge to design, implement and evaluate. Unfortunately, there are several obstacles from competing forces that may cancel the intended effect!

The questionable constitutional status of the Federal Sentencing Guidelines adds additional strain to the investigation, prosecution, and adjudication of criminal conduct by organizations. According to the Association for Corporate Counsel (2005), there will be "strong interest in proposing new mandatory Guidelines . . . it is likely that they will only get tougher, not more lenient" (p. 5). In the interim, organizations accused of criminal activity after the *Booker* and *Fanfan* decisions are less likely to cooperate, even though self-reporting and cooperation are requirements of the Guidelines.

The utility of a well designed, implemented, and evaluated compliance and ethics program is questionable given that fines have stayed the same (or increased depending upon the research one cites) and not decreased as promised under the Guidelines. Very few organizations are submitting compliance programs for evaluation by federal prosecutors and judges. Those that do submit their programs for review run the risk of being judged insufficient, thus negatively impacting culpability calculations.

The lack of a credible external reference, such as the *Program Evaluation Standards* (Sanders, 1994) makes the review of such programs a roll of the dice. Federal prosecutors and judges are steeped in the statutes, laws, and procedural rules that guide their practice. They do not have rigorous training in evaluation and measurement theory, nor are they uniformly informed on what constitutes effective program development. The potential for disparate conclusions on similarly situated compliance programs flies in the face of the purpose of the Federal Sentencing Guidelines. According to Hutchinson, Hoffman, Young, and Popko (2006), that there will "likely be litigation about the meaning of an effective program" (p. 2014) is inevitable.

Issues like those raised above prompted the following remark by Eliot Spitzer, Attorney General of the State of New York: "It's not altruism, and it's probably not the paperwork. It's enforcement. One jail term is worth a lot of compliance officers. And it doesn't require you to create a whole new bureaucracy" (Obrien, 2004, p. 75).

Epilogue

After years of researching and publishing on the topic of training liability, I am amazed at the lack of attention that this subject has received in the theoretical and practical literature. Feuer (1985) was the first to ask how much training is enough when it comes to protecting the public. By the mid-1990s, enough litigation had permeated the practice of training and development such that articles in practitioner journals began to surface (Eyres, 1990; Mathiason & de Bernardo, 1998; Sample, 1993). Eyres's (1998) comprehensive text, *The Legal Handbook for Trainers, Speakers and Consultants* placed the issue front-and-center for the all adult educators, human resource development specialists, and instructional designers to ponder. More recently, Clardy (2003, 2004) has attempted to elevate the nature of inquiry from general practice issues to generating useful theories and models that guide practice. In spite of these good works by various writers, mainstream survey textbooks on adult education, human resource development, or instructional design either ignore the topic, or only provide limited and incomplete coverage (Noe, 2006; Werner & DeSimone, 2006).

The following questions set the stage for further research and thoughtful reflection by practitioners and academicians alike.

Is court-mandated training the answer to reducing liability and protecting employees and the public? Bisom-Rapp (2001) argued that court-mandated training from a civil-rights perspective is designed to protect the employer, more so than employees and the public, from litigation, settlements, and judgments. Organizations that provide a clear antiharassment policy, communicate and train to the policy, and provide progressive discipline for wayward employees may mount an affirmative defense that prevents or reduces liability (EEOC, 1999). A similar argument has been mounted by some who believe that the code of ethics and training program mandates in the revised federal sentencing guidelines are designed to shield or rescue senior managers and executives from criminal prosecution and exorbitant fines against their businesses (Wellner, 2005).

How effective has training been in reducing the potential for liability? The often dreaded question of evaluating program effectiveness sends trainers and instructional designers into arrhythmia (Swanson, 2005). Evaluations can be labor intensive, time consuming, and ill-defined in terms of purpose, benefits and stakeholders. Little empirical research is available to guide trainers and instructional designers in the area of regulatory compliance and liability. What does exist is disheartening.

As discussed in Chapter 2, diversity training and related initiatives demonstrate mixed and controversial results (Grace, 1994; Hemphill & Haines, 1997; Hite & McDonald, 2006; Sanchez & Medkik, 2004; Von Bergen, Soper & Foster, 2002).

The recent Enron debacle and related business scandals (Petrick & Scherer, (2003) have placed an emphasis on codes of ethics. Ethical codes of conduct are addressed in some form of documentation in 98 percent of *Fortune* 1000 businesses, and of those, 78 percent distribute their policies throughout their organizations. Ethics and compliance training is available, and reporting avenues such as hotlines are used in many businesses. Corporate ethics officers and legal professionals agree that such codes are important (Trevino et al., 1999). Unfortunately, empirical research fails to unequivocally establish significant relationships between codes of ethics and compliance training with improved employee conduct. Several research efforts explore this nature of these phenomena.

Schwartz (2001) used an in-depth qualitative process to interview 57 employees in several Canadian companies. Some of those interviewed could not recall instances of behavior change due to a code of ethics, and most indicated that their individual behaviors were not modified by their employer's code of ethics. Schwartz (2001) concluded that given the potential for codes of ethics to guide behavior that "this appears to take place on very rare occasions" (p. 253). These findings are consistent with a litany of studies cited by Krawiec (2003, p. 511).

A study by McKendall, DeMarr, and Jones-Rikkers (2002) researched the potential for corporate compliance programs to reduce criminal activity in corporations. The researchers wanted to determine if "ethical codes, communication about ethics, ethics training and incorporating ethics into human resource practices would result in fewer OSHA violations" (p. 367). A survey research questionnaire was sent to key informants in 315 companies. Usable responses were received from 108 high-ranking human resource personnel. Regression analysis indicated that ethical compliance programs did not reduce OSHA-related violations. The one "main *effect* suggested the possibility that ethics programs may serve as window dressing to deflect attention [hide management involvement] and/or culpability [reduce corporate liability] resulting from illegal actions" (p. 367).

A study published in 1987 researched the frequency of civil and regulatory actions taken by four federal regulatory agencies against more than 480 corporations during the time period 1973 to 1980. Matthews (1987) concluded that there was very little relationship between ethical codes of conduct and compliance conduct of employees. This study did report a positive correlation between required affidavits of compliance or codes that require "maintaining the reputation of the corporation" and employee conduct (p.125-126).

Given these dismal and controversial findings, it is difficult to imagine corporate life without training programs that focus on issues of diversity, ethical conduct, and safety and health issues. We really have no way of knowing how many lives are enriched or saved from injury or death because of these programs!

Should organizations focus more on comprehensive risk-management strategies? According to Clardy (2004), risk associated with noncompliance with regulatory laws is only one of several factors impacting training and development units within organizations. Other risks include increased costs for benefits (hospitalization, medical expenses, increased workers' compensation costs and taxes); untrained employees that cause increased production costs; losses associated with business reputation and goodwill; direct financial losses from untrained employees who handle or manage cash or investment opportunities; managerial malpractice related to lack of training and development; failure to use standard "best practices" in the planning, development and evaluation of programs, and ineffective administration of the training and development function. These additional risks will likely result in costs that equal or exceed any settlements or judgments from noncompliance with regulatory laws.

Risk management is best viewed as a policy and management tool, rather than as a technical means for reducing insurance costs. In this context, risk management becomes a broad-based strategy, that when embedded with other strategies, will result in reduced costs and increased productivity. Archbold (2006) concluded that a wide variety of organizations utilize these strategies: medicine, athletic training, psychology, social work, banking and finance, engineering and architecture, schools and universities, and governmental agencies (including law enforcement and corrections).

Although risk management strategies will vary with business culture and context, there appears to be agreement that the following five steps are fundamental (Ashley & Pearson, 1993; Clardy, 2004; Conrow, 2000; Wong & Rakestraw, 1991).

1. Identify potential risks and liabilities in terms of frequency and severity. Clardy (2004) has identified the following descriptors useful for establishing a risk management database: peril, hazard, risk, and loss. Sources of information include any history of lawsuits, incidents resulting in regulatory compliance actions and fines, insurance and workers' compensation payouts and tax rates, incidents involving violence in the workplace and employee assistance referrals.
2. Analyzes approaches to manage exposure from identified risks. The organization conducts a thorough audit of current organizational practices, policies, and procedures. Training in all forms (orientation, on-the-job training and coaching, formal classroom instruction) and supervision practices are essential to risk analysis.
3. Select strategies most likely to reduce exposure to risk. The organization devises a comprehensive strategy to revise and update vision, mission, and strategy initiatives that make managing risk an integral part of the organization. These strategies guide the design and development of training for managers and employees.
4. Implement strategies that reduce exposure to risk. Use a change-management process that fits the culture and context of the organization to implement policies, training and supervision. This includes attention to selecting employees who regard risk management as an important job duty, as well as progressive discipline for those employees who place the organization at risk.
5. Continuously monitor and evaluate effectiveness of the risk management program. Given that risks change over time, it is necessary that an organization adopt a continuous improvement approach which can only be accomplished with monitoring and evaluation.

Appendix A
Glossary of Basic Legal Terems

Accreditation of educational institutions. In copyright law and specific to the TEACH Act, a requirement that post-secondary colleges and universities be either regionally or nationally accredited or recognized by the U.S. Department of Education; accreditation is at the institutional level, not course-by-course.

Affidavit. A statement in writing and made under oath before a notary public or some other official or officer of the court.

Affirmative action. Preferential hiring or promotion on the basis of membership in a protected category, such as race or gender; may be voluntary or based on a court-approved consent decree.

Affirmative defense. An explanation proffered by a defendant to explain or minimize liability and damages.

Agency – A legal relationship in which an agent acts under the principal's direction.

Americans with Disabilities Act (ADA) – An extension of the Vocational Rehabilitation Act of 1973 which protects employees in the private sector who are deemed to have a qualified disability (medical, mental, or emotional).

Appellant. One who appeals the decision of a trial court to a higher court for review.

Author. In copyright law, an author is one of the following: the person who created the work, the business or person that pays another to create the context of employment (see *work for hire*), or the person or business that commissions the work under a valid work for hire contract.

Brightline rule. Case law that makes a clear legal distinction, or that resolves a criminal case, or proves facts needed to support a claim or crime. A preponderance of the evidence is required in civil cases and proof beyond a reasonable doubt is necessary for criminal cases.

Case law. Decisions from the courts that interpret *statutes*, regulations, and constitutional provisions; it is also known as decisional law.

Cause of action. A legal claim that is the basis for a lawsuit.

Certiorari. A request by a lower court that a higher court accept an appeal from the lower court; if an appeal is accepted for review, the higher court (i.e., the U.S. Supreme Court) will issue a writ of certiorari.

Circuit court. In the federal system, an appellate court between the district trial court and the U.S. Supreme Court. In some state judicial systems, a higher level trial court.

Civil trail. Court proceedings governed by laws of evidence (preponderance of evidence rule) in which civil (noncriminal) disputes between parties are resolved.

Class action. A lawsuit brought on behalf of many people who are all asserting a common legal claim against a *defendant.*

Code of Federal Regulations (CFR). The systematic compilation of federal laws and regulations, organized by titles and sections.

Common law. Non-statutory law based on precedent and derived from centuries of case law compiled by judges.

Compensatory damages. Compensation to the plaintiff for direct losses from an injury.

Complaint. Legal papers filed by a *plaintiff* about actual injuries done to him or her by the *defendant*; the initial pleading by the plaintiff stating why the defendant is being sued, what damages were sustained by the plaintiff, and what relief is sought by the plaintiff.

Constructive discharge. Occurs when an employee finds the workplace to be so hostile that the only alternative is to quit and is considered that same as an unlawful termination.

Continual training requirement. An OSHA rule that requires an employer to provide safety training to all new employees and to all employees who have been transferred into new positions.

Contributory negligence. Someone who contributes to harm from the negligence of another is barred from recovering damages.

Copyright. Legal protection provided to the authors of original works of authorship that are fixed in a tangible form of expression, including literary, dramatic, musical, artistic, and certain other intellectual works.

Copyright owner. Individual who is listed as the owner of a copyright with the U.S. Copyright Office; one who has one of the following exclusive rights: the right to reproduce a copy of the work, the right to prepare derivative works, the right to distribute copies of the work, the right to perform the work, and the right to display the work.

Copyrighted work. Any work that is registered with the U.S. Copyright Office and/or any original work that is fixed in a fixed tangible medium; registration with the U.S Copyright Office is not necessary to secure the rights of copyright, but does afford additional protection.

Credit line. In copyright, the acknowledgment of authorship that is provided when permission has been issued allowing the work of the copyright holder to be used by a second party; credits the original work to the author.

Criminal trial. Court proceeding brought by prosecutor in the name of the state for a statutory offense (crime) committed by an individual in which the rule of evidence (beyond a reasonable doubt) is required for a finding of guilty.

Defendant. The person, institution, or organization being sued by a *plaintiff(s)*.

Deliberate indifference. In negligence, the intentional or reckless disregard of the consequences of someone's or an organization's acts or omissions.

De minimus. A trivial matter not worthy of the court's attention; an innocent or insignificant infringement on a copyright would likely be dismissed.

Deposition. A statement made under oath by a witness recorded electronically or in writing as part of pretrial discovery.

Derivative work. In copyright, when a preexisting copyrighted work is recast, transformed or adapted in such a manner as to create a new original work, then considered a derivative work for which permission from the original copyright holder must be received; examples include an English translation of a novel written in German; a computer program translated into a different programming language; a television script based on a book.

Directed verdict. A verdict entered by the trial judge when the plantiff has failed to present sufficient evidence for a jury to consider.

Disparate impact. The effect of what appears to be a neutral policy or employment practice that impacts members who are protected by a state or federally protected right; a reading comprehension test as a selection predictor in which everyone passes excepts members in a particular group, such as Hispanics.

Disparate treatment. Treatment of people at work differently because of a state or federally protected right; treating a woman differently from a man in a term, condition, or privilege of employment.

Display. In copyright law, means the nonsequential showing of a copy of a work directly or by means of some technology, such as television, slide, or film.

Due diligence. Actions taken by reasonable people to reduce liability or to avoid harm to self or others; to investigate thoroughly before entering into an agreement, such as an acquisition or merger.

Due process. A constitutional requirement that state and federal governments conduct themselves fairly under the law and that they avoid arbitrary behavior.

Effect. A statistical conclusion indicating the strength of a relationship between variables; converts the findings of a research study to an effect size (i.e., comparing the effects of an experimental group and a control group).

Evidence. Testimony and other sources of fact used by either party to prove legal questions in dispute; rules of law that determine what testimony is to be admitted or rejected in each case and the weight given to such testimony.

Fair use. In copyright, the use of protected works without the permission of the owner that does not materially impact market of profits for noncommercial purposes.

Indictment. Formal charge of the grand jury resulting in a criminal *defendant* standing trial.

Interrogatories. A series of pretrial questions drawn up to determine from witnesses or parties to the case if they have information about the case.

Judgment. An order that finalizes the resolution of a lawsuit.

Jurisdiction. The authority of a court to act, either over a particular person or with regard to a particular cause of action.

Liquidated damages. An agreement between parties to a specified sum of money recovered by the injured party in the event of a breach of a contract.

Make whole relief. To make whole again; remedy for discrimination in which the aggrieved party is placed in a position that he or she would have had but for the discrimination.

Mediated instructional activity – In copyright law and specifically the TEACH Act, the use of copyrighted works in an online course in which the works are essential to the goals of the course (not tangential), under the control and supervision of the instructor, and equivalent to what would be lawfully used in a traditional face-to-face class; excludes supplemental sources such as "coursepacks" that are designed for sale to students.

Negligence. Conduct that falls below the legal standard of care expected by a reasonable and prudent person under the same or similar circumstances.

Negligent hiring. A cause of action against an employer who failed to check references and criminal history of convictions and selected an employee who subsequently injures another employee or third party.

Negligent referral. A cause of action against a previous employer for failing to disclose to another employer that a current or previous employee has a record of workplace violence or harassing behaviors.

Negligent retention. A cause of action against an employer who maintains on payroll an employee who has a documented work history of serious safety violations, criminal activities, workplace violence, or harassment of others.

Negligent supervision. A cause of action in which a supervisor or manager failed to direct or instruct an employee in the safe operation of a task resulting in injury and or damages.

Negligent training. A cause of action in which employees who are trained improperly or not trained at all, are injured themselves or injure third parties.

Organizational policies. Policies that direct managers and employees in the performance of strategic, operational, and compliance-related duties and tasks.

Pecuniary gain (or loss). Regarding the Federal Sentencing Guidelines, the "before tax profit to the defendant resulting from the relevant conduct of the offense" (USSG, 2005, § 8A1.2).

Plaintiff. One who files a lawsuit against a *defendant* in court.

Pleadings. Documents filed by plaintiff and defense attorneys that state claims and counter claims at the beginning of a civil case; complaints and answers to complaints are examples.

Preponderance of evidence rule. A general rule in civil litigation in which evidence is more probable than not (more believable than not); see *reasonable doubt* standard for criminal cases.

Pretrial discovery. The process of uncovering evidence prior to a trial (see *depositions* and *interrogatories*).

Principal. Based on agency law, an agent operates under the direction of the principal for the benefit of the principal.

Proximate cause. The direct or immediate cause, without which an injury would not have occurred, and sufficient to support an action of *negligence.*

Public domain. Works not protected by copyright are in the public domain, meaning that anyone may use the work without obtaining permission from the originator. Works created by the U.S. federal government are not subject to copyright, therefore in the public domain.

Punitive damages. Damages assessed beyond actual losses due to injury; also known as exemplary damages designed to make an example of or punish the defendant for outrageous negligence or conduct.

Reasonable doubt standard. The standard used in criminal cases to establish a guilty verdict; beyond and to the exclusion of a reasonable doubt.

Reasonable person standard. Used in civil cases as a measure of what a reasonable person under the same or similar circumstances would have done; varies by expertise as professional accountants have a different standard from a book keeper, or a physician from a nurse.

Recklessness. Willful or conscious disregard for the safety of others.

Respondeat superior. Holding the employer responsible for negligence of employees as part of the business; liability imposed, usually by a regulatory statute, on managers for the conduct of their employees.

Section 1983 proceeding. A proceeding based on the Civil Rights Act of 1871 in which governmental entities, such as police and correctional agencies, may be sued in federal district court for a civil rights violation occurring under "color of state law."

Service of process (summons). Notice served upon a defendant and others in a civil action that requires presence in court.

Stare Decisis. A principle of law stating that cases already decided must serve as precedents to govern later cases.

Statutory law. A body of law created by acts of state and federal legislatures and takes the place of *common law.*

Strict liability. Legal responsibility placed on an individual for the results of his or her actions irrespective of whether at fault.

Summary judgment. A decision by the trial court judge dismissing the cause of action without hearing any evidence or proceeding to trial.

Supreme Court. The highest and final level for appeals. The U.S. Supreme Court may decide conflicts between the circuit court of appeals and rule on constitutional issues. In certain jurisdictions, the original *trial court.*

Testimony. Statements by those testifying under oath in court or through depositions.

Tort. A civil wrong, such as negligence, that may be basis for an action brought by a plaintiff against a defendant for damages or injunctive relief. A tortfeasor is someone who commits a tort.

Trade secret. A secret that provides a business with a competitive advantage, and includes any secret formula, pattern, process, program, method, device, technique or compilation of information that is proprietary.

Trial court. The court of original jurisdiction with authority to hear civil and criminal cases, including testimony and other evidence.

Vicarious liability. Liability imposed on one party (an employer) for the wrongs of another (an employee); based on master-servant or principal-agent theories of law.

V*oir dire.* An examination of prospective jurors by attorneys for the plaintiff and defendant to determine their qualification to be on a jury in a civil and criminal case.

Workers' compensation. A state-by-state no-fault system for compensating employees for job-related injuries; employers pay tax that funds the insurance pool.

Work for hire. In copyright law, any work prepared by an employee for his or her employer as part of the employees job responsibilities; from a training and development perspective, this would include ". . . an instructional text, as a test, as answer material for a test . . . if the parties expressly agree in a written instrument signed by them that the work shall be considered a work made for hire" (17 U.S. Code, § sec 101).

Writ of mandamus. An order by a higher court commanding a lower court, public entity, or corporation to perform a nondiscretionary legal duty; an extraordinary judicial proceeding when other remedies are insufficient.

Appendix B
Summary of Federal Statutes That Require or Imply Training

This summary is a partial listing of federal statutes that require or imply training; however, it should not be considered a complete listing as statutes are added every year. Check state statutes for similar training requirements.

Statute	Comments
Civil Rights Acts (CRA) of 1871, 1964, and 1991	CRA of 1871, 42 U.S.C.§ 1983. "Every person who, under color of any [state, county, or municipal] statute, ordinance, regulation, custom, or usage, of any State . . . subjects, or causes to be subjected, any citizen of the United States . . . [to be deprived] of any rights, privileges, or immunities secured by the Constitution and laws, shall be liable to the party injured in an action at law . . ." CRA of 1964. Prohibits discrimination in all aspects of employment based upon race, color, national origin, religion and sex. 42 U.S.C. § 2000(e). CRA of 1991. Amends CRA 1964 allowing jury trials, award of punitive damages, disallows race-norming, clarifies mixed motives by employer, and other provisions.
Drug-Free Workplace Act of 1988	41 U.S.C. § 701. Applies to employers who seek or have contracts with the federal government of $25,000 or more, as well as recipients of federal grants (municipalities and not-for profit organiza-

	tions). Training requirements include publishing a drug free workplace policy and a "drug-free awareness program.
Occupational Safety & Health Training Act of 1970	29 U.S.C. § 654. Ensures safety and health of America's workers by setting and enforcing standards; providing training, outreach, and education; establishing partnerships; and encouraging continual improvement in workplace safety and health.
Fair Labor Standards Act of 1938 (Wage and Hour Requirements, Child Labor Laws)	29 U.S.C. § 201. Establishes a federal minimum wage and conditions under which overtime is payable to employees. The act exempts certain administrative and professional employees. Establishes requirements for minimum age and hours worked by children, and the conditions under which they work.
Americans with Disabilities Act of 1990	42 U.S.C. § 1211. Prohibits employment discrimination on the basis of qualified physical or mental disabilities. Employers are required to make "reasonable accommodations" to assist employees in the performance of the essential functions of the job..
The Age Discrimination in Employment Act of 1967	29 U.S.C. § 621. Prohibits discrimination against employees based on age, unless age can be shown to be a bona fide occupational qualification, meaning that a person over a certain age cannot perform the job in question. Applies to those 40 years of age and over, with no upper age limit.
Equal Pay Act of 1963	29 U.S.C.§ 206. "No employer . . . shall discriminate . . . between employees on

	the basis of sex by paying wages . . . at a rate less than the rate at which he pays wages to employees of the opposite sex . . . for equal work on jobs the performance of which requires equal skill, effort, and responsibility, and which are performed under similar working conditions . . . Exceptions include a seniority system, a merit system; a system which measures earnings by quantity or qual-ity of production; or a differential based on any other factor other than sex . . ."
Immigration Reform and Control Act of 1986	8 USCA 1324B. Controls unauthorized immigration to the United States, including employer sanctions, enforcement, and amnesty provisions. The employer sanctions provision designates penalties for employers who hire aliens not authorized to work in the United States.
The Family Medical Leave Act of 1993	29 U.S.C. § 2601. Requires employers of more than 50 employees to provide up to 12 weeks of unpaid leave to employees, after giving notice, to care for self, spouse, or child with a serious health condition as well as for a birth or adoption.
Sarbanes-Oxley Act of 2002	15 U.S.C. 7201. Establishes the Public Company Accounting Oversight Board which oversees, regulates, inspects and disciplines accounting firms in their auditing role. The law addresses auditor independence, corporate governance, and financial disclosure.
Foreign Corrupt Practices Act of 1977	15 U.S.C. § 78dd-1. Prohibits corrupt payments to foreign officials for the purpose of obtaining or keeping business by any individual, firm, officer, director, or

	other third parties. Criminal, civil, and other governmental actions may be imposed on violators.
Vocational Rehabilitation Act of 1973	29 U.S.C. § 701. Prohibits discrimination in employment against disabled individuals by the federal government.
Pregnancy Discrimination Act of 1978	42 U.S.C. § 2000(k). The Pregnancy Discrimination Act is an amendment to Title VII of the Civil Rights Act of 1964. Discrimination on the basis of pregnancy, childbirth, or related medical conditions constitutes unlawful sex discrimination under Title VII. Women affected by pregnancy or related conditions must be treated in the same manner as other applicants or employees with similar abilities or limitations.
The Fair Credit Reporting Act of 1970, The Consumer Credit Reporting Reform Act of 1996, and The Fair and Accurate Credit Transactions Act of 2003	15 U.S.C. § 1681. The Fair Credit Reporting Act regulates the activities of credit reporting bureaus such as TRW Information Services, Equifax Credit Information Services, and Trans Union Credit Information Company. This law, which is administered by the Fair Trade Commission, regulates and punishes unauthorized persons who obtain credit reports, as well as employees of credit reporting bureaus who furnish credit reports to unauthorized persons. The law also places responsibilities on those who supply the reporting bureaus with the initial information. Subsequent amendments strengthen the FCRA.
National Institute for Occupational Safety and Health (NIOSH)	29 U.S.C. § 669. NIOSH is a division of the Centers for Disease Control within the U.S. Department of Health and

	Human Services. NIOSH is the U.S. government's occupational safety and health research agency.
Toxic Substances Control Act of 1976	15 U.S.C. 2601. Provides the Environmental Protection Agency the ability to track 75,000 industrial chemicals currently produced or imported into the United States. EPA repeatedly screens these chemicals and can require reporting or testing of those that may pose an environmental or human-health hazard. EPA can ban the manufacture and import of those chemicals that pose an unreasonable risk.
Copyright Act of 1976	17 U.S.C. § 100. Establishes the rights of intellectual ownership of performances and displays fixed in some tangible form or expression.
Digital Millennium Copyright Act of 1998	17 U.S.C. § 201. Criminalizes production and dissemination of technology that can avoid measures taken to protect copyright and heightens the penalties for infringement on the Internet.
TEACH Act of 2002	17 USC § 110. The TEACH Act amends the Copyright Act of 1976 by clarifying what uses are permissible with regard to the digital transmission of mediated instructional activities. Applies mostly to online and distance education programming.
Uniform Trade Secret Protection Act of 1998 and The Economic Espionage Act of 1996	18 U.S.C. § 1831. Proprietary information of a competitive nature that is held secret by a business and has commercial value, the disclosure of which would weaken the competitive nature of the business and devalue its products or services. The UTSA is a model act that has been adopted

by over forty states. The Economic Espionage Act makes theft or possession of a trade secret a federal crime.

Appendix C
Summary of Federal and State Requirements for Harrassment Prevention Training

NO FEAR Act of 2002 (Notification and Federal Employee Antidiscrimination and Retaliation Act)	The NO FEAR Act requires that all federal agencies must train employees on their rights and remedies under the federal discrimination, retaliation, and whistle-blower laws. New employees must be trained during their employee orientation program, or in the absence of such a program, within 60 business days of the new employees' appointment. Agencies must provide refresher training to all employees "on a training cycle of no longer than every 2 years." (Johnson, 2005).
California	This new law requires employers who operate in California and who employ 50 or more persons to provide all supervisory employees two hours of sexual harassment training every two years. Employers must complete the first round of training for supervisors by January 1, 2006
Colorado	The Colorado Sex Discrimination Rules, as adopted by the Colorado Civil Rights Commission, encourage employers to "sensitize" employees regarding issues relating to sexual harassment. *See* 3 Colo. Code Regs. § 708-1, Rule 80.11(C).
Connecticut	The Connecticut Human Rights and Opportunities Act requires all private and

	public employers with 50 or more employees to provide two hours of sexual harassment training to all supervisory employees within six months of the assumption of a supervisory position. Conn. Gen. Stat. § 46a-54(15)(B). The sexual harassment training must cover topics such as the laws prohibiting sexual har-assment, the definition of sexual harassment and examples of prohibited conduct, remedies available for sexual harassment, and strategies for avoiding sexual harassment in the workplace. The state has also promulgated regulations describing in detail the sexual harassment training requirements. Conn. Agencies Regs. § 46a-54-204.
Florida	The Public Personnel Rules of Florida's Administrative Code require all supervisors in Florida executive branch agencies to receive training on affirmative-action and equal opportunity, which would include sexual harassment training. *See* Fla. Admin. Code, Title 60L, § 33.007.
Illinois	The Illinois Human Rights Act requires every public employer to provide sexual harassment training as part of all new employee training programs. Ill. Comp. Stat., Chap. 775, § 2-105(B)(5).
Maine	Maine's Sexual Harassment Training and Education in the Workplace Law requires all private and public employers with 15 or more employees to provide sexual harassment training to all new employees within one year of beginning employment. Me. Rev. Stat. § 807(3).

Massachusetts	The Massachusetts Fair Employment Practice Act requires all employers to promote "a workplace free of sexual harassment." Thus, the law encourages employers to provide sexual harassment training to all new employees within one year of beginning employment. Supervisors and managers should receive additional sexual harassment training on their responsibilities for preventing sexual harassment and responding to sexual harassment complaints. In addition, employers must distribute a written version of their sexual harassment policy annually to all employees and to each new employee at the beginning of employment. See Mass. Gen. Laws, Chap. 151B, § 3A.
Michigan	Michigan's Disability Bias Law requires the department of civil rights to offer training programs, which would include sexual harassment training, to employers, labor organization and employment agencies to assist in understanding the requirements of the Act. See Mich. Comp. Laws Ann., § 37.1212.
New Jersey	In the 2002 case Gaines v. Bellino, 173 N.J. 301 (2002), the New Jersey Supreme Court held that, in judging whether an employer has been negligent in pre-vent-ing sexual harassment under state law, state courts should consider whether the employer made sexual harassment training available to all employees in its organization. The court stated that an employer that provides sexual harassment training helps demonstrate the employer's "unequivocal commitment

	from the top" to preventing sexual harassment.
Oklahoma	Oklahoma's "Fair Employment Practices Act," through its Rules of Personnel Management and Administration, requires that all state personnel who investigate complaints of discrimination be trained in the areas of equal employment opportunity, discrimination, and burdens of proof. See Okla Stat., tit. 74, § 840.21(F.1); tit. 530, § 10-3-20. Thus, investigators should receive sexual harassment training and training on all other equal opportunity laws.
Rhode Island	Rhode Island's Sexual Harassment, Education and Training Law encourages employers to provide sexual harassment training to all new employees within one year of beginning employment. Employers are further encouraged to provide sex-ual harassment training to new supervisory and managerial employees with-in one year of their assumption of a supervisory position. Supervisory sexual harassment training should specifically address the responsibilities of supervisory and managerial employees to prevent sexual harassment and respond appropriately to sex-ual harassment complaints. See R.I. Gen. Laws, Chap. 118, §§ 28-51-2(c), 28-51-3.
Tennessee	The Tennessee State Employees' Sexual Harassment Law obligates the state department of personnel to provide sexual harassment training to all public employees. See Tenn. Code § 4-3-1703.

Texas	Texas's Employment Discrimination Law mandates that each state agency provide its employees with employment discrimination training (which should include, among other things, sexual harassment training) within 30days after being hired and then on a supplemental basis every two years. See Tex. Lab. Code § 21.010.
Utah	The Utah Department of Human Resource Management Rules obligates all public employers to provide sexual harassment training consistent with standards established by the Department. See Utah Admin Code § 477-25-7.
Vermont	The Vermont Fair Employment Practices Act encourages employers to provide sexual harassment training to all current employees and to provide sexual harassment training to all new employees within one year of commencement of employment. Supervisory sexual harassment training should specifically address the responsibilities of supervisory and managerial employees to prevent sexual harassment and respond appropriately to sexual harassment complaints. See Vt. Stat. § 495h(f).

* Adapted and modified from Brightline Compliance (www.brightlinecompliance.com). Reprinted with permission of Brightline Compliance.

Appendix D
Summary of OSHA General Industry Training Requirements

The following summary of general industry training requirements is not meant to be exhaustive. Consult the appropriate CFR—Code of Federal Regulation—for specific requirements. Note that OSHA also has standards for the maritime and construction industries, which are not summarized here. These standards will be found at the OSHA website (www.osha .gov).

Part 1910.1030 Bloodborne Pathogens Program

- Methods used to perform hazard assessments and inspections.
- Engineering and work practice controls used to reduce exposure.
- Procedures that ensure use of "universal precautions" and good housekeeping.
- Personal protective equipment selection, use and maintenance procedures.
- Decontamination and waste disposal procedures.
- Incident reporting and response procedures.
- Postexposure medical evaluation and follow-up.
- Procedures for hepatitis vaccinations.
- Procedures for periodically evaluating program effectiveness.
- A written program is required.

Part 1910.38 Emergency Action Plans

- Designated program administrator or other persons who can respond to questions.
- Internal and external emergency phone lists.
- Describe escape routes from each work area.
- Emergency equipment locations and procedures for use.
- Procedures for employees who remain behind to shut off critical

equipment before evacuating.
- Procedures for taking headcounts after evacuation.
- Rescue and medical assignments.
- Incident reporting procedures.
- Alarm systems use, maintenance and testing.
- Content and frequency of employee training and instruction.
- Procedures for periodically evaluating program effectiveness.
- A written program is required.

Part 19190.23 & 132 Fall Protection Requirements for General Industry

- Employer must prove safety training for employees who work with specified equipment.
- Demonstrate proper selection based on task-specific hazard analyses.
- A written program is required in some instances.

Part 1910.38 Fire Prevention Plans

- Potential fire hazards and control measures.
- Potential ignition sources.
- Names of persons assigned to maintain fire prevention and firefighting systems.
- Names of persons assigned to control accumulation of combustible materials.
- Housekeeping procedures to prevent accumulation of combustible materials.
- Content and frequency of employee training and instruction.
- Standard operating procedures for equipment and alarm testing.
- Procedures for periodically evaluating program effectiveness.
- A written program is required.

Part 1910.151 First Aid and Medical Services

- Absent an infirmary or hospital in proximity to workplace, provide an adequately trained person to render first aid.
- A written program is not required.

Part 1910.1200 Hazard Communication

- Educate employees about the nature of hazards with which they work.
- Train employees in measures to protect their health.
- A written program is required.

Part 1910.120 Hazardous Waste Operations and Emergency Response

- Employee training is required for all employees potentially affected by release of any hazardous substances.
- Training for emergency responders and those involved in hazardous waste operations.
- A written program is required.

Part 1910.95 Hearing Conservation Program

- Methods used to perform hazard assessments and inspections.
- Methods used to measure employee exposures.
- Engineering and work practice controls to reduce exposure.
- Procedures and frequency of remonitoring for exposures.
- Procedures and frequency of hearing tests.
- Procedures for responding to and notifying employees of documented hearing loss.
- Procedures for selection, fitting, and maintenance of hearing protection.
- Content and frequency of employee training and instruction.
- Procedures for periodically evaluating program effectiveness.
- Procedures for cleaning, storage, and waste disposal procedures.
- Content and frequency of employee training and instruction.
- Procedures for periodically evaluating program effectiveness.
- A written program is required.

Part 1910.119 Process Safety Management (PSM)

- Equipment-specific work practices and emergency control required as well as employee training.
- A written program is required.

Part 1904 Recordkeeping

- Inform employees of how they are to report an injury or illness.
- A written program is not required.

Part 1910.134 Respiratory Protection Program

- Identify a designated program administrator.
- Methods used to perform task-specific hazard assessments and inspections.
- Engineering and work practice controls used to reduce employee exposure.
- Medical evaluations and examinations fit testing procedures for employees.
- Procedures for selecting, fitting, using, and maintaining respirators.
- Cleaning, storage, and maintenance procedures.
- Content and frequency of employee training and instruction.
- Procedures for periodically evaluating program effectiveness.
- A written program is required.

Part 1910.107 Storage and Handling of Combustible Liquids, Including Cooking Oils and Cleaning Solvents.

- Employers must be able to document employee training and understanding of safe work practices.
- Employers advised to have written safe work practices for these activities.
- A written program is not required.

Part 1910.252 Welding and Cutting Safety Requirements; General Requirements for Safe Use, Handling, and Storage of Compressed Gas Cylinders, Including Welding Gases.

- Written safe work practices advisable.
- Employers must be able to prove task-specific employee training.
- A written program is not required, but is recommended.

OSHA Guidelines Workplace Violence Prevention Program

- This program is recommended by OSHA guidelines for health care and social service workers, late night retail establishments, and taxi drivers.
- Identification of a designated program administrator.
- Responsibilities for each job title.
- Measures to ensure employee compliance.
- Methods used to communicate with employees.
- Content and frequency of employee training and instruction.
- Methods for anonymous hazard reporting.
- Methods used to perform hazard assessment and inspections and to correct hazards.
- Incident reporting and investigation. Emergency response procedures.
- Recordkeeping procedures.
- Procedures for periodically evaluating program progress

OSHA Ergonomics Program

- Methods used to perform hazard assessments and inspections.
- Engineering and work practice controls used to reduce exposure.
- Procedures and frequency of reevaluating exposures.
- Content and frequency of employee training programs.
- Procedures for periodically evaluating program effectiveness.
- A written program is required.

Source: OSHA (n.d.) General Industry Standards. (www. osha.com)

Appendix E
Summary of Safety and Workplace Violence Training Resources

The following resources are available from the Internet and include several types of media (print, streaming video, teleconferences, slide presentations, and case studies). Many of these resources were developed by various state and federal agencies.

Workplace Safety

- OSHA Making the Business Case for Safety http://www.osha.gov/dcsp/products/topics/businesscase/index.html
- OSHA Free Posters and Publications http://www.osha.gov/Publicationsworkplace_poster _page.html
- OSHA. (n.d.). Draft Model Training Program for Hazard Com munication http://www.osha. gov/dsg/hazcom/MTP101703.html
- OSHA. (2001). How to Plan for Workplace Emergencies and Evacuations (document # 3088). www.osha.gov/Publicationsosha 3088.pdf
- OSHA Multimedia – a combination of Power Point slides and streaming videos. http:/www. osha.gov/SLTC/multimedia.html
- OSHA eTools and Electronic Products for Compliance Assistance http://www.osha.gov/dts/osta/oshasoftindex.html#PowerPoint %20Presentations
- OSHA "$$afety Pays" interactive software program to assess costs associated with safety violations. http://www.osha.gov/dts/osta/oshasoft/safetwb.html
- National Institute for Occupational Health and Safety, NIOSH Publication No. 97-140: NIOSH Pocket Guide to Chemical Hazards. http:/www. cdc.gov/niosh/npg/npg.html
- Society for Chemical Hazard Communication http://www.schc.org/schcnewsite/home.php

Drug-Free Workplace

- Office of National Drug Control Policy http://www.whitehouse

drugpolicy.gov/prevent/workplace/

- eLaws Advisor—Drug- Free Workplace http://www.dol.gov/elaws/drugfree.htm
- Drug Free Work Place Training Kit for Employers http://workplace.samhsa.gov/WPWork it/workitindex.html

Violence in the Workplace

- American Bar Association, Domestic Violence and the Workplace http://www.abanet.org/dom viol/workviolence.html
- Dealing with Workplace Violence. This handbook was developed by the U.S. Office of Personnel Management and the Interagency Working Group on Violence in the Workplace. http://www.opm.gov/employment_andbenefits/worklife/official documents/handbooksguides/WorkplaceViolence/intro.asp
- Domestic Violence Model Workplace Policy Initiative http://www.opdv.state.ny.us/workplace/
- Federal Bureau of Investigation. (2003). Workplace Violence—Issues in Response. www.fbi. gov /publications/violence.pdf
- National Institute for Occupational Health and Safety, NIOSH Publication No. 2004-100d: Program #1 Violence on the Job and Program #2Violence on the Job Case Study (streaming video). http://www.cdc.gov/niosh/docs/video/violence.html
- National Institute for Occupational Health and Safety, NIOSH Publication No. 2003-114d: Working with Stress (streaming video). http://www.cdc.gov/niosh/docs/video/stress1.html
- OSHA. (2004). Guidelines for Preventing Workplace Violence for Health Care and Social Workers (document # 3148-01R). www.osha.gov/Publications/osha3148.pdf
- Workplace Violence—Health Care and Social Service Workers (Power Point slide presentation and participant handout). http://www.osha-slc.gov/SLTC/workplaceviolence/healthcare/index.html

Appendix F
Supervisory Audit of Training Related Liability

Training and development units in businesses have a responsibility to make sure their supervisors and managers understand their responsibilities regarding the employers' human resource management policies and employment laws (both federal and state). Such personnel are also the first-line trainers in their organizations, and failure to train could result in allegations of negligent supervision and negligent training. This reproducible audit form will allow the employer to review each supervisor or manager for gaps in knowledge—gaps that cold result in liability.

Name_______________Department___________________Date ________

Training Topic	Has Training	Needs Training	Date Training Completed
■ Fair Labor Standards Act (federal and state equivalent)	________	________	________
• Hours and overtime requirements (exempt and nonexempt employees).	________	________	________
• Child labor laws.	________	________	________
■ Equal Employment Opportunity and Americans with Disability Act Laws Federal and state equivalent laws.	________	________	________
• Illegal discrimination (all forms).	________	________	________
• Sexual harassment and hostile work environment.	________	________	________

- Specific issues:
  - o Recruits, selects, trains, and supervises employees using job-related requirements. ________ ________ ________
  - o Provides reasonable accommodations for applicants and employees who have a qualified disability. ________ ________ ________
  - o Provides a zero-tolerance approach to hostile work environments. ________ ________ ________
  - o Seeks advice from the HR department in a timely manner when necessary. ________ ________ ________

■ OSHA and Safety Concerns ________ ________ ________

- Hazard communication. ________ ________ ________
- Personal protective equipment. ________ ________ ________
- Machine safety. ________ ________ ________
- Lockout/tagout. ________ ________ ________
- Confined spaces. ________ ________ ________
- Bloodborne pathogens. ________ ________ ________
- Emergency evacuations. ________ ________ ________
- Signage and notices. ________ ________ ________
- Industry specific requirements (construction, chemical, utility, etc). ________ ________ ________

■ Violence in the Workplace ________ ________ ________

- Recognizes unusual change in behaviors of potentially violent employees (previous threats against others and restraining orders; preoccupation with violence, knives, guns). ________ ________ ________

- Knows the employer's policy regarding confronting a violent situation (what to do, who to contact, keeping employees safe). ________ ________ ________
- Conducts terminations and other personnel and union disputes in a way to avoid violence. ________ ________ ________
- Knows to avoid heroic acts during violent confrontations with employees and others. ________ ________ ________

■ Intellectual Property (copyright and trademarks) ________ ________ ________

- Knows what materials the business copyrights and how to protect that copyright. ________ ________ ________
- Knows how to handle proprietary and competitive information or information that is copyrighted by other businesses. ________ ________ ________
- Knows the employer's policy on software piracy and requires employees to conform. ________ ________ ________
- Knows the purposes of nondisclosure agreements and the importance of having employees adhere to such guidelines. ________ ________ ________

■ Due Diligence

- Knows that employees who are involved in criminal activities on the job ________ ________ ________ could establish liability for the employer.

- Monitors employees, supervisors, Managers, and professional staff for possible criminal behavior and ethical breaches. ________ ________ ________
- Takes corrective actions if suspected criminal activity by an employee, and knows the employers policy for failure to report criminal and ethical breaches. ________ ________ ________

■ Documentation

- Documents employee performance using critical incidents or other reliable and valid method. ________ ________ ________
- Documents on-the-job training and coaching of high risk work. ________ ________ ________

■ Other Areas of Concern

- ____________ ________ ________ ________
- ____________ ________ ________ ________
- ____________ ________ ________ ________

Appendix G
Checklist for Compliance with the TEACH Act

The complexity and policy-driven nature of the TEACH Act (2002) require educational institutions and governmental agencies to carefully monitor the use of copyrighted materials for "mediated instructional activities" that are digitally transmitted over the Internet. The following checklist will be useful for adult educators who are employed by governmental agencies that market and deliver noncredit continuing education programs over the Internet for employees and the public. Note that adult educators employed by educational institutions continue to have fair use privileges under the Copyright Act of 1976; employees of governmental agencies only have educational fair use under the TEACH Act, which limits fair use to digitally transmitted instruction over the Internet.

- I am employed by a nonprofit accredited educational institution or a governmental agency.
- My employer has an agency policy on the use of copyrighted materials that complies with the requirements of the TEACH Act and the Copyright Act of 1976.
- My employer provides accurate information about use of copyrighted materials to instructional personnel (adult educators), employees (adult learners), and other personnel about copyright.
- My employer has adequate security safeguards on computer networks and Internet programs that protect outsiders from accessing copyrighted materials.
- The educational materials that I have designed are specifically for employees that I instruct, and only those employees who are registered for my course will have access to copyrighted instructional materials.
- Instructional materials will be provided under my direct control or supervision of others that I direct.
- Any copyrighted instructional materials are directly related and

necessary for my instruction.

- Instructional programs that I deliver by digital transmission are part of the instructional offerings by my employer.
- I am required to provide a complete notice on any instructional materials that are protected by copyright.
- My employer has technology that limits the employee's ability to retain or further distribute the materials.
- Employees who are registered for my courses are directed by course policy not to retain or further distribute copyrighted instructional materials.
- My instructional materials are stored on my employer's secure server and will be transmitted only as allowed under the TEACH Act.
- The copyrighted materials that are digitally transmitted are in proportional amounts as would be used in a face-to-face instruction of the same program.
- The materials that I use are not among those the TEACH Act specifically excludes from use:
    - instructional materials designed and marketed for use in a digital online format;
    - copies I know or should have known are illegal;
    - textbooks, coursepacks, electronic reserves and similar materials required for purchase by individual students for use outside the classroom or class session.
- If I am using an analog original, before digitizing I will be sure to
    - only copy the proportional amount that I am authorized to transmit
    - make sure there is no digital copy of the analog version available for use, and if so, will use the available digital version.

Appendix H
Checklist for Compliance with the Fair Use Privilege for Educators

Educators who wish to claim a fair use privilege under the Copyright Act of 1976 are allowed to make "multiple copies for classroom use" (17 U.S.C. §107). This privilege has evolved over the years through case law and agreements between representatives for the publishers and nonprofit educational institutions.* A set of guidelines has evolved for educators; however, it must be understood that there is no specific number of words or pages that may be used without permission, and acknowledging the source with a notice is no substitute for obtaining permission. Any interpretation of what constitutes fair use must be made in relation to the four factors enumerated in § 107, the most important of which is the extent to which there is the possibility for impact on the potential market and lost commercial value.

Adult educators in public agencies, other than nonprofit educational institutions, have no fair use privilege other than explained in §107 of the Copyright Act of 1976. They must seek permission to use copyrighted material just as their counterparts in the private sector. Adult educators do have a fair use privilege when using "mediated instructional activities" in a distance learning (online) application under the TEACH Act (see Appendix G Checklist for Compliance with the TEACH Act.)

The following checklist is interpretative and summarizes factors typically taken into consideration by educational institutions. It is strongly recommended that educators review the applicable copyright policies for their institution.

- ◆ Educators may make one copy of copyrighted materials (a book chapter, magazine or journal article, news report) for purposes of planning instruction.
- ◆ Educators may make multiple copies for distribution in a class (only one copy per student) as long as spontaneity and brevity requirements are met.
- ◆ Use must be inspired or spontaneous, meaning that the teacher

could not be expected to request and obtain permission in a timely manner.

- Brevity is defined in the following manner:

  - poem less than 250 words
  - articles, stories, or essays less than 2,500 words
  - one chart, picture, diagram, graph, cartoon or picture per book or periodical issue
  - excerpts from a longer work (like a book) of not more than 10 percent of 1,000 words, whichever is less

- Consumables such as workbooks, test booklets, and answers sheets may not be copied and may be used only once..
- Educators are limited to making copies in nine instances per class term; same copies may not be used semester to semester.
- Copying cannot be a substitute for having students purchase educational materials required for a class (text books, lab materials and exercises).
- Copies must be from a legally acquired original source.
- Proper credit must be given to the owner of the copyright somewhere on the material.

* The recommendations stated above are based on a letter to Congressional Subcommittee Chair Kastenmeir dated March 19, 1976. That letter summarizes an agreement the Ad Hoc Committee of Educational Institutions and Organizations of Copyright Law Revision and the Authors League of America, Inc. and the Association of American Publishers, Inc.

Appendix I
Example of a Permission Request Letter

Permissions Editor (or name of author) Date
Publisher (books or periodicals)
Address
City, State, ZIP

To whom it may concern,

I am requesting permission to copy the following (quote, paragraph, passage, pages, chapters, figure, table, diagram, scientific notation or formula) for use (in my academic course; in my publication submission; in my employee training workshop):
Title: title of publication
Copyright Owner (author or publisher):
Material to be duplicated: list and provide a photocopy, such as "chapter 3 and 4" or "pages 356-390"
Number of Copies: state number of copies
Distribution: state how used (distributed to students in my class who will only pay for cost of copying; included in my manuscript submission to (name of publication); distributed to employees in my training workshop at no charge
Intended Use: as supplementary reading material

Appendix J
Guidelines for Registering a Copyright

Employers and consultants who create original works are advised to copyright their materials. Note that minimal creativity of a work may be copyrighted. A formal registration will take some time to complete and the cost is minimal for the protection afforded by the copyright.

Consider the following for copyright: needs assessment and performance analysis protocols; training manuals, electronic performance support systems (EPSS) and job aids; program evaluations, pre- and posttests (including administration instructions and answers); survey instruments, modular instructional materials; video and audio recordings used to support instruction; computer-assisted learning programs, including CD and DVD and other software; and Internet or Intranet screens, graphics, and related programs.

Once you have identified the works for copyright application, do the following (17 U.S.C. 407):

1. Prominently display a copyright notice on the material within three months of creation, if not immediately. Use the form "© (year) by (author)" or "Copyright (year) by (author)" for notice of publication.
2. Select and complete the correct application available from the U.S. Copyright Office. Form "TX" is for literary material, including computer programs and databases; form "PA" is for audiovisual material. Note that fees not only vary by type of application, they are subject to change over time. Check the Copyright Office website for increases in fees. Forms at no cost are available by mail, online fill-in, or download in Adobe format from the Copyright Office (http://www.copyright.gov/forms/).
3. The following three items must be included in the mailing to the Copyright Office:

- a properly completed and signed application form,
- a nonrefundable check or money order in the amount of $30 for a single work payable to the Register of Copyrights, and
- a deposit of the works being submitted for registration.

4. Deposits of works to the Copyright Office are mandatory. Deposit of literary works (Form TX) refers to a copy of the complete work to be registered (regardless of length) and includes a printout, audiocassette, or videotape. Use the following address to submit an application:

   Library of Congress
   Copyright Office
   101 Independence Avenue, S.E.
   Washington, D.C. 20559-6000

Works developed for digital transmission (online and distance education applications) may be sent using one of two options. (1) The deposit may be made on a computer disk that clearly identifies the author. Longer works may meet the deposit requirement by submitting five representative pages or three representative minutes, or short works submitted in entirety. (2) A complete copy (no disk required) of the entire work, regardless of length, submitted to the above address.

Appendix K
Example of a Nondisclosure Agreement for Training Material

____________________________ (name of business)
____________________________ (name of instructional program)
____________________________ (date, location, and instructor name)

The information in this [describe specifically the document—training publication, manual, instructor guide, checklist, survey and evaluation instruments, on-the-job training guide, job aid or electronic performance support system] is the sole property of __________________ (employer) and shall not be duplicated, reproduced or stored electronically without the written permission of ____________ (employer). The contents and information in this document are provided for the sole use of _________________ (employee) in the performance of job related duties and responsibilities, and shall not be disclosed to parties outside the business unless approved in advance by _______________ (employer). This notice must be signed and returned to the instructor prior to the start of instruction.

____
Employee Signature Date

Appendix L
Example of a Nondisclosure of Trade Secrets Agreement

As a condition of employment, __________ (Employee) agrees that he/she will not during any time of employment with __________ (Employer), in any direct or indirect manner, use, communicate, disclose or divulge to any individual, business, or corporation, any secret, privileged, or confidential information of any kind by any means that describe the nature of the business, the methods and processes used further the competitiveness of the business, further referred to as "Confidential Information."

Confidential Information includes, however is not limited to, the following: [specify trade; costs of materials; secrets], as well as the names, buying habits, or practices of the Employer's customers; the Employer's sales and marketing plans and related data; names of the Employer's vendors or suppliers; details of services (or product) pricing structure, manufacturing costs, customer lists and related information (email addresses, telephone numbers), details or training and development methods; new service (or product innovations), licensing agreements, computer programs and employee performance support systems, or any other confidential data of any kind, nature, or description.

The Employee and the Employer concur between them that Confidential Information is important and material to the success of the Employer and the Employee, and that trade secrets be of the will be respected. Additional Confidential Information may from time to time be developed and obtained, and shall automatically be included within the terms of this Agreement.

Prior to employment, Employee had knowledge of the following information which is specifically excluded from this Agreement [specify].

All equipment, notebooks, documents, training materials, memoranda, reports, files, sample books, correspondence, lists, other records affecting the course of the Employer's business, including that which the Employee shall prepare, use, possess or control is the sole property of the Employer.

If any Confidential Information is sought by legal process, the Employee will promptly notify Employer and will cooperate in preserving its confidentiality.

____

Signature of Employee Date

Appendix M
Example of a Noncompete Agreement

While ________________________ (employee) is employed by ______________ (employer), the employee agrees not to directly or indirectly own an interest in, operate, participate in, or be associated as an officer, employee, agent, independent contractor, partner, shareholder, or principal of any corporation, partnership, proprietorship, firm, association, providing, selling or marketing products or services that directly or indirectly compete with employer's products or employer's business for a period of ______ (years) and is limited to the geographic locations within a 300-mile radius of the employer.

References

Abelson, R. (2002, January 9). Surge in bias cases punishes insurers, and premiums rise. *New York Times*. Retrieved September 12, 2005 from http://www.nytimes.com

Alexander, C. R., Arlen, J. & Cohen, M. A. (1999). Regulating corporate criminal sanctions: Federal guidelines and the sentencing of public firms. *Journal of Law and Economics*, *42*(1), 393-423.

American Educational Research Association, American Psychological Association & National Council on Measurement in Education. (1999). *Standards for educational and psychological testing.* Washington, DC: American Educational Research Association.

American Library Association. (n.d.). *Distance education and the Teach Act*. Retrieved August 20, 2006 from, http://www.ala.org/ala/washoff/woissues/copyrightb/distanceed/Default3685.htm

Anonymous. (2002). Drama brings diversity to life at Phillips Petroleum. *Industrial and Commercial Training*, *34*(6/7), 239-241.

Anonymous. (2003). Fatal workplace violence claims 13 lives. *Occupational Hazards*, 65, 8, 14.

Archbold, C. A. (2005). Managing the bottom line: Risk management in policing. *Policing: An Interdisciplinary Journal of Police Strategies and Management*, *28*(1), 30-48.

Ashford, N. (1976). *Crisis in the workplace.* Cambridge, MA: MIT Press.

Ashley, S., & Pearson, R. (1993). Fundamentals of risk management. Retrieved January 30, 2006 from www.sashley.com/articles.htm

Association of Corporate Counsel. (February, 2005). *The federal sentencing guidelines*. Washington, DC: Author. Retrieved September 10, 2006, from http://www.acca.com

Attran, M. (2000). Managing legal liability of the net: A ten step guide for IT managers. *Information Management and Computer Security*, *8*(2), 98-100.

Awadalla, C. A., & Roughto, J. E. (1998). Workplace violence prevention: The new safety focus. *Professional Safety, 43(12), 31-35.*

Badaracco, J. L., & Webb, A. P. (1995). Business ethics, a view from the trenches. *California Management Review*, *37*(2), 8-28.

Barnes, J. A., Dworkin, M. T., & Richards, E. L. (2003). *Law for business*. Boston: McGraw-Hill/Irwin.

Barrett, G. V. & Kernan, M. C. (1987). Performance appraisal and terminations: A review of court decisions since *Brito v. Zia* with implications for personnel practices. *Personnel Psychology*, *40*, 489-503.

Barrineau, H. E. (1987). *Civil liability in criminal justice*. Cincinnati, OH: Anderson.

Barron, M. (2006). Excellence in administrative innovation. *Journal of Housing and Community Development, 63*(1), 22-27.

Bartlett, C. J, (1978). Equal employment opportunity issues in training. *Human Factors*, *20*(2), 179-188.

Barton, D. (August, 2003). Release of liability. *Michigan Bar Journal*, 22-25.

Bennett-Alexander, D. D., & Hartman, L. P. (2001). *Employment law for business* (3rd ed.). New York: McGraw-Hill/Irwin

Berringer, H. G. (1987). *Civil liability and the police*. Evanston, IL: The Traffic Institute, Northwestern University.

Bhalala, M. (2006). Compliance dashboards for regulated industries. *Quality Digest*, 26(8). Retrieved August 12, 2006 from, http:/www.qualitydigest .com/currentmag/articles/03_article.shtml.

Biegelman, M. T., & Bartow, J. T. (2006). *Executive roadmap to fraud prevention and internal controls*. Hoboken, NJ: Wiley

Bigler, M. (2003). The high cost of software piracy. *The Internal Auditor*, *60*(3), 64-65.

Bisom-Rapp, S. (2001). An ounce of prevention is a poor substitute for a pound of cure: Confronting the developing jurisprudence of education and prevention in employment discrimination law. *Berkeley Journal of Employment and Labor Law, 22*(1), 1-47.

Blackburn, M. (1999). Organization 2005: New strategies at P & G. *Diversity Factor*, *8*(1), 16-20.

Blakeley, G. L., Blakely, E. H., & Moorman, R. H. (1998). The effects of training on perceptions of sexual harassment allegations, *Journal of Applied Social Psychology, 29*, 71-83.

Bowie, V., Fisher, B. S., & Cooper, G. L. (2005). *Workplace violence: Issues, trends, strategies*. Portland, OR: Willan Publishing.

Bowman, F. O. (2004). Drifting down the Dnieper with Prince Potemkin: Some skeptical reflections about the place of compliance programs in federal criminal sentencing. *Wake Forest Law Review, 39,* 671-690.

Brinkerhoff, R. O. (2006). *Telling training's story.* San Francisco: Berrett-Koehler.

Broad, M. L., & Newstron, J. W. (1992). *Transfer of training.* Cambridge, MA: Perseus Books.

Browell, S. (1996). Training and development specialists and the law. *Journal of European Industrial Training, 20*(2), 25-32.

Brown, T. J. (1999). Adventure risk management. In J. C. Miles & Simon Priest (Eds.), *Adventure programming* (pp. 273-284). State College, PA: Venture Publishing.

Brown, T. J., & Wood (1997). J. (1997). *Uluru-Kata Tjuta national park: Visitor risk management assessment and visitor safety plan.* Brisbane, Australia: Griffith University Centre for Leisure Research and EDAW.

Bureau of Justice Statistics. (2001). Violence *in the workplace, 1993-1999.* Washington, DC: U.S. Department of Justice. (Report # ncj-190076). Retrieved September 20, 2006, from http://www.ojp.usdoj.gov/bjs/

Bureau of Labor Standards. (2005b, September 1). MLR: Editor's desk. (2005, September 1). *Workplace homicides declined in 2004.* U.S. Department of Labor. Retrieved October 13, 2006 from http://www.bls.gov/opub/ted/2005/aug/wk5/art04.htm

Burnett, D., & James, K. (1994). Using the outdoors to facilitate personal change in managers. *The Journal of Management Development, 13*(9), 14-24.

Busco, C., Firgo, M. L., Giovannoni, E., Riccoboni, A., & Scapens, R. W. (2005). Beyond compliance: Why integrated governance matters today. *Strategic Finance, 87*(2), 34-43.

Business Software Alliance. (2005). Business Software Alliance Fact Sheet, retrieved June 8, 2006, from http://www.bsa.org/.

Campbell, I. (1995). Stress litigation and training. *Management Development Review, 8*(4), 21-22.

Cannon, L., Kruse, L., Owen, R., Simkin, R., & Wood, W. (2006). *Third Annual Litigation Trends Survey Findings.* Retrieved February 25, 2007 from http://www.fulbright.com/indexcfm?fuseaction=publications.detail&pub_id+2463&siteid=494&detail=yes

Carbonell, J. L., Higginbotham, J., & Sample, J. A. (1990). Sexual harassment of women in the workplace: Managerial strategies for understanding, preventing, and limiting liability. In J. W. Pfeiffer, (Ed.), *The 1990 annual: Developing human resources* (pp. 225-240). San Diego, CA: University Associates.

Cardani, C. L. (1986). Municipality liability after *City of Oklahoma City v. Tuttle*: A single incident of police misconduct may establish municipal liability under 42 U. S. C. Sec. 1983 when based on inadequate training or supervision. *Suffolk University Law Review. 20,* 551- 578.

Carlisle, K. E. (1986). *Analyzing jobs and tasks.* Englewood Cliffs, NJ: Educational Technology.

Carrell, M. R., Mann, E. E., & Sigler, T. H. (2006). Defining workforce diversity programs and practices in organizations: A longitudinal study. *Labor Law Journal, 57*(1), 5-12.

Carroll, S. C.,& Miller, S. R. (2006). Equal employment opportunity commission issues new compliance manual. *Employment Relations Today*, 33, 2, 67-74.

Cascio, W. F. (2000). *Costing human resources* (4th ed). Cincinnati, OH: South-Western/Thomson Learning.

Cascio, W. F., & Aguinis, H. (2005). *Applied psychology in personnel management.* Upper Saddle River, NJ: Prentice Hall.

Ceausu, J. (2005, August 23). US employers stand up to domestic abuse at work. *Personnel Today*, p. 6.

Census of Fatal Occupational Injuries: Table A-6 Fatal occupational injuries by worker characteristics and event or exposure, 2000. U.S. Dept. of Labor, Bureau of Labor Statistics. Washington DC. Retrieved October 29, 2006 from http: www.bls.gov /iif/oshwc/cfoi/ cftb137.txt.

Chapman, M. H. (2003). The return on investment for training. *Compensation and Benefits Review, 35*(1), 32-38.

Clardy, A. (2003). The legal framework of human resource development: Overview, mandates, strictures, and financial implications. *Human Resource Development Review, 2*(1), 26-53.

Clardy, A. (2004). Toward an hrd auditing protocol: Assessing hrd management risk practices. *Human Resource Development Review*, 3, 2, 125-150.

Clarke, R. A. (2006). OSHA citations: Understanding their potential long-term impact. *Professional Safety, 51*(1), 46-48.

Clement, R. W. (2006). Just how unethical is American business? *Business Horizons, 49*(4), 313-327.

Cody, N. (1990). Preparing for your day in court. *Small Business Reports, 15*(1), 56-59.

Conrow, E. H. (2000). Effective risk management: Some keys to success. Reston, VA: American Institute of Aeronautics and Astronautics.

Copeland, J. D. (2000). The Tyson story: Building an effective ethics and compliance program. *Drake Journal of Agricultural Law, 5*, 305-15.

Cordle, I. P. (2000, July 21). ValuJet claims settled for $262 million. *Miami Herald*, p. 3A.

Cordle, I. P. (2001, December 8). ValuJet crash: Case closed. *Miami Herald*, p. 1C.

Cordle, I. P. (2002, August 8). SaberTech sentenced to probation, $5,000,000 fine in '96 ValuJet Crash. *Miami Herald*, p. 1C.

Cotterell, B. (1999, November 17). State workers hurt on military obstacle course. *Tallahassee Democrat*, p. A1.

Craven, C. P. (1998). New software offerings. *Occupational Health and Safety, 67*(7), 24.

Curtis, R. (1995). Outdoor action guide to outdoor safety management. Retrieved August 15, 2006, from http://www.princeton.edu/~oa/safety/safeman.html

Cutright, S. (2005). Ethics and compliance training: Reporting to the board. *The Corporate Compliance & Regulatory Newsletter, 2*, 1, 4-6.

Dainty, P., & Lucas, D. (1992). Clarifying the confusion: A practical framework for evaluating outdoor development programmes for managers. *Management Education and Development, 23*(2), 106-122.

Dames, M. (2005). Copyright Clearances: Navigating the teach act. *Online, 29*(2), 25-30.

Daniel, M. D. & Farb, B. G. (2005). Workplace violence guidebook. Los Angeles: University of Health Care Publishing.

Davis-Berman, J., & Bermon, D. (2002). Risk and anxiety in adventure programming. *The Journal of Experiential Education, 25*(2), 305-310.

Dawson, M. (2005). Raising awareness of the benefits of diversity at ING. *Human Resource Management International Digest, 13*(2), 20-22.

Day, M. (2006). *Designing residential wilderness programs for adults.* Malabar, FL: Krieger.

Delbecq, A. L., Gustafson, D. H., & Van de Ven, A. H. (1986). *Group techniques for program planning.* Glenview IL: Scott-Foresman.

DeMaria, R. H. & Gardiner, D. (August 16, 2002). Anti-harassment training is mandatory for managers and supervisors: New Jersey supreme court rewrites Lehmann, establishes a bright-line rule for the standard of negligence required in sexual harassment claims. *New Jersey Law Journal*, 29-30.

Desio, P. J. (2004). Introduction to organizational sentencing and the U.S. sentencing guidelines. *Wake Forest Law Review*, *39*(3), 559-563.

Dewey, J. (1938). *Experience in education.* New York: Macmillan.

Dick W., Carey, L., & Carey, J. O. (2004). *The systematic design of instruction.* Boston: Allyn & Bacon.

Dobbs, K. (2000). The lucrative menace of workplace violence. *Training*, *37*(3), 54-60.

Donahue, J. J., & Seligman, P. (1993). Law and macroeconomics: Employment discrimination litigation over the business cycle. *Southern California Law Review*, *66*, 709-765.

Employment Law Learning Technologies and Littler Mendelson. (2002). *Compliance Training Brings Superior ROI to Organizations*, April 11, 2002. Retrieved May 7, 2005, from http://www.elt-inc.com/roi.html

Erickson, P. A. (1996). *Practical guide to occupational health and safety.* New York: Academic Press.

Ethics Resource Center. (2005). National business ethics survey. Retrieved September 15, 2006 from http://www.ethics.org/research/nbes-2005.asp

Eyres, P. S. (September, 1990). Keeping the training department out of court. *Training*, 27, 9, 59 -67.

Eyres, P. S. (1998). *The legal handbook for trainers, speakers, and consultants.* New York: McGraw-Hill.

Eyres, P. S. (2004). Businesses beware: Copyright infringement on your intranet can be costly. *Business Credit*, *106*(5), 67-68.

Eyres, P. S. (2005). *Keep your email from becoming a legal pain in the net* (Session # M214). Paper presented at the meeting of the American Society for Training and Development Conference, Dallas, TX.

Fenton, J. W., Ruud, W. N., & Kimbell, J. A. (1991). Negligent training suits: A recent entry into the corporate negligence arena. *Labor Law Journal*, 46, 6, 351-356.

Feuer, D. (1985). Protecting the public: How much training is enough? *Training, 22* (11), 22-28.

Fields, G., & Cohen, L. P. (February 11, 2005). Judges maintain sentence formula despite ruling. *Wall Street Journal* (Eastern Edition), p. A5.

Fine, S. A., & Cronshaw, S. F. (1999). *Functional job analysis: A foundation for human resource management.* Mahwah, NJ: Erlbaum.

Fishman, S. (2004). *The copyright handbook* (8th ed.). Berkeley, CA: Nolo Publications.

Freedman, J. C. (2002). The fair labor standards act today: A primer. *Compensation and Benefits Review, 34*(1), 49-57.

Gahin, F. S., & Chesteen, S. S. (1988). Executives contemplate the call of the wild. *Risk Management, 35*(7), 44-51.

Gallagher, G. P. (1990a). Risk management for police administrators. *The Police Chief*, 18-28.

Gallagher, G. P. (1990b). The six-layered liability protection system for police. *The Police Chief*, 40-43.

Gallaway, L. K. (2006). E-learning winter showcase and learning symposium highlights best practices and innovative approaches. *T & D, 60*(2), 14.

Gass, M. A. (1999). Accreditation and certification: Questions for an advancing profession. In J. C. Miles and Simon Priest (Eds.), *Adventure Programming* (pp. 247-251). State College, PA: Venture Publishing.

Gold, M. (2003). IRS goes e. *T & D, 57*(5), 76-82.

Goldsborough, R. (1994). Computers and the law. *PC Today, 8*(5), 18-24.

Gosen, J., & Washburn, J. (2004). A review of scholarship on assessing experiential learning effectiveness. *Simulation & Gaming, 35*(2), 270-290.

Gould, L. J., Stapley, L. F., & Stein, M. (2004). *Experiential learning in organizations: Applications of the Tavistock group relations approach.* New York: Karnac.

Grace, P. (1994). Danger—diversity training ahead: Addressing the myths of diversity training and offering alternatives. In J. W. Pfeiffer (Ed.), *The 1994 annual: Developing human resources* (pp. 189-200). San Diego, CA: Pfeiffer.

Griggs, L., & Louw, L. (1995). *Valuing Diversity.* New York: McGraw-Hill.

Grollman, W. K., & Cannon, D. (2003). A better chalkboard. *Financial Executive, 19*(8), 45-47.

Gurchiek, K. (2006). Domestic abuse: Serious, hidden workplace problem. *HR Magazine*, 51, 3, 38.

Gutman, A. (2005). Adverse impact. In F. J. Landy (Ed.), *Employment discrimination litigation* (pp. 20-46). San Francisco: Jossey-Bass.

Gutek, B. A., & Stockdale, M. S. (2005). Sex discrimination in employment. In F. J. Landy (Ed.), *Employment discrimination litigation* (pp. 229-255). San Francisco, CA: Jossey-Bass.

Halan, J. M. (2004). Protecting trade secrets. Steps every trade secret owner should know. *Employee Relations Law Journal, 30*(3), 22-28.

Handoo, O. (2005). Association training program expense reimbursement. *Association Management, 57*(4), 19-21.

Hartley, D., Biddle., E. A., & Jenkins, E. L. (2005). Societal cost of workplace homicides in the United States, 1992-2001. *Amcrican Journal of Industrial Medicine, 47*, 518-527.

Hartman, G. S., Homer, G. W., & Reff, A. H. (1998). *Personnel law handbook: 1998 edition*. Winston-Salem, NC: Wake Forest CLE.

Harvey, M. G., Heames, J., Richey, R. G., & Leonard, N. L. (2006). Bullying: From the playground to the boardroom. *Journal of Leadership and Organizational Studies*, 12, 4, 1-11.

Hasnas, J. (2006). *Trapped: When acting ethically is against the law*. Washington, DC: Cato Institute.

Hatcher, T. G. (2002). *Ethics and HRD: A new approach to leading responsible organizations*. Cambridge, MA: Perseus.

Hattie, J., Marsh, H. W., Neill, J. T.,& Richards, G. E. (1997). Adventure education and Outward Bound: Out of class experiences that make a lasting difference. *Review of Educational Research, 67*(2), 43-87.

Hayles, R., & Russell, A. M. (1997). *The diversity directive: Why some initiatives fail and what to do about it*. Alexandria, VA: American Society for Training and Development.

Hemphill, H., & Haines, R. (1997). *Discrimination, harassment, and the failure of diversity training*. Westport, CT: Quorum Books.

Henszey, B. N., Myers, B. L., Phalan, R., Bagby, J., & Sharp, J. (1994). *Introduction to basic legal principles*. Dubuque, Iowa: Kendall/Hunt Publishing Company.

Hicks, P. H.,& Alexander, N. M. (1997, April). Negligent training, supervision and retention in Nevada. *Nevada Lawyer, 5*, 10-14.

Hicks, T. (2001, April 4). *Mediation in sexual harassment cases.* Retrieved May 5, 2005, from http://www.hr.com.

Hightower, A. S. (2004). Employment practices liability coverage: Time to reevaluate coverage to consider expanded liability laws. *Employee Relations Law Journal. 30*(1), 65-80.

Hill, D., & Phillips, J. (1997). Preventing sexual harassment Health Care Inc. In J. J. Phillips (Ed.), *Action: Measuring return on investment (Vol. 2)* (pp. 17-36). Alexandria, VA: American Society for Training and Development.

Hite, L. M., & McDonald, K. S. (2006). Diversity training pitfalls and possibilities: An exploration of small and mid-size US organizations. *Human Resource Development International*, 9, 3, 365-377.

Holmes, T. A. (2005). How to connect diversity to performance. *Performance Improvement, 44*(5), 13-17.

Hood, J. B., Hardy, B. A., & Lewis, H. S. (1999). *Workers' compensation and employee protection laws.* St. Paul, MN: West.

Hospital chain ends fraud case. (2002, December 19). *New York Times.* Retrieved from http://query.nytimes.com gst.fullpage.html?see= health&res=9D04E2D7133DF93AA2575 on October 10, 2006.

HR Focus. (2005). How HR can facilitate ethics. *HR Focus, 82*(4), 11-12.

Hume, S., & Teinowitz, I. (1990, December 3). $1.1 m verdict in Chilko. *Advertising Age*, 1.

Hutchison, T. W., Hoffman, P. B., Young, D., & Popko, S. G. (2006). *Federal sentencing law and practice.* Cleveland, OH: Thomson West.

Ibbetson, A., & Newell, S. (1999). A comparison of a competitive and non-competitive outdoor management development programme. *Personnel Review, 28*(1/2), 58-76.

Isaccs, L. (2003). Online lessons. *American City and County, 118*(4), 40-45.

Janis, I. L. (1972). *Victims of groupthink.* Boston: Houghton Mifflin.

Jasper, M. C. (2005). *Injured on thejob: Employee rights, workers' compensation and disabilities.* Dobbs Ferry, NY: Oceana.

Jenero, K. A. & Galligano, M. L. (2003). Courts continue to emphasize importance of policy development and training. *Employee Relations Law Journal, 28*(4), 113-124.

Jennerette, P. R., & Strong, M. H. (2003). Linking O*NET job analysis information to job requirement predictors: An O*NET application. *Personnel Psychology, 56*, 465-492.

Johnson, M. W. (2004). Harassment and discrimination prevention training: What the law requires. *Labor Law Journal, 55*(2), 119-129.

Johnson, M. W. (2005). *No FEAR Act requires federal agencies to train all employees on discrimination, whistleblower, and retaliation laws by September 30, 2005.* Retrieved May 11, 2005 from http:/www.brightlinecompliance.com/training/articles.html

Johnson, P. R., & Gardner, S. (1999). Domestic violence and the workplace: Developing a company response. *Journal of Management Development*, 18, 7, 590-597.

Jones, P. J., & Oswick, C. (1993). Outcomes of outdoor management development: articles of faith. *Journal of European Industrial Training, 17*(3), 10-18.

Jordan, K. S., & Murphy, J. E. (2004). *Course handbook. Compliance programs: What the government really wants. PLI's Corporate Compliance Institute 2004.* New York: Thomson RIA.

Keller, T. & Olson, W. (2000). The advisability of outdoor leadership training: Caveat emptor. *Review of Business*, 21, ½, 4-6.

Kahn, R.A. (2004). Records management and compliance. *Information Management Journal, 38*(3), 28-36.

Kamp, J., & Krause, T. R. (1997). Selecting safe employees: A behavioral science perspective. *Professional Safety*, 42, 4, 24-28.

Kaplan, R., & Norton, D. (1996). *The balanced scorecard: Translating strategy into action.* Boston: Harvard College.

Kennedy-Glans, D. (2005/2006). Achieving a single ethical standard in a globalized world. *Corporate Responsibility Management, 2*(3), 24-29.

Kezman, S. W., & Connors, E. K. (1993). Avoid legal pitfalls in nontraditional training. *HR Magazine, 38*(5), 71-74.

Klane, J. (2005). Really effective training. *Occupational Health and Safety, 73*(9), 190-195.

Knowles, M. S. (2005). *The adult learner.* Boston: Elsevier.

Kolb, D. A. (1984). *Experiential learning: Experience as the source of learning and development.* Englewood Cliffs, NJ: Prentice Hall.

Kosidlak, J. G. (1987). DACUM: An alternative job analysis tool. *Personnel, 64*(3), 14-18.

Kouzes, J., & Posner, B. (2002). *The leadership challenge.* San Francisco: Jossey-Bass.

Krawiec, K. D. (2003). The future disclosure system: Cosmetic compliance and the failure of negotiated governance. *Washington University Law Review, 81*, 487-544.

Kriesberg, S. M. (2006). Proceed with caution: International trade compliance in lending transactions. *The Banking Law Journal, 123,* 7, 579-604.

Kubal, D., Baker, M., & Coleman, K. (2006). Doing the right thing: How today's leading companies are becoming more ethical. *Performance Improvement, 45*(3), 5-8.

Landy, F. J. (Ed.). (2005). *Employment discrimination litigation.* San Francisco, CA: Jossey-Bass.

Langewiesche, W. (1998). The lessons of ValuJet 592. *The Atlantic Monthly, 281*(3), 81-97.

Ledvinka, J., & Scarpello, V. (1991). *Federal regulation of personnel and human resource management* (2nd ed.). Boston: Kent.

Littler & Mendolsen. (2005). Chapter 15 Training really is the law: The rise of mandatory training. *The national employer 2005-2006 edition.* Retrieved from www.elt-inc.com/law-of-training.html on October 15, 2006

Loescher, K. J. (2006). Before you train, reframe: Elements of effective ethics training programs. *Employee Relations Today*, 33,3,91-102.

Logsdon, J. M., & Wood, D. J. (2005). Global business citizenship and voluntary codes of ethical conduct. *Journal of Business Ethics, 59,* 55-67.

Lubove, S. (1997, December 15). Damned if you do, damned if you don't. *Forbes, 160*, 122-134.

Lunt, P. (1994). Should you do diversity training? *ABA Banking Journal, 86*(8), 53-54.

Malkin, L. (1991, August 19). Five top officers leave Solomon as Buffett takes control of the firm. *International Herald Tribune.* Retrieved from http://www.iht.com/articles/1991/08/19/resi.php

Malos, S. B. (1998). Current legal issues in performance appraisal. In J. W. Smither (Ed.), *Performance Appraisal: State-Of-The-Art Methods for Performance Management* (pp. 49-94). San Francisco: Jossey-Bass.

Manuele, F. A. (2000). Task analysis for productivity, cost efficiency, safety & quality. *Professional Safety,45*(4), 18-22.

Mathiason, G. G., & de Bernardo, M. (1998). The emerging law of training. *The Federal Lawyer, 45,* 4, 2536.

Matthews, M. (1987).Codes of ethics: Organizational behavior and misbehavior. In W. Fredrick (Ed.), *Research in Corporate Social Performance* (pp. 107-130). Stamford, CT: JAI Press.

Mazany, P., Francis, S., & Sumich, P. (1995). Evaluating the effectiveness of an experimental "hybrid" workshop strategy development and team building in a manufacturing organization. *The Journal of Management Development, 14*(1), 40-52.

McAvoy, L., & Lais, G. (1999). Programs that include persons with disabilities. In J. C. Miles and Simon Priest (Eds.), *Adventure Programming* (pp. 403-414). State College, PA: Venture Publishing.

McCalman, L., Bates, P. T., Morris, N. T., & Wilder, M. R. (1996). Workplace success for adults with learning disabilities. *Employment Relations Today, 23*(2), 77-84.

McConnaughhay, J. N., & Collier, J. E. (2000). *2000 workers' compensation desk manual.* Tallahassee, FL: Author.

McDonald, J. J. (2004). You're looking at me like I'm crazy! *Employee Relations Law Journal, 30*(3), 74-87.

McKendall, M., DeMarr, B., & Jones-Rikkers, C. (2002). Ethical compliance programs and corporate legality: Testing the assumptions of the corporate sentencing. *Journal of Business Ethics*, 37(4), 367-384.

McKenzie, M. D. (200). How are adventure education programs achieved?: A review of the literature. *Australian Journal of Outdoor Education, 5*(1), 19-28.

McLaughlin, E., & Mershasin, C. (2001, January 29). Training becomes important step to avoid liability. *National Law Journal*, B10.

Means, R. (2005). The history and dynamics of section 1983. *The Police Chief, 71*(5), 10-14.

Miles, J. C., & Priest, S. (Eds.). (1999). *Adventure Programming.* State College, PA: Venture Publishing.

Mills, J. E., Srikanth, B. H., & Clay, J. (2001). Cyberslacking! A liability issue for wired workplaces. *Cornell Hotel and Restaurant Administration, 42*(5), 34-48.

Miner, J. (1999). The creation of outward bound. In J. C. Miles and Simon Priest (Eds.), *Adventure Programming* (pp. 55-63). State College, PA: Venture Publishing.

Miner, T. (1999). Adventure in the workplace. In J. C. Miles and Simon Priest (Eds.), *Adventure Programming* (pp. 395-414). State College, PA: Venture Publishing.

Mitchell, C. E. (July, 1990). Newage training programs: In violation of religious discrimination laws. *Labor Law Journal*, 410-416.

Montante, W. M. (1994). An ergonomic approach to task analysis. *Professional Safety*, *39*(2), 18-22.

Moyer, R. S., & Nath, A. (1998). Some effects of brief training interventions on perceptions of sexual harassment. *Journal of Applied Social Psychology*, *28*, 333-354.

Murphy, J. E. (1997). Training "in a practical manner." *PLI's course handbook, corporate compliance: After Caremark*. New York: Thomson RIA.

National Institute for Occupational Safety and Health. (2004). Workplace violence prevention strategies and research needs. Report from the conference, Partnering in workplace violence prevention: Translating research to practice. November 17-19, 2004. Baltimore.

National Transportation Safety Board. (August 19, 1997). Aircraft Accident Report. *In*-flight Fire and Impact with Terrain, VALUJET airlines Flight 592, DC 9-32, *N904VJ, Everglades, Near Miami Florida, May 11, 1997*. NTSB/AAR-97/06. Washington, DC: Author.

Navran, F. (1992). Hiring trainers with disabilities. *Training*. *29* (7), pp. 24-26, 31.

Noe, R. (2006). *Employee training and development* (4th ed.). New York: McGraw-Hill.

Nontraditional training. (1994, March). *Fair Employment Practices Guidelines, 355,* 3-6. Waterford, CT: Bureau of Business Practice.

Norton, R. E. (1993). *DACUM and Tech Prep: Dynamic duo*. Paper presented at the Mid-America Competency-Based Education Conference, Bloomington, MN. (ERIC Document Reproduction Service No. ED359 339).

Obrien, L. (2004). How to restore the fiduciary relationship: An interview with Eliot Spitzer. *Harvard Business Review, 82(*5), 70-78.

Paap, K. (2006). *Working construction: Why white working-class men put themselves—and the labor movement—in harm's way*. Ithaca, NY: Cornell University Press.

Paine, L. S. (1994). Managing for organizational integrity. *Harvard Business Review, 72*(2), 106-117.

Papinchock, J. M. (2005). Title I of the Americans with disabilities act. In F. J. Landy (Ed.), *Employment discrimination litigation* (pp. 294-335). San Francisco: Jossey-Bass.

Parker, J. S., & Atkins, R. A. (1999). *Journal of Law and Economics, 42*(1), 423-453.

Paskoff, S. M. (2006). Behavior matters: Building a legal, ethical workplace culture. In R. C. Preziosi (Ed.), *The 2006 Pfeiffer human resources annual* (pp. 223-233). San Francisco: Pfeiffer/Jossey-Bass/Wiley.

Pell, G. (1996). Corporate compliance programs: Leading edge practices. *Corporate Conduct Quarterly*, 5(3). Retrieved August 13, 2006, from http://camden-www.rutgers.edu/~ccq/pell53.html

Perline, I. H. & Goldschmidt, J. (2004). *The psychology and law of workplace violence*. Springfield, IL: Charles C. Thomas.

Perrow, C. (1999). *Normal accidents: Living with high-risk technologies.* Princeton, NJ: Princeton University Press.

Petrich, M., & Moon, E. (September, 2005). The role of technology in effective compliance programs. *The Metropolitan Corporate Counsel*. Retrieved August 12, 2006, from http:/www.metrocorpcounsel .com/

Petrick, J. A., & Scherer, R. F. (2003). The Enron scandal and neglect of management integrity capacity. *Mid-America Journal of Business, 18*(1), 37-49.

Pierce, F. D. (2003). Low English proficiency & increased injury rates. *Professional Safety, 48*(8), 40-45.

Piskurich, G. M. (2000). *Rapid instructional design: Learning ID fast and right.* New York: Wiley.

Pohlman, R. A. & Mujtaba, B. G. (2007). The impact of the Sarbanes-Oxley Act on human resource management. In R. C. Preziosi (Ed.), *The 2007 Pfeifferan-nual human resource management*. San Francisco: Pfeiffer/Jossey-Bass/Wiley. 179-194.

Policy, S. J. (2000). Employer monitoring of employee internet and email use: An effective litigation avoidance tool. *The Computer and Internet Lawyer, 17*(11), 21-23.

Prevette, S. S. (2006). Charting safety performance. *Professional Safety, 51*(5), 34-41.

Reid, R. L. (1992). On target: Tools to train people with disabilities. *Technical & Skills Training, 3*(5), 8-20, 31.

Risser, R. (1993). *Stay out of court: The manager's guide to preventing employee lawsuits*. Englewood Cliffs, NJ: Prentice Hall.

Roberson, L., Kulik, C. T., Pepper, M. B. (2003). Using needs assessment to resolve controversies in diversity training design. *Group and Organization Management, 28*(1), 148-174.

Robinson, D. G., & Robinson, J. C. (1991). *Training for impact*. San Francisco: Jossey-Bass.

Robinson, D. G., & Robinson, J. C. (2004). *Strategic business partnering: Aligning people strategy with business goals*. San Francisco: Berrett-Koehler.

Rohnke, K. (1999). Ropes courses: A constructed adventure environment. In J. C. Miles and Simon Priest (Eds.), *Adventure Programming* (pp. 347-371). State College, PA: Venture Publishing.

Rosen, J. (2000). Assessment of training needs for occupational safety and health personnel in the United States: A labor perspective. *AIHAJ, 61*(4), 456-460.

Ross, D. L. (2000). Emerging trends in police failure to train liability. *Policing: An Interdisciplinary Journal of Police Strategies and Management, 23*(2), 169-193.

Rothwell, W. J., & Kazanas, H. C. (2003). *Mastering the instructional design process. A systematic approach*. San Francisco: Pfeiffer/Jossey-Bass.

Russell, J. S. (1984). A review of fair employment cases in the field of training. *Personnel Psychology, 37*, 261-275.

Rynes, S., & Rosen, B. (1995). A field survey of factors affecting the adoption and perceived success of diversity training. *Personnel Psychology, 48*(2), 247-270.

Sage, J. E. (1990). Safe attitudes minimize trainer liability. *Technical & Skills Training, 1*(4), 9-13.

Sample, J. A. (1993). *INFO-LINE Legal liability & HRD: Implications for trainers*. Washington, DC: American Society for Training and Development.

Sample, J. A. (1995a). Liability and the technical trainer. In L. Kelly (Ed.), *The ASTD technical and skills training handbook* (pp. 175-210). New York: McGraw-Hill.

Sample, J. (May, 1995b). Using subject matter experts to identify high liability tasks. *Performance & Instruction, 34*(5), 34-37.

Sample, J. A. (July, 1997). Training programs: How to avoid legal liability. *Supplement to the Fair Employment Practices Guidelines*. New York: Bureau of Business Practice.

Sample, J. A. (2006). Developing and using behaviorally based rating scales: A tool for appraising human resources. In R. C. Preziosi (Ed.), *The 2006 Pfeiffer annual: Human Resources*. San Francisco: Pfeiffer/ Wiley. 235-261.

Sample, J. A. (2007a). Are you at risk *T & D, 61*, 6, 42-46

Sample, J. A. (2007b). HR's other legal nightmare: Liability and the training and development function. In R. C. Preziosi (Ed.), *The 2007 Pfeiffer annual human resources management*. San Francisco: Pfeiffer/ Jossey-Bass/Wiley. 205-234.

Sample, J. A. (2007c). The compelling argument for harassment prevention training: Implications for instructional designers. *Performance Improvement, 47*, 7, 17-24.

Sample, J. A., & Hylton, R. (1996). Falling off a log and landing in court. *Training, 33*(5), 66-69.

Sanchez, J., & Medkik, N. (2004). The effects of diversity awareness training on differential treatment. *Group and Organization Management, 29*(4), 517-536.

Sanders, J. R. (1994). *The Program Evaluation Standards*. Thousand Oaks, CA: Sage.

Schultz, G. A. (2004). Conveyor safety—Task analysis procedure helps identify, reduce risks. *Professional Safety. 49*(8), 24-27.

Schwartz, M. S. (2001). The nature of the relationship between corporate codes of ethics and behavior, *Journal of Business Ethics, 32*(3), 247-263.

Schwartz, V. E., Kelly, K., & Partlett, D. F. (2000). *Torts: Cases and materials*. (10th ed.) New York: Foundation Press.

Seibert, K. W., Hall, D. T., & Kram, K. E. (1995). Strengthening the weak link to strategic executive development: Integrating individual development and global business strategy. *Human Resource Management, 34*(4), 549-567.

Senosk, E. M. (1977). *An examination of outdoor pursuit leader certification and licensing within the United States in 1997*. Unpublished master's thesis, University of Oregon, Eugene.

Sims. R. R. (1990). *An experiential approach to employee training systems*. New York: Quorum Books.

Siskind, L. (2003). How to prosecute and defend hot issues in copyright cases. *Computer and Internet Lawyer, 20*(6), 25-35.

Skalak, S., & Nestler, C. (2005). 2005 Price Waterhouse Coopers global economic crime survey 2005. Retrieved August 7, 2006 from http://www.pwc.com/extweb/insights.nsf/docid/D1A0A606149F2806852570C0006716C0

Society for Industrial and Organizational Psychology. (2003). *Principles for the validation and use of personnel selection procedures* (4th ed.). Bowling Green, OH: Author.

Souissi, M. (2006). Going beyond compliance: The role of the balanced scorecard. *The Journal of Corporate Accounting and Finance, 17*(4), 75-81.

Soverign, K. L. (1999). *Personnel Law* (4thed.). Upper Saddle River, NJ: Prentice Hall.

Spector, P. E. (2006). *Industrial organizational psychology* (4th ed.). New York: Wiley.

Stape, C. (2005). Overcoming OSHA. *Training, 42*(3), 74.

Steer, J. R. (2001). Changing organizational behavior – The federal sentencing guidelines experiment begins to bear fruit. Unpublished paper presented at the Twenty-ninth Annual Conference on Value Inquiry, Tulsa, Oklahoma (April 26, 2001), 21 pages.

Steinglass, S. H. (1988). *Section 1983 litigation in state courts.* New York: Clark Boardman.

Steingold, F. (2000). *The employer's legal handbook* (4th ed.). Berkeley, CA: Nolo.

Stimson, B. (1998, October). Operating highly complex and hazardous technological systems without mistakes: The wrong lessons from ValuJet 592. *The Manitoba Professional Engineer*, retrieved June 25, 2005, from, http://www.cns-snc/branches/Manitoba/valujet.html

Stokes, P. P., Stewart-Hill, S., & Barnes, J. M. (2000). The supreme court holds class on sexual harassment: How to avoid a failing grade. *Employee Responsibilities and Rights Journal, 12*(2), 79-91.

Strickland, L. S. (2003). Part 2: The DCMA, the Teach Act and other e-copying considerations. *Bulletin of the American Society for Information Science and technology. 30*(2), 18-23.

Stuller, J. (1995). Doing what comes unnaturally. *Across the board, 32*(6), 27-30.

Sunoo, B. P. (1998). Sexual harassment: After everything else—buy insurance. *Workforce, 77*(10), 45-50.

Swanson, R. A. (2005). Evaluation, a state of mind. *Advances in Developing Human Resources, 7*(1), 16-21.

Swerdow, J. (1991). Negligent referral: A potential theory for employer liability. *Southern California Law Review, 64*, 1645.

Tarullo, G. M. (1992). Making outdoor experiential training work. *Training, 29* (8), 47-49, 50.

Tebo, M. G. (2005, September). When home comes to work. *ABA Journal*, 91, 42-47.

Trevino, L. K., Weaver, G.R., Gibson, D. G., & Toffler B. L. (1999). Managing ethics and legal compliance: What works and what hurts. *California Management Review, 41*(2), 131-151.

Tuttle, M. A. & Winokur, M. N. (2003). Using technology to prove and defend against punitive damages. 2003 ABA annual meeting—Section of labor and employment law. Retrieved May 16, 2005 from http://www.bna.com/bnabooks/ababna/annual/2003/mallery.doc

United States Sentencing Commission. (2000). Annual Report. Retrieved August 1, 2006, from http://www.ussc.gov/guidelin.htm

United States Sentencing Commission. (2005). United States Sentencing Guidelines, Chapter 8. Retrieved August 1, 2006, from http://www.ussc.gov/2005guid/TABCON05.htm

U.S. Department of Justice. (June 26, 2003). Largest health care fraud case in U.S. history settled HCA investigation nets record total of $1.7 billion. News release retrieved September 25, 2006 from http://www.usdoj.gov/opa/pr/2003/June/03_civ_386.htm

van der Smissen, B., & Gregg, C. R. (1999). Legal liability and risk management. In J. C. Miles and Simon Priest (Eds.), *Adventure Programming* (pp. 285-297). State College, PA: Venture Publishing.

van der Smissen, B., & Liddle, J. B. (1997). *Accreditation of adventure-based experiential education policy and procedure manual.* Boulder, CO: Association for Experiential Education.

Vogel, J. (1991). Manufacturing solidarity: Adventure training for managers. *Hofstra Law Review*, 19, 657-724.

Volis, P., Roper, M. J., & Decker, K. (2005). Avoiding the legal aftermath of workplace violence. *Employee Relations Law Journal*, 31, 3, 65-71.

Von Bergen, C. W., Soper, B., & Foster, T. (2002). Unintended negative effects of diversity management. *Public Personnel Management, 31*(2), 239-251.

Vroom, V. H. (1964). *Work and motivation.* New York: Wiley.

Waddington, P. A. J., Badger, D., & Bull, R. (2006). *The violent workplace.* Portland, OR: Willan Publishing.

Wallstein, K. (1998). Tower records uses games to boost training results. *Workforce, 77*(10), 115-116, 118.

Ward, G. (1988). *High-risk training: Managing training programs for high risk occupations.* New York: Nichols.

Weigand, R. (1995). Experiential learning: A brief history. In C. Roland, R. Wagner, and R. Weigand (Eds.), *Do it . . . and understand* (pp. 2-4). Dubuque, IA: Kendall/Hunt.

Weisman, B. R. (2006). Handling BBP requirements in manufacturing and service industries. *Occupational Health & Safety, 75*(4), 22-24.

Wellner, P. A. (2005). Note: Effective compliance programs and corporate criminal prosecutions. *Cardozo Law Review, 27,* 497-505.

Werner, J. M., & DeSimone, R. L. (2006). *Human resource development* (4th ed.). Belmont, CA: Thomson Southwestern.

Whitt, S. (1990). *Note - City of Canton v. Harris:* Municipality liability under 42 U.S.C. Section 1983 for inadequate police training. *George Mason University Law Review, 12,* 757-724.

Whitten, A. D. & Mosley, D. M. (2000). Caught in the crossfire: Employers' liability for workplace violence. *Mississippi Law Journal, 70,* 505-55.

Wick, C. W., Pollock, R. V. H., Jefferson, A. M., & Flannagan, R. D. (2006). *The six disciplines of breakthrough learning.* Hoboken, N.J: Pfeiffer/Wiley.

Wildermuth, C., & Gray, S. (2005). *Diversity training.* Alexandria, VA: ASTD Press.

Williamson, J., & Gass, M. (1993). *Manual of Accreditation Standards for Adventure Programs.* Boulder, CO: Association for Experiential Education.

Wong, K-S. R., & Rakestraw, K. M. (1991). The a, b, c's of risk management. Washington, DC: International City Council Management Association.

Working Life. (May 1991). *Training and Development,* p. 93.

Zimmerman, D. S. (2005). Is OSHA important? *Employee Relations Law Journal,* 30, 4, 42-55.

Zink, D. L., & Gutman, A. (2005). Statistical trends in private sector employment discrimination suits. In F. J. Landy (Ed.), *Employment discrimination litigation.* San Francisco, CA: Jossey-Bass.

Zinkewicz, P. (2006). EPLI innovators. *Rough Notes, 149*(6), 104-107.

Statutes

Americans with Disabilities Act of 1990.
Civil Rights Act of 1871, 1964 and 1990.
Copyright Act of 1976.
Economics Espionage Act of 1996.
Foreign Corrupt Practices Act of 1977.
Occupational Safety and Health Act of 1970.
Sarbanes-Oxley Act of 2002.
Uniform Trade Secrets Act of 1985.
TEACH Act of 2002.

Regulatory Guidelines

EEOC. (1983). EEOC Dec. No. 83-7, ¶ 6836 (CCH).

EEOC. (2006). Section 15 Race and Color Discrimination. EEOC Compliance Manual revised April 19, 2006 retrieved from http://www.eeoc.gov/policy/docs/race-color.html on November 9, 2006.

EEOC. Policy Statement on Training Programs Conflicting With Employees' Religious Beliefs. Issued February 22, 1988.

EEOC. Guidelines on Employee Selection Procedures. 29 CFR 1607 1993 - Selecting employees for training.

EEOC. v. Ford Motor Company, Inc. No. 1:04-CV-00845 (S.D. Ohio June 16, 2005)

EEOC. (1999, June 18). Enforcement guidance: Vicarious liability for unlawful harassment by supervisors, No. 915.002.

EEOC. (1980). Guidelines on discrimination because of sex.

EEOC. (1998). Facts About Religious Discrimination, February, 22, 1988.

OSHA. (n.d.). General Industry Standards. Retrieved from http://www.osha.gov/pls/oshaweb/owastand.display_standard_group?p_toc_level=1&p_part_number=1910&v_description=General+Industry+-+%28Standards+-+29+CFR%29 October 25, 2006.

OSHA. (1998a). Industrial hygiene #4143. Washington, D.C: U.S. Department of Labor.

OSHA. (1998b). Recommendations for workplace violence prevention programs in late-night retail establishments. Washington, D.C: U.S. Department of Labor.

Uniform Guidelines on Employee Selection Procedures. 29 C.F.R. § 1607.

U.S.S.G (1991). Case N0. 88-266. Supplemental Report on Sentencing Guidelines for Organizations.

Case Citations

Albamarle Paper Co. v. Moody, 422 U.S. 405 (1975).

American Geophysical Union v. Texaco, Inc., 105 Lexis 40 (S.D. New York, 1992).

Arthur Anderson v. U.S., 544 U.S. 696 (2005)

Burlington Industries v. Ellerth, 524 US 742 (1998).

Cadena v. Pacesetter Corporation, 224 F.3d 1203 (10th. Cir. 2000).

Caggiano v. Fontoura, NJ. Supar., LEXIS 367 (App. Div 2002)

City of Canton v. Harris, 109 S. Ct. 1197 (1989).

Cleveland Electric Illuminating Company v. Occupational Safety Health Review Commission, Docket # 91 2198. (1984)

Dobrich v. General Dynamics Corporation, 106 F.Supp 386 (D Conn. 2000).

Kim v. The Dekalb Farmers Market, Inc. Civil Action No.- 88CV2767HTW (D. Northern District of Georgia, filed December 7, 1988).

Ellerth v. Burlington Industries, Inc., 524 U. S. 742 (1998).

Faragher v. City of Boca Raton, 524 U. S. 775 (1998).

Fasules v. DDB Needham Worldwide, Inc., No 89 C 1078; (1988 U.S. Dist Court)

Fitzgerald v. Mountain States Tel. & Tel. Co., 68 F3d 1257 (10th Cir. 1995).

Gaines v. Belino, 2002 NJ LEXIS 1083 (2002).

General Dynamics v. Occupational Health Review Commission, 599 F 2d 453 (1977).

Goldstein, et al. v. DDB Needham World Wide, Inc., et al., 740 F.Supp 461 (SD Ohio, 1990).

Granite Construction Co. v. Mendoza, 816 S. W. 2d 756 (1991).

Green v. Coach, 218 F. Supp 2d. 440 (SD NY 2002).

Griggs v. Duke Power Company, 401 U.S. 436, (1971).

Hartman v. Pena, 914 F.Supp. 225 (1995).

Hiatt v. Walker Chevrolet Co., 822 P. 2d 1235 (1987).

ICS Bunker Ramo Corporation v. Altech, Inc., 765 F. Supp. 1310 (ND Ill. 1990).

Kolstad v. American Dental Association, 527 U. S. 526 (1999).

Langston v. Kidder, 670 So. 2d. 1 (1995).

Lowry's Reports Inc. v. Legg Mason, 221 F.Supp.2d 737 (D. Md. 2003).

Mann v. Rhino Linings USA, Inc., Cal., Los Angeles County Super. Ct., No. VC 036135 (Feb. 9, 2004).

Meritor Savings Bank v, Vinson, 477 U.S. 57 (1986).

Moller v. Department of Social Services, 1995 WL 464903 (N. D. Cal 1995).

Monell v. Department of Social Services of the City of New York, 436 U.S. 658, 56 L Ed 2d 611, 98 S Ct 2018 (1978)

Orlando v. Alarm One, Inc., Superior Court of California, Fresno County, Case No. 04 CE CG 01288 DSB (May 2, 2006).

Pennsylvania State Police v. Suder, 124 S. Ct. 2342 (2004).

Pittard v. Four Seasons Motor Inn, 688 P2d. 33 (N.M. App. 1984).

Sager v. Woodland Park, 543 F.Supp. 282 (D.C. Colorado, 1982).

Stacy v. Truman Medical Center, Unpublished Supreme Court of Missouri, July 21, 1992; 1992 Mo. LEXIS 113 (1992).

Stallworth v. Monsanto Co., 13 FEP Cases 827 (1984).

State of Wisconsin v. Shoreline Support Corporation, Unpublished Supreme Court of Wisconsin. April 11, 1989; 443 N. W.2d 310; 1989 Wisc. LEXIS 358 (1989).

Steen Construction v. Federal Mines Safety and Health Review Commission,.Docket no LAKW 89-68-M and 89-93-M (1992).

Stender v. Lucky Stores Inc., 760 F.Supp. 1486 (2001).

Tampa Shipyards, Inc, 15 Occupational Safety Health Center1533 (1992).

United States v. SabreTech, Inc., 11th Circuit Court of Appeals (October 31, 2001).

U.S. v. Booker, 375 F.3d 508 (7th Cir. (2004).

U.S. v. Fanfan, 543 U.S. ____ (2005)

Vaughn v. Edel, *918 F.2d 517, 522 (5th Cir. 1990).*

Wagenseller v. Scottsdale Memorial Hospital, 147 Ariz. 370 (1985).

Waterston Brick Co. v. Hercules Powder Co., 265 FSupp 268 (M.D. Pa 1967).

Watson v. Fort Worth Bank and Trust, 487 U.S. 977(1988).

Index